AN ENGLISHWO

ANTHONY SATTIN is a writer and freelance journalist who lives in London. He has an MA in Creative Writing from the University of East Anglia, is a contributor to the Times Literary Supplement and the Literary Review, and has had short stories published in the Fiction Magazine. He is the editor of Florence Nightingale's *Letters From Egypt: A Journey on the Nile, 1849–1850*.

AN ENGLISHWOMAN IN INDIA

THE MEMOIRS OF HARRIET TYTLER

1828–1858

Edited by

ANTHONY SATTIN

With an Introduction by

PHILIP MASON

Oxford   New York

OXFORD UNIVERSITY PRESS

1988

Oxford University Press, Walton Street, Oxford OX2 6DP

Oxford New York Toronto
Delhi Bombay Calcutta Madras Karachi
Kuala Lumpur Singapore Hong Kong Tokyo
Nairobi Dar es Salaam Cape Town
Melbourne Auckland

and associated companies in
Beirut Berlin Ibadan Nicosia

Oxford is a trade mark of Oxford University Press

First published 1986
First issued as an Oxford University Press paperback 1988

British Library Cataloguing in Publication Data

Tytler, Harriet
An Englishwoman in India: the memoirs
of Harriet Tytler 1828–1858.
1. Women—India.   2. British—India
3. Women—England.   4. India—Social
life and customs
I. Title.   II. Sattin, Anthony
954.03'1'0924   HQ1742
ISBN 0-19-282100-8

Library of Congress Cataloging in Publication Data
Data available

Set by Rowland Phototypesetting Ltd.
Printed in Great Britain by
The Guernsey Press Co. Ltd.
Guernsey, Channel Islands

CONTENTS

ILLUSTRATIONS

MAPS

INTRODUCTION
BY PHILIP MASON

HARRIET TYTLER became famous because she gave birth to a son on the ridge before Delhi at the height of the hot weather in 1857. He was born in a bullock-cart with no shelter but a temporary thatching of straw. It was often said that she was the only woman to be present with the Delhi Force throughout what is generally called the Siege of Delhi. She is more accurate herself; 'I was the only lady,' she says. Her Breton maid was with her throughout. But she had no baby clothes, no bed linen, nothing to lie on but straw covered with a razai, a quilt of coarse cotton. The only water available to her for washing or drinking came from the canal, which was used by every camel, elephant, bullock, horse and mule of an army based entirely on animal transport. Yet she and her three children survived. So much, she remarks triumphantly, for the theory that disease is carried by water.

The Siege of Delhi was not really a siege. The British force held only the ridge, on the north-west of the walled city; the south-eastern approaches were open and the mutineers in the city received reinforcements and supplies throughout. They outnumbered the investing force by at least four to one and had heavier artillery. They had no lack of courage and determination. All they lacked was unity and officers with experience of commanding anything more than a platoon. That is why they failed to use their great superiority in numbers to full advantage by any large-scale outflanking movement that would have cut the British force's communications with the North-West. But they kept up a constant fire on the investing force and made numerous assaults. Harriet became inured to danger. She tells of a visit by a relation of her husband who had only just arrived in the camp. As they sat talking, a shell landed near them and he was startled. 'It is only a shell,' she said reassuringly, and the phrase became a byword in the camp.

Her husband, a captain in the 38th Native Infantry, was with his regiment in Delhi on the fatal 10 May when the Mutiny broke out in Meerut, only forty miles away. But it was not till next day that the British in Delhi learnt something of what was happening. There were no British troops in Delhi—and throughout northern India it was the same tale over and over again. In regiment after regiment, officers would not believe that *their* men would ever turn against them. Often they believed this until they were actually shot down. So it was on that dreadful 11 May.

Harriet was there, in the eighth month of her pregnancy, with two other children of two and four years old. Perhaps only someone who knows what Delhi can be like in May and has also experienced the sense of security the English usually felt in India can fully live with her through the shocks of that day, the succession of hopes dashed, the agonized waiting in the searing heat.

Harriet was between seventy-five and seventy-seven years old when she wrote down her memories. On the whole, she is surprisingly accurate, though she is not always to be relied on about dates and the exact order of events; she is wrong, for example, about her father's promotions. Her reconstruction of Hodson's capture and execution of the King of Delhi's sons is not quite right; Hodson *did* get a grudging consent from Archdale Wilson, he made two expeditions, one for the King and one for his sons, and he had more men with him than Harriet thinks. But her guess at the bargain made by the King's wife may well be a good one and her memories of what happened to herself and of what she felt at the time are vivid and are good evidence.

No adventure story could be more exciting than her account of her escape from Delhi on 11 May, when almost the entire British population was slaughtered. But the interest of her memories lies not only in the horrors and hardships of the Mutiny, sharply though she brings them to life. Her childhood in India makes absorbing reading too; so does the bitterness of separation from her parents and life in Birmingham under the iron rule of a cruel aunt. She had to practise the piano for two hours before breakfast every morning, surreptitiously wiping the blood from her chilblains off the keys. There was no heating in the schoolroom all through the winter. Breakfast was cubes of bread, thinly buttered on one side, and each chunk had to be snatched from a table in the garden while passing at the run. Fifty times round the garden at the run was the rule, varied only by skipping a thousand times in the schoolroom when there was snow. But the hardships—even the cold mutton six days a week—were easier to bear than the snubbings and scoldings.

From all this, Harriet emerges as an engaging and endearing personality, enormously courageous, resilient after misfortune, delighted and surprised by success, never spiteful. At an early stage of the aunt's terrible régime, she was sent every morning to play in the cemetery and almost every day was in tears over the funeral of a baby. It was 'to this early training among the graves' that she put down her lifelong sympathy with the misfortunes of others.

She had misfortunes enough of her own. Released from her aunt's tyranny, she blossomed on the way back to India and, in spite of being in the company of the 'sweetly pretty' Miss Moresby, she had 'her share of the gentlemanly attentions' of the young men, and radiantly enjoyed the change from constant snubbing. But at Aden she was prostrated by news of the death of her beloved father. She would not show herself in public for several days, though later she shocked the lady passengers by uncontrollable laughter at the sight of portly Mrs Onslow squatting on the deck and rolling about in a storm. It was most unseemly. Not only was she in mourning but they were all in danger of their lives!

There was a fresh blow awaiting her at Calcutta. Her mother had decided to take the younger children to England. But Harriet, being eighteen, would lose her pension if she left India. So she was left behind, truly an orphan now. She 'could have married many times over in Calcutta', but would not marry for security, and started out by herself on a 900-mile journey to an uncle in the North-West, travelling by palkee dak. That is, she was carried in a litter by eight men; each team took her ten or twelve miles to the next staging-post, where another team of bearers would take over.

Bandits—a tiger sleeping on the road—exorbitant bearers—over-persistent admirers—she survived these hazards and the more serious business of falling in love with a penniless Irishman—of good family, for his sister was married to an earl, but with no hope of a pension, so her mother would never consent. She was very sad and he was heart-broken but she knew it was no use. Though still not twenty when she married Captain Tytler, Harriet was by then a very different character from the girl who had left the schoolroom and sailed from London two years earlier. She is never dull and to read her memoirs is like reading a brisk letter from a friend.

That she is entertaining is a good enough reason for reading

Harriet's tale. But it is of historical value too. She was born in 1828, before Queen Victoria's reign began. It was towards the close of a period of transition for the British in India. Gone altogether were the days when the average Englishman in India was the wicked Nabob —'with a bad liver and a worse heart', as Macaulay wrote—the merchant suddenly turned ruler, whose one thought was to get rich quickly. That had been a surprisingly short period and by the beginning of the century the civil servants of the Company were boasting that they were 'minutely just, inflexibly upright' and the equals of any civil service in the world. The East India Company was a corporation exercising its powers on behalf of Parliament, and that fact was more important than the fiction that their powers were delegated by the King of Delhi.

These shifts of intention and responsibility in the exercise of power were reflected in the tone of the society into which Harriet was born, a brotherhood of army officers and civilians, often linked by birth or marriage. Harriet's parents were clearly very different from the kind of people known by William Hickey, the Calcutta diarist of fifty years before. Her father, John Lucas Earle, born in 1791, was still a captain when Harriet was born. Profuse only in the begetting of children, he was austere over personal expenditure and expected his children to amuse themselves without expensive toys. He was severe with his children but just, and with Harriet he clearly came first; her more permissive mamma made a favourite of her younger brother and Harriet does not feel separation from her as she did the loss of her father. He was clearly what was then called an earnest or serious man and also a good officer; Harriet inherited from him an unquestioning faith in a simple religion rather like the Queen's.

The previous generation had included far more men who drew their beliefs from the scepticism of the eighteenth century, men who were agnostic or vaguely theistic in their outlook. John Earle's successors, the contemporaries of her husband, Robert Tytler, were many of them—like Nicholson, Edwardes and the Lawrences— fiercer and more positive in their religion. Some of them believed it was their duty to convert to Christianity the men under their command or influence. Others, such as Thomason, the great Lieut-enant-Governor of the North-Western Provinces, himself no less fervent a believer, thought it would be wrong to use secular power to enforce a religious belief which he held as ardently as the militants. Thomason's view was the official view of the Government.

This religious climate, among officers both civil and military, was one of the causes of the Great Mutiny; in the days of William Hickey, it would hardly have been possible for anyone to believe that the British would have made elaborate plots for the conversion of the native army to a religion which they did not appear to believe in themselves.

In all this, Harriet provides good evidence of the feelings and attitudes of her contemporaries. Of courage, liveliness and generosity, she may have more than her share, but she does not exceed the others in depth of insight or understanding of the native population. She illustrates very well, though quite unconsciously, the aloofness from their surroundings that always marked the British in India, an aloofness which made possible the withdrawal of 1947, but which did not always endear them to their subjects, and which made possible the Mutiny. Consider the confidence with which she sets out, aged eighteen, on the journey from Calcutta to Landour! She takes it happily for granted that everyone will do as she tells them. She is ready in her sympathy for individuals, particularly those she knows, like the old bearer Dabi, of whom she is really fond; she understands the feelings of the Afghan who had saved the life of Mrs Leeson but was suspected by Nicholson of being a spy. She sits and eats with him to show her confidence. She is no racist. She sends her husband to save a carter when she sees British soldiers dragging him off to hang him on suspicion of being an enemy. These are individuals. But she has no sympathy for 'natives' in general; she does not think of them as people. At the elephant fight in Lucknow, when the defeated monster bolted, she remarks unfeelingly: 'The best part of this scene was the stampede among the natives, all terrified out of their lives lest the creatures should tread them down.'

Nor does she understand—how could she?—the general feeling of insecurity among the higher castes and people of property. Dalhousie—of whom her picture is illuminating—believed that the benefits of British rule were such that he should take every possible chance of annexing a princely state. He would not permit a prince without natural heir to adopt an heir according to Hindu custom. Seven states lost their independence during his reign by this 'doctrine of lapse'. That filled all the princes with apprehension. But the insecurity was far more widespread. There was contempt among the highest ranks of the British for every custom not defensible by reason according to the principles of Jeremy Bentham and manifestly 'for the greatest good of the greatest number'. Throughout the North-Western Provinces—later the United Provinces—where most of the Bengal Army were recruited, the man who actually tilled the soil paid rent to a zamindar who paid Land Revenue to the Government. These zamindars were often far from wealthy; some ploughed holdings of their own. It was the small zamindars who were the backbone of the army; they were a kind of impoverished nobility, like d'Artagnan and his companion musketeers. But the principle of zamindari was offensive to Dalhousie and such men as John Lawrence. They wanted no intermediary between the Government and the tillers of the soil. They were the Levellers; they were eager for progress; they hated caste and privilege; they would have liked to carry out much of the reforming programme put through by the Congress after Independence 100 years later—and they took every chance to do it piecemeal. But they were before their time and they caused unhappiness and insecurity, particularly among the very classes upon whom they most depended, the high-caste villagers of the North-West.

Harriet says nothing of this, but she understands very well indeed one aggravation of it, a specialized case. The annexation of Oudh* as a penalty for misgovernment came on top of the seven annexations which resulted from want of an heir. Oudh was the second largest state; its ruler had always been a faithful ally and had been granted the title of king; the annexation added to the general feeling of insecurity; who was safe now? But there was a special effect in Oudh. Most of the Brahmin and Rajput infantry of the Bengal Army came from Oudh and, so long as it was an independent state, the Company's soldiers were a highly privileged class. A soldier had only to complain to his commanding officer that a local official was not giving him due attention for a message to go to the British Resident and the King would send a reprimand to reach the official. The other party to the dispute did not matter. But when British rule was introduced and Oudh became part of the North-Western Provinces, the soldier was no longer a privileged favourite; he was a subject like

* Oudh is really A-wadh and in English is best pronounced to rhyme with 'proud', not with 'food', as often on the BBC. Harriet spells it 'Oude'.

others and both sides of the dispute must be heard. Understandably, if not very laudably, he regarded this as a grievance.

Another cause of distrust and insecurity was the shortage of good officers with their regiments. Often only a third of the full strength was present. There were many opportunities for staff and political appointments away from the regiment; pay was much higher and prospects much better in these appointments and a man who stayed with his regiment far too often felt that he was a failure. Senior officers were too old; even Harriet, good-natured though she is, knows this and it was an important factor, not only in the causes of the Mutiny but in the course of events. On 11 May, 200 men were willing to obey Tytler, but not the colonel.

Thus for some time before the Great Mutiny, there had been an atmosphere of diminishing trust. Religion seemed threatened and the old hierarchical system of caste and privilege and precedence at home in the village. In the army, which had seemed a second home, the British officer, who had once been a father and mother, seemed to have lost interest in his men, to have turned his eyes to marriage and children and fashions from England. Gone was the colonel's brown wife, who could be bribed. Gone were the officers who came to watch wrestling or dancing in the lines, who found their amusement in things Indian. Quite a little grievance could be the spark to set such material in a blaze.

Good officers knew something of this. Tytler had known the danger. Napier had known the danger as long ago as the conquest of Sind, thirteen years before the Mutiny. Financial pedantry had then caused a number of little mutinies which were quickly suppressed. The ancient institution of batta—a hard-lying allowance for discomfort and extra expense, which might double a man's pay if he was far from home—had been admissible in full when the Company's troops marched into Sind. Men from Oudh hated Sind, the climate and the people, and it was a long way from home—but they could send back twice as much to the village. They won some hard-fought battles, Sind was annexed, and their reward was a heavy loss. Quite logically to a financial mind in Calcutta, *batta* became inadmissible. Hence the mutinies.

Harriet says nothing of this but her husband must have known. The spark for the Mutiny of 1857 was of course the question of the famous greased cartridges. This trouble arose near Calcutta in

January. The new cartridge, for a new weapon, had been devised by ordnance officers in Britain, of course without a thought for India, and was sent to ordnance depots in India before any officers in touch with Indian troops knew the implications. The cartridges had to be broken with the teeth and were smeared with tallow coming both from cows and pigs. They would therefore have been deeply defiling both to Hindus and Muslims. But their issue was stopped within five days of the facts coming to notice, by 23 January 1857. Units were told to grease their own cartridges with beeswax and linseed oil. No one was ordered to use the offensive cartridges.

Harriet, of course, like everyone else, has heard of the cartridges but does not seem to have known that the original offensive cartridges were withdrawn. Like every other young wife in India at the time, she thinks that the Mutiny was a deep-laid plot, instigated by the sons of the king—the princes who were shot by Hodson—and spread by wicked Muslims who played on the fears of the simple and gullible Hindus. The spirit of man hankers for a demonology; ninety years later many of the British in India cherished a picture of wicked Hindu agitators deceiving the simple Muslims. But plots are not so easily organized as is sometimes supposed. Undoubtedly there were many interested people trying to foment trouble, both Hindu and Muslim, but the most sensible verdict on that question was Sir Bartle Frere's. He was Chief Commissioner in Sind throughout the Mutiny and soon afterwards became a member of the Governor-General's Executive Council and later Governor of Bombay. 'A plot,' he wrote, 'such as Mazzini and his friends would call a plot, we have no evidence of, and I think it is a waste of time to seek for one.'

There was another belief, widespread and almost universal among the British during the Mutiny, that English women who fell into the hands of the mutineers invariably suffered 'a fate worse than death'. Harriet alludes several times to this belief and kept a bottle of poison for herself and the children for use if the British were defeated in the final assault. But Kaye, much the best historian of the Mutiny, enquired carefully into the legend and found no evidence whatever of systematic rape and only one case—that of Miss Wheeler, Eurasian daughter of the general commanding at Cawnpore—of a woman carried off to be the mistress of a mutineer.

Harriet was quite right, however, in thinking that the assault on Delhi would be decisive. When it succeeded, waverers all over India made up their minds to come in on the British side and there could no longer be any doubt that the mutineers would be defeated. If it had failed, the powerful forces still uncommitted would have gone the other way and India could only have been retaken step by step after a long and expensive war.

There will always be controversy about that year. The interpretation of the facts available will always be a matter of art, of sympathy with the spirit in which statements were made and the systems of belief which caused men to act as they did. On many points, Harriet Tytler adds her fragments of evidence to a varied pile; she saw instances of the thoughtless ferocity of British troops to 'the enemy' —any Indian they did not know—of their kindness to a good officer, of the rough delicacy with which they greeted the arrival of her baby. She gives examples of the injustice and inefficiency of the system of purchase for steps in rank. Her value to a historian lies in the fact that she was so representative of her class and period. She increases one's admiration for Victorian women and leaves me with a strong feeling that I should like to have known her, which I hope many readers may share.

PHILIP MASON

January 1985

EDITOR'S NOTE

FROM references in the text, it seems likely that Harriet Tytler wrote her memoirs between 1903 and 1906 (the year before her death in Simla, aged seventy-nine). Adelaide Rogers Calkins wrote that 'It was to her daughter Edith that Mrs Tytler consigned this manuscript, written while she was on a visit to Canada in 1894, and it has been kept as a precious memorial of her',* but since Harriet refers, amongst other things, to a book that was not published until the turn of the century, it seems that the date suggested by Mrs Calkins is incorrect.

Harriet Tytler remembered and vividly recorded many of the exciting and remarkable events that she took part in or witnessed, but although she gives a detailed description of her everyday existence during her stay in England, she omits to tell us of the drudgery and boredom that often faced her as a memsahib, especially up-country, in India.

Mostly marrying young, because they were always in demand, greatly outnumbered by the single men around them, English girls in India often chose husbands considerably older than themselves who were better able to provide for them, the starting salaries in the East India Company's army being particularly low. Harriet was married when she was nineteen. Her husband, ten years older than herself, had already been married once before. His first wife, Isabella Neilson, whom he had married in 1843, when she was only seventeen, died in January 1847. Robert married Harriet on 3 March 1848.

The routine existence of a memsahib was often exceptionally dull. 'In her drawing-room for the chief part of her day, the Anglo-Indian lady is as much a prisoner by reason of the heat as the zenana woman is by custom. She is by herself all day long and thrown on her own resources.'† Her day started early, between four and five, seeing to the household and then perhaps taking a short ride around the station before breakfast at eight. Visited by the 'ladies' on her own social level during the late morning and early afternoon (the wives of the Other Ranks were referred to as 'women' and seldom mixed with),

* *Chambers's Journal*, 7th Series, p. 1.
† Pat Barr, *Memsahibs*, London, 1976.

she would then have her lunch and sleep through the heat in the whitewashed rooms of her screen-darkened bungalow. The early evening drive was invariably taken over the same route, acknowledging the greetings of people encountered every day. Then it was back to the bungalow for dinner and an early retreat to bed, or out to a party or to dine with the other officers and their ladies.

Her household responsibilities seldom demanded too great an exertion. The children were generally over-cared for by their ayahs; the kitchen, once the food and daily instructions had been supplied, usually ran smoothly enough; and in addition, there were the tailor, bearer, groom, steward, table servant, watchman, water carrier and sometimes a whole host of other servants, all waiting for the word of command. And if she appeared trapped by domestic conventions, the memsahib was no less constrained by a lack of privacy, which was especially a feature of the smaller stations.

But it was the heat, added to the lack of any great necessity for action, that was the downfall of so many English ladies in India. Even when a retreat to the Hills became an integral part of the calendar, the climate was taxing. The English grew old before their time. 'Everybody looks more than fifty!' Emily Eden had complained.*

Harriet was lucky on two accounts. Firstly she had a lively mind, tempered by a great sense of the value of time. Consequently she was always involved in one project or another, raising money for charities, collecting information for an architectural book, painting, taking photographs, and so on. Secondly, she travelled a great deal. She had seen much of Bengal before she married, but even after her wedding she never stayed long enough in any one place for inertia or the quirkily named disease 'Sand in the Head' to overcome her. 'The native nurse', she remembers, 'noticed in giving me my first bath a mole on the sole of my left foot, from which she predicted I should travel till I died—so far her prediction has come true.' But it should be remembered that part of the reason why Harriet was able to travel so widely, both before and after her marriage, was that she did so within an official and social hierarchy that protected her almost as well as if she had stayed at home. When she travelled alone from Barrackpore to Landour, she moved along a network of friends and

* Barr, op. cit., p. 25.

relatives who looked after her. And when she was alone on the road, she was protected by the arrogance and belief in her own superiority that characterized so much of the British raj in India. 'Knowing the world as I do now,' she recalls, 'I have often wondered how my friends could have allowed me, a girl of eighteen, to travel a journey of 900 miles alone. It was an awful risk, but in those days the peasants of India would no more have thought of harming an English woman than of flying, for they knew they could not have escaped punishment.'

The period before the Mutiny was undoubtedly one of innocent belief in British supremacy. For a long time, the Company's European and native forces had been regarded, along with the Queen's troops on duty in India, as invincible. Their record was impressive. But when their Army of the Indus was completely destroyed in the campaign in Afghanistan in 1841–2, the myth of British infallibility became severely tarnished, and this loss of conviction was an important factor in the outbreak of the Mutiny only fifteen years later.* But old beliefs die hard, and though the native forces inside the city of Delhi at the outset numbered more than 40,000 well-trained troops, they still believed themselves to be besieged by a force which at its height numbered less than 9,000 men, including the wounded.

After the Mutiny, during her journey from Simla to the Andaman Islands where Robert had been posted as Superintendent of the settlement, Harriet noted the changed attitude of the natives towards the memsahibs:

One night the coolies had to be changed. After waiting a whole hour or more, I got into perfect despair that we would never arrive in time to catch the mail steamer, which only went once a month. So I got out of the carriage with my husband's tiny revolver and made my way, groping in the dark, to where I thought I could see the glimmer of a light . . . I ordered them to come out immediately, but no one took the least notice of me, so I decided it was time to frighten them. I held up the revolver—of course they did not know it wasn't loaded—and said, 'If you don't obey me at once, there will be six dead men among you!' This . . . had the desired effect. Ellen [the maid] thought I was very brave, but I would have considered myself braver if I had been holding a loaded revolver, and probably shot myself by mistake! I shall never forget that journey of ours. You see, it was after the Mutiny and the natives had learnt to be very cheeky to lone women.

* Cf. note 8, Part 2.

Harriet thus quietly reaffirms her belief in her own superiority and, interestingly, in the greater protection afforded by a man.

The remarkable confidence exhibited by many English ladies —Harriet was by no means alone in this—was invariably a reflection of the attitude of their generally more active husbands. It was a rare occurrence for Harriet, after her marriage, to go out without Robert. Her knowledge of the native character was therefore mainly acquired through her contact with servants and traders and, in an even more limited sense, through Robert and his 'fine men'. She claims that, 'Indeed, all I ever learnt was from him', but perhaps she was being unduly modest.

It is easy to forget, when reading Harriet's memoirs, how completely protected she was for most of her life, another reason why the destruction of her life-style, brought on by the Mutiny, shook her so much. But even in those troubled times she was shielded as much as possible. Throughout the three months of the siege she only 'ever saw fought with [her] own eyes' one encounter between the British and the rebel forces. Similarly, although she was in Delhi after its recapture, she is telling 'second-hand' stories, because she herself spent 'those monotonous days after the siege' in 'a little hot-weather sleeping room on the second storey above the present Diwan-i-am, where the King's mother had lived and died'.

It is perhaps especially because of her limited perspective that her narrative is disturbing at times. In times of action, there were rigidly observed regulations for the men; women were expected to keep out of the way.

Although she wrote her memoirs with a view to publishing them, there were very few paragraphs in the original manuscript and the sentences tended to be extremely long; these therefore have been punctuated. Great care has been taken not to intrude on the idiosyncrasies of Harriet's writing style, and most of the original chapter breaks have been kept.

It has been impossible to corroborate all of Harriet's claims, but wherever information was available—generally from contemporary sources—her version has been checked, and her spelling of proper names corrected where necessary. When she made a mistake in recollecting the order of events, for instance her father's promotion in 1839, this has been pointed out in the notes.

Harriet's spelling was erratic, especially when she was using Anglo-Indian words adopted from Hindi, or referring to native names. No absolute rule has been adopted here in order to preserve the original spelling wherever possible. So 'Oudh' has been left as 'Oude', 'Ambala' as 'Umballa', and many words usually ending in '-i' have been left as '-ee', as Harriet wrote them. The spelling of words that are in general usage has been changed, however: hence 'Hindoostanee' becomes 'Hindustani'. Harriet's spelling of native names has generally been left alone: her Munsoorali could have been Munsur Ally, and there were several ways of spelling the name of the famous mutineer Mungal Pandee. She refers to Bahadur Shah as both the King of Delhi and the Emperor. He was called the King of Delhi by the British, although even that title was in name only for he received a pension from the East India Company and his powers only extended, effectively, as far as the walls of his own palace. The title of Emperor was an even more flattering one, recalling the glorious days of his ancestors—he was descended from the great Jenghiz Khan and Tamerlane, and from the Emperor Babur who established Mogul rule at Delhi in the sixteenth century. But his titles still commanded great reverence and authority amongst the native population. The first step the mutineers took to consolidate their rebellion was to march to Delhi from Meerut and proclaim him king. Bahadur Shah sat on his silver throne for the first time in fourteen years. It seems unlikely that the Mutiny, in Bengal at least, would have been so widespread or dangerous had the King not served as a rallying emblem, reminding the natives of past glories.

Harriet's memoirs were given to her daughter, Mabel Tytler, who married Captain Benbow of the 1st King's Dragoon Guards, and were handed on to their descendants. The manuscript was acquired by my father, Gerald Sattin, for his collection. Unfortunately a great number of Harriet's letters and other papers were destroyed at that time, and I believe that the manuscript is the only important material to have survived.

Robert Tytler's account of the outbreak of the Mutiny at Delhi has been included as an appendix to Harriet's narrative. It was written immediately after the Mutiny and was referred to during the trial of the King of Delhi, to prove that the Delhi sepoys knew, on 10 May, that the Mutiny had broken out at Meerut that day, and that the mutineers were on their way to Delhi. It was published in 1859 in N. A. Chick's *Annals of the Indian Rebellion*.

The photographs included amongst the illustrations in this volume belong to a series of Calotypes that Harriet and Robert produced during 1858. The series, nearly 500 negatives in all, contained views of all of the most important locations connected with the Mutiny. The entire collection was exhibited to the Photographic Society of Calcutta and was described as 'unquestionably the finest ever exhibited in Calcutta'. It won them the Society's Gold Medal and they were voted honorary life members. Queen Victoria asked to see their collection, but on the appointed day of their meeting she was obliged to attend her mother who was ill at Windsor. A part of the collection has survived and is preserved in the India Office Library.

In the course of my research I have been helped by many people and I owe a debt of gratitude to them all. I am most indebted to the India Office Library and Records, the British Library and the Guildhall Library for the use of their material and facilities, to Anna Houghton for her help with the research, and especially to my parents, Mona and Gerald Sattin, for providing me with the manuscript, for endless advice, and for giving me access to their own library and resources.

ANTHONY SATTIN

March 1985

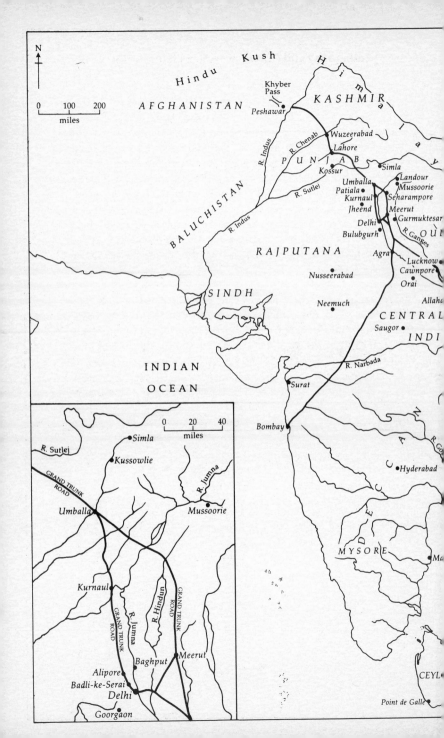

India, 1857 and (inset) the Routes from Delhi

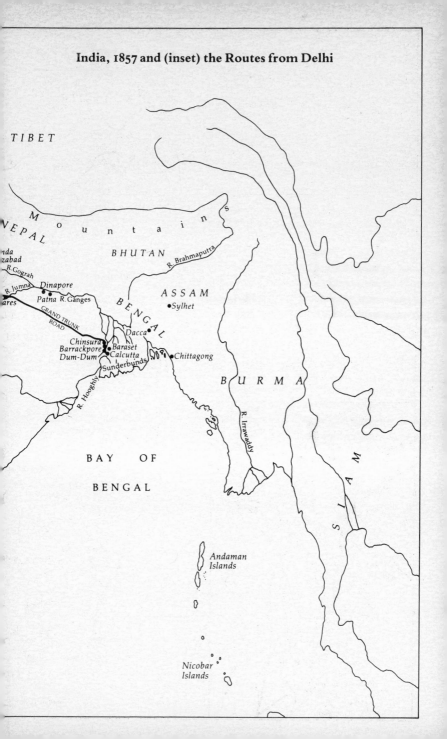

THE MEMOIRS OF
HARRIET TYTLER
1828–1858

PART ONE

MOTHER told me I was born on the 3rd of October 1828, in Secrora, once a small station in Oude, and that the native nurse noticed in giving me my first bath a mole on the sole of my left foot, from which she predicted I should travel till I died—so far her prediction has come true. Years ago I was weary of so much travelling with a number of little children and often threatened to burn out the mole, whereupon my husband would exclaim, 'Oh Harrie don't do any such thing, it may really mean the end of your travelling!' The mole is still there, and no rest yet, as far as I can see, to the soles of my weary feet.

At the great age of thirteen days I began my first journey. The regiment[1] had to march from Secrora to Nusseerabad (where it stayed nearly three years), and my mother, with my little self and the others, three older children, marched with the troops,[2] getting up every morning between two and three o'clock, going ahead of the regiment in palankeens carried by bearers. The children of course slept soundly travelling thus, but not so the poor mothers, who had little rest I fear day or night. After leaving Secrora the regiment went to Neemuch, where my baby brother was born, now a retired colonel of the artillery.

Of course I recollect nothing of my life till I was a little over two years old, when my father and mother decided to send my eldest sister and two eldest brothers home to England, not only for their education, but more principally on account of the climate being so trying to English children, for in those days we had no Himalayas to go to. My mother was twenty-six years in India, and I might almost say had never heard of the Hills, not that they did not exist, but simply we had no sanitoriums so far back as the early days of my parents' sojourn in India. Nowadays everybody goes to the Hills, as we call these gigantic mountains. Consequently, children can be kept in India in as perfect health as in the Mother Country, by a summer's visit to any of the Hill stations.

Father and mother thought it best to leave me with my uncle and aunt till they returned from Calcutta. Mother said she could not understand how it was, but I seemed to have a presentiment of her leaving me, and nothing would persuade me to go out of her arms for a moment, until overcome with sleep I was deposited in my cot, only to awake in the morning to call for mamma. Getting no response I gave way to bitter tears and cried out, '*Hum janta mamma chulla gia, chulla gia!*' ('I know Mamma has gone away, has gone away'). I recollect that scene perfectly; no one could comfort me, till I sobbed and sobbed myself to sleep again. Strange, I have no recollection of their coming back.

The next excitement in my life was that of being stung by a scorpion, fortunately a little, tiny brown one. I could not have been three years old. My brother being only a small baby, I had no one to play with, and so had to amuse myself as best I could. Father never allowed any of us toys. He used to argue it was just throwing money away, and that children ought to find their own amusements. I think he was right, for when we were older it was astonishing with what ingenuity we manufactured our amusements. I remember my doll at Chittagong was a narrow plank with a pinafore tied round it. On the occasion of the scorpion episode, the drawing room grate contained many little treasures of broken odds and ends, amongst others the brass end of an infantry scabbard. I recollect I went to play with these treasures and, always being fond of bright, pretty things, reached over for the brightest. No sooner had I handled the scabbard end, than out ran the scorpion and stung me in the palm of my tiny hand. Over sixty years later, I was stung by another, somewhat similar one, and can vouch for the agony that mite of a child must have suffered. A piercing cry brought the whole household to my aid. The little rascal was discovered chivvying away as hard as he could for his life and was promptly slaughtered. The servants ran here and there, each bringing some antidote in the shape of a herb and applying it to the wounded spot, all however to no avail until the sting had taken its course. They say the sting of a full-grown scorpion of this species, which never exceeds four inches, takes twenty-four hours before the pain begins to subside. When I was stung the second time, I could not sleep the whole night, the slow heavy throb from the tip of the fingers to the top of the shoulder causing much excruciating pain. At the end of twelve hours the pain left me suddenly, and there was not a vestige of a mark to be seen on the tip of the finger where I had been stung.

Not many years ago, when I was staying in Bombay, I heard of the death of a poor little English baby. The parents had gone out for their evening drive, as is customary in India, leaving the baby with the ayah and other servants to look after it, and to put it to bed at its regular time. The ayah bathed the child and put on its nightdress as usual, when the poor little thing gave a fearful cry. The ayah never thought of anything being wrong with the nightdress and tried to pacify the child by hugging it closer and closer, but each time she did so, the child gave a fresh scream, until it went into violent convulsions and died. When the parents came home, they would not believe the ayah's story that the child had cried without any fault of hers and then died so quickly. However, when the poor little one was undressed to be laid out in its coffin, they found the scorpion and knew what it all meant. Evidently the ayah disturbed it each time she clasped the child to comfort it, resulting in a fresh sting, till the agony was more than the little life could bear.

While I am on the subject of scorpions, I may as well mention a very strange fact which came under the notice of my husband. After the annexation of Oude, my husband's regiment was ordered to a newly formed station called Gonda in Oude. It was a jungle place, with little or no habitation, and full of snakes and scorpions, not small brown ones, but huge creatures of some six or seven inches long and almost black in colour, loathsome-looking brutes. Every mud-bank was full of holes, either round or narrow oblong ones. The former were the habitation of snakes, mostly of the deadly cobra, the latter the abode of scorpions alone. Now, in our regiment one of the soldiers in my husband's company, a young sepoy, was noted for catching scorpions without ever being stung. My husband, a naturalist, knowing much about the habits of all kinds of living creatures, was not disposed to believe this, and put the man to the test. Strange to say, he never failed to pull out one of these awful creatures and place him in the palm of his hand. My husband could not detect what he did so dexterously, but the animal seemed powerless to sting and did not even attempt to run away. According to the present theory, people will say it was hypnotism. The feat was performed over and over again, each time with equal success. A scorpion when not asleep is always on the aggressive tack, with his tail well cocked up, ready to sting, which he does with a backward dart. Whatever the sepoy did while dragging the animal out of his hole seemed to paralyse him, for he never attempted, so my husband said, to cock up his tail even, but lay in the man's hand quietly as if asleep, though wide awake in all other respects.

My next experience was a quarrel with my baby brother (I must have been about three at the time) over some tiny pieces of broken china, kept near the filter. I don't think there is a better and simpler filter in all the world. It consists of three ghurras—the top one has the unfiltered water with a tiny hole at the bottom in which is a small piece of rag, through which the water from the top drips, drop by drop, into the second which contains pounded charcoal and under this, in equal quantities, river sand. This filter also has a small hole with a piece of rag from which the filtered water drips, drop by drop, into the third and last ghurra, from which it is poured into sorais (goblets), ready for use. The two pieces of broken china over which we two quarrelled were kept for the purpose of cleaning the sorais every day, by shaking them well inside of the goblets. All little children in those days of scarcity of toys were fond of playing with these bright little things. Childlike, I would not give them up to my little brother, who wanted them, so he crawled up to me and gave me a fearful bite on my bare arm. It resulted in my giving him a hard slap, which made us howl in concert. Of course my mother scolded me and took away the coveted things, giving them to my injured brother, heedless of the pain from my bleeding arm. I resented the injustice and cried all the more. I do think as a rule mothers are hard on their girls where a darling son is concerned, engendering selfishness in men in after-life, specially towards their daughters and wives.

A later experience was that of going down the river Ganges in a houseboat with a thatched roof. This was a common mode of travelling in those days. There were two kinds of boats, ooluks and puttailas. The former were sharp-keeled with high sterns and had the advantage of speed, combined with the disadvantage of being easily overturned in a squall. The latter, on the other hand, were shallow and flat-bottomed, and slow, but quite safe in any weather, though if by chance they sprang a leak they filled and settled at once. Going down to Calcutta was not quite so tedious as coming up, for the current took us down in six or eight weeks, over a distance of some 800 miles as the crow flies. But coming up against the current, the boat had to be dragged along by men just as a canal barge is towed by horses, each boat having as many men as its tonnage needed. These men would rise at daybreak, loosen their craft from its moorings, and then start off, either to float down with the current or to walk along the shore upstream, as the case might be, in water often knee deep and even waist-deep, dragging the boat at a rate of sometimes only one mile an hour, never more than two even if the current was slack.

These boatmen in the North-West are Hindus, hardy fellows, accustomed to an aquatic life, who rise early and work all day till sunset, when they moor their boat for the night alongside of some low-lying shore. Indian rivers often have on one side a high bank composed of perpendicular limestone rocks called kunkur, the opposite one being low and subject to annual overflowing in the rainy season. The current is strongest on the limestone side, where the river has cut its way from time immemorial to its present wall-like form, for which reason it is usually avoided when going up stream, though of course preferred when coming down, unless by doing so they can save a long detour caused by shifting sandbanks, using long poles to keep their craft at a respectable distance, lest a bump against some sharp corner should cause them to settle down before they could reach a safe landing place. Should such a catastrophe happen, the crew would not in most cases lose their lives, for they would at once take to the water and swim to the nearest landing, though always with the possibility of being eaten up by an alligator or crocodile, with which these rivers abound. As I said before, these boatmen moor their boats every evening, and set to work at once preparing their one hot meal on shore, as no Hindu will cook his food anywhere except on terra firma, which is the reason why they have such an objection to travelling by sea. After finishing their meal, they wash up their brass utensils and put by some of the unleavened bread (chupattees) to eat the next day on board—doing so does not imperil their caste—and then retire for the night, sleeping on plain boards with only a blanket or razai for covering, many even without the pretence of a pillow. All the same, a king might envy their sound sleep, so much for habit. At dawn, they are up and away again.

This time on our way to Calcutta we came across a terribly sad sight. We saw numbers of famine-stricken people, never to be forgotten. When my father saw them, he gave orders to the boatmen to draw near to the shore to enable him to speak to these poor people. It appears these unhappy Hindu peasants had left their village to die on the banks of the Ganges, so that when the holy river rose, as it was sure to do, either through the melting of the snows in the Himalayas or the deluges of rain caused by the monsoon, their bones might be carried away into the stream and so ensure for their souls the blessing of reincarnation. Many of the unfortunate men, women and children were already dead from starvation. My father offered the living food, but one and all made the same reply, 'Sir, if you will give me food cooked by a Brahmin I will eat, if not I must die!' My dear father was grieved beyond measure for he had no Brahmins on board. He told them so, but they only replied, 'Well sir, then we must die.' I was at this time standing on the prow of the boat, looking on with childlike curiosity, when I observed a little infant crawl up to its dead mother and try in vain to obtain some nourishment from her. I recollect perfectly well the whole scene, little child as I was, for I could scarcely have been six years old, and I said to myself, 'When I grow up to be a woman I will save all the little starving children and bring them up as Christians'—an aspiration which never left me until thirty-three years later, when God permitted me in his good-ness to carry out my heart's desire.

When my father returned to the boat after failing to persuade the poor dying creatures to eat our prepared food, they being too weak to cook any for themselves, a young Brahmin lad came up and said, 'Sir I will eat, give me to eat.' Immediately the order was given to bring him some of our own dinner, which was ready waiting for us. The poor boy went close to the water's edge and, putting up his hands in prayer, took off the Brahminical cord from his neck, muttering something, and threw it into the holy Ganges, which meant renouncing his faith, and said, 'Now sir, give me to eat.' The dish was placed before him; he ate voraciously and died half an hour afterwards. My dear father, in his desire to help the helpless, never thought of the serious consequences of giving the lad food, which in his weak state he could not digest. Thus ended the sad day's experiences, but the result of it was the founding of my Himalayan Christian Orphanage in Simla, now known as the Mayo School, which thank God is doing so much good. Here is a proof of how God in His mercy can bring good out of evil.

On our return journey from Calcutta to Agra, our bearer Gunga asked my father's permission to go and bathe in the river, saying he would join us further on. There being no objection, he undressed himself and jumped into the river, while we went on our course up a long sandbank shore. These Indian rivers are always changing their course, owing to the sand shifting and making new land where there was none before, much to the inconvenience and delay of travellers and commerce generally. These sandbanks are often full of quicksands too—I once got into one while running about playing in the evening when the boat was moored for the night. I cannot describe the awful feeling. I just screamed with terror till the servants ran to my help and dragged me out. Of course a grown-up person could in most cases have extricated himself without assistance, whereas a small child could not. Woe to the poor creature who is within reach of an elephant's trunk when he finds himself on a 'dull dull' (quicksand). His natural instinct makes him catch hold of anything: not straw, but a human being, a plank, a branch, anything to put under his feet, and so to raise himself up till he can get out of his serious predicament. The mahouts know their danger and slip off backwards as fast as possible; they then bring the elephant boughs of trees, and whatever else they can find to assist him, taking good care to keep well out of reach of his trunk.

It is the winding of these rivers which makes travelling in India by water so slow and tedious, but in those days we could only choose between three modes of travelling, by palankeen dak, by water, or by marching ten miles a day on the trunk road. The latter mode had to be adopted if you wished to carry all your belongings with you in patriarchal style – such as your horses, cows, goats and household goods. What a different life to what it is now. In those days officers used to get six months' leave from Meerut or Delhi to reach Calcutta, the only port of embarkation for the Bengal army, before sailing for England, and the same when they returned from furlough to rejoin their regiments. Now they only get one week's leave from either that port or Bombay, the same distance being reached in the present day by train in forty-eight hours.[3] In spite of such rapid travelling, I have often seen men lose their tempers because the train was ten minutes behind time. I firmly believe in many respects we were happier in those days than we are now. Certainly we had better servants, less expectations, less luxuries, and cheaper food. Everything now is doubled and trebled in price and servants by no means as good or as faithful as they used to be. Yet I cannot say I would desire a retrograde movement, after having tasted the pleasures of speed and the said civilization, to go back to those days when it took a year and often more before we could hear of our children's safe arrival in England or get a reply to a letter. Certainly we were quite fifty years behind European countries in everything.

To return to Gunga and his ablutions, we had not gone very far as the crow flies on our journey, skirting the long sandbank, when the bearer was seen swimming for his dear life. As soon as he reached father's boat—for we always travelled with two, one for ourselves, the other for the servants and the cooking—he called out breathlessly, 'Sahib, Sahib! I have just seen such a dreadful sight, a fakir[4] killing a man and burying him in the sand.' Gunga then scrambled up and, after dressing himself, gave father the details of the murder. When later on we reached the other side of the said sandbank, which was only a short distance across although a long way round, Gunga called out, 'There Sahib, see the murderer is now washing the dead man's clothes, and that is the hut the fakir came out of.' True enough, there was a solitary little grass hut on a spur of land above the sandbank we had skirted, and there too was a man washing some very bloody clothes. Poor Gunga was very excited, evidently realizing the narrow escape he had had from the Thug (a garrotter). We were several days' journey from any place where the information could have been lodged, and then only to a native official, who probably would have taken no notice of the murder. What father did, I do not recollect, but I think he would have been justified, under the circumstances, to have shot him, if only to have stopped his killing and robbing more unfortunate men who might have to pass that lonely way.

In the course of time we reached Agra, the birthplace of my younger sister Emily (now Mrs Comfrey). As you all know, Agra is the town in the suburbs of which stands that lovely tomb, the Taj Mahal, a striking monument of an emperor's devotion to the memory of a beloved wife.

A very sad tragedy took place when I was there as a child. The Taj gardens used to be a great resort for picnics in those days. On one of these occasions, the whole station was there, when after lunch some of the officers and their wives proposed to run a race to the top of one of the beautiful white marble minarets. There was a poor young English woman, a Mrs Monkton, a civilian's wife, who won the race and was so excited over it that she fell backwards over the very narrow parapet and was smashed into atoms. It was a terrible shock to all present. Her poor remains were placed in our doctor's palan-keen and taken back to cantonments.

In those days of no European shops up-country, there lived a very enterprising man of the name of Myers, who used to carry on an extensive business during the cold season by importing a quantity of English goods and bringing them up as far as the river was navigable, stopping at each station, small or great, wherever there were Euro-peans to purchase them. Everybody, on hearing of Myers' arrival, used to go as quickly as possible to him to get the first choice of these antiquated articles, but which were of course quite modern to us. I remember so well Myers' arrival in Agra on this occasion because father was going to break through his rules and buy me a doll, and my little brother a bugle. My joy was so great that it knew no bounds. To think that I was to have a real English doll. But alas for the vicissitudes of this life. As soon as my father and mother drove back to the house I ran out saying, 'Papa, have you got my doll?' Their grave faces prepared me for the worst. 'My child, we could not buy one, they were so expensive.' I cannot express my feelings properly. It was real grief, because I loved dolls so much. Of course I shed many tears over the disappointment.

Some two or three hours later a buggy drove up and a lady and gentleman came to call on my mother. The lady, who was a hunchback, brought with her two little parcels. They also had paid Myers a visit that morning and had probably overheard my father saying the doll was too expensive and poor little Harriet must do without one. Anyhow, judge of my joy when lo and behold I was called to witness the unpacking of these two parcels, in one of which was the identical doll which my father would have bought, but for its price of twelve rupees, equal to twenty-four shillings in those days. My joy now was as extreme as my sorrow had been. The doll was a beauty so I thought, all dressed in the fashion of the day. The other parcel contained the six rupee brass bugle for my brother. It is a merciful providence that enables us to forget sorrows sooner than we can forget joys. The latter will last our lifetime thank God. I am sure that dear Mrs Baker must have had her reward for giving so much pleasure and happiness to two little children. If we would but try to do things to forget self and make others happy, I feel sure from my own experience we would then know what real happiness meant. How well I recollect philosophizing with myself as I played with my doll that day. 'How did Mrs Baker know I loved a doll so much, and how could she know that Edward wanted a bugle?' This was a many days' wonder to me, only seven years old at the time. Of course poor father could not afford eighteen rupees for just two toys, on a captain's pay, with six children to provide for, three of whom were in England.

From Agra, our regiment, the 9th Native Infantry, was sent down to Barrackpore, a military station on the banks of the Hooghly, sixteen miles from Calcutta. For some reason, mother and the children did not march with the regiment, but went by water again. Nothing particular happened on this journey, except that our English tortoiseshell cat, which had come out from England with mother seventeen years before, gave birth to a lot of kittens. They were all born without legs, or rather with only apologies for such. Mother, on hearing of this, gave orders to have them all drowned. I begged for their lives to be spared, saying, 'Mamma, the legs will grow, I know they will grow', but she would not listen to my entreaties. How cruel I thought her, yet it was the kindest thing she could do. Had she only reasoned with me a little, I would not have felt so badly about it.

When we reached Dinapore, a military station some 300 miles from Calcutta, the boat was moored as usual for the night. Without any warning the evening gun was fired, which so startled my mother that it made her very ill. However, by the time father joined us in Barrackpore she had quite recovered.

Barrackpore has a lovely park, beautifully laid out. We used to take our daily morning walks there. With my passion for flowers (in this I took after my father) I could never resist gathering one or two. Lord Auckland, the Governor-General in those days, was a very disagreeable, austere old bachelor. The servants used to terrify me by saying, 'There comes the Lord Sahib, if he knows you have been gathering his flowers, he will assuredly put you into prison.' Believing this, through my conscience smiting me, I used to hide behind the ayah and scarcely breathe till the great man on his elephant had passed by.

The first strawberry plants that ever grew in India were grown in the Barrackpore gardens. This must have been in 1836. My father and mother, with some friends, went to see these wonders, and I was allowed to accompany them. Two of the plants had one ripe berry each. Of course everyone was delighted at the novel sight. No one touched them, but all expressed the desire to be Lord Auckland to have the pleasure of eating the first Indian strawberries. There were lovely nasturtiums out too, also a novelty sixty-one years ago. No sooner had my father and his friends gone on, chatting away, than I thought I really must taste the strawberries. Accordingly, I picked and ate them both. I did not dare let my parents know of my wickedness. My father would, I really believe, well nigh have killed me, for he was very severe with us. First to *steal*, and then to eat the fruit were crimes unheard of in our home, but, child as I was, through fear I kept my own council.

In Barrackpore I used to ask my father for his watch so that I might time myself to see how much needlework I could accomplish in five minutes. From childhood I seemed to have a natural instinct for the value of time, through God's goodness in putting it into my heart to do so, and as I grew older I felt a certain responsibility to answer to Him for every moment I wasted, which has conduced to make me a very hard worker all my life.

It was in Barrackpore when I was eight years old that my youngest sister was born. Mother used to give her to me a great deal to nurse and feed with a bottle, just such a one as babies use nowadays. So I was kept pretty hard at work, what with lessons, sewing, and looking after the baby. She taught me to embroider, being a beautiful worker herself. I recollect the Christening robe I made for this little sister, in French embroidery, which I couldn't do now. I have loved needlework all my life, but I did hate grammar. Lindley Murray was my abhorrence.[5] Many a time I was punished, some-times even whipped, for not knowing my bit of grammar by heart. What lovely books children have now. *Little Mary's Grammar* for instance—so easy for a child of five to understand. If I escaped a while, I used to be punished by being kept in of an evening and deprived of my pony ride, which my brother and I took alternately. On one of these occasions I was left alone, to cry my heart out, when a sparrow flew in at the window. Immediately I set to work to catch it, and kept throwing up towel after towel as it flew round the room, till at last, worn out, he fell to the ground and I caught my bird. 'Poor little bird,' I said. 'You and I are both prisoners, but I will be kinder to you than papa is to me. I will take you out and give you a walk in the garden.' I took him by the tail, and just as I was stooping down to let him reach the ground, expecting him to hop along, while I held on quite happily, he was off like a shot, leaving like Bo Peep's sheep the whole of his tail behind him. I was so astonished that I stood gaping, transfixed to the spot.

From Barrackpore, the regiment was sent to Chittagong, now no longer a military station, but full of tea plantations. Recollecting how the wild coffee, with its little, white, star-like flower, grew there, I have often wondered if it would not have paid better to have cultivated coffee instead, especially as the once famous Ceylon plantations had had to be given up on account of a destructive pest appearing, which until then had been unknown on the island. This calamity had caused the planters to give up coffee and turn to tea.

Chittagong was a hilly place, full of low jungle and tigers in-numerable. Each European house was built on the top of a hillock, and I presume Chittagong must have been a station of not long standing from the fact that each house was built of wattle and daub with a thatched roof. At this time my father was suffering terribly from insomnia. Night after night he could not sleep a wink. In the thatch of our house there lived a large lizard called a tucktoo. This species is a common also in Burma. The tucktoo has red spots down each side of his body, and the natives believe a new spot is added every year, to those he had before, as also another tucktoo to his call. Our lizard used to repeat tucktoo, tucktoo seven times, thus proving to the native mind that he was seven years old. What his age was mattered little, but to my father he was unbearable. At last he determined to get rid of him at any cost and had the thatch taken off, expecting to find and kill him. But tucktoo was not found, his fairy godmother evidently having warned him of impending danger. The roof was put on again, when he reappeared and called out tucktoo, tucktoo as before.

Chittagong is quite tropical and full of fireflies. On a dark night they are a sight to behold, flitting about everywhere in thousands. One of our great amusements used to be catching fireflies; on one particular occasion I proposed to my brother and sister that we should go out with our nets and catch a lot and loosen them in the house to make it a fairy land. We started off, expecting to have a good time, but fireflies do not show themselves until light is beginning to disappear. We did not reckon upon this, but went on and on, expecting to find them somewhere. When they did appear, we were unconscious of the lateness of the hour and of the distance we had strayed from home. There is no twilight in India, so darkness came on and the fireflies increased in numbers and in brilliancy. We ran after them further and further, getting with every step deeper into the jungle, till at last I began to get frightened of father being angry with us for being out so late and tried to retrace our steps. But we had lost our way and found ourselves on the borders of a swamp, through the centre of which ran a narrow road dividing it. We made for the road till struck with fear at the thought of not knowing where it might lead to. Night too was getting blacker and blacker. Terror took entire possession of us all. We did not dare take another step for fear of tumbling into the swamp on either side, and here we were alone in a jungle where tigers abounded. The jackals began to howl, which according to native tradition was a forerunner of immediate danger, the tiger being close at hand. My brother and sister cried bitterly in spite of my begging them not to do so for fear the tiger should hear us, but to no purpose; they cried all the more, and added to my misery by saying, 'It's all your fault, you brought us here, and now we shall be eaten up by the tigers.' It was too true. Here again, my love for the beautiful had brought me into trouble.

No one could understand the agony of mind we three went through. Our highly wrought imaginations even made us believe we could hear a tiger sniffing close at hand, and but for the glistening swamp on either side, reflecting the beautiful stars shining so peacefully above, I am sure that we would have run further into danger in the hopes of delivering ourselves from the tigers. At last, after a very lengthy suspense, I imagined I saw the figure of a man in the distance walking towards us. Presently he stopped and called out, '*Yahan kya karte? Tum log kaun hain?*' I replied, '*Ham log Major Sahib ke baba log hain.*' ('What are you doing here? Who are you?' 'We are the Major Sahib's children' and have lost our way.)

It turned out that he was one of our sepoys and was coming across this short cut from the lines. You may imagine how narrow the path was when we could not walk two abreast. The sepoy took my little sister in his arms and said to my brother and myself, '*Baba log, mera kuppra kapra pakarke, pichehe ab.*' ('Children, hold on to my clothes and follow me.')

He did not venture to take us back through the jungles, the way we had come, on account I presume of the tigers, but took us through the lines, making for the parade ground, on the other side of which stood our house, where our parents were passing moments of agony. The servants were all out looking for us with torches and lanterns. As the sepoy neared the grounds and saw the lanterns flitting about, he called out in a stentorian voice, 'The children are safe, I, your sepoy, am bringing them with me.' I was sure father would whip me well, and he would have too, if joy at seeing us again had not softened his heart and filled it with thanksgivings to the giver of all good, for having delivered us from the jaws of the tigers. As soon as we reached home, we were greeted with 'You wicked children, you deserve to be well whipped', but instead of a whipping, we were packed off to bed without any supper. It was quite nine o'clock by this time, so they must have gone through three hours of cruel suspense. Never did I attempt wandering after fireflies again.

The tigers were so numerous in Chittagong in those days, and so bold, that they were often seen actually in broad daylight, bounding across a public thoroughfare which led to the seashore three miles from where we lived, after some unfortunate cattle grazing on the other side of the road and, pouncing upon one, carrying it off across the same road to their own eating grounds. Fortunately, up to the time that we were there, not a case had been known of a man, woman or child being attacked by any one of these Chittagong tigers, for had any one of them once tasted human blood, that road would have been impassable.

We had two great sportsmen in our regiment, a Captain Thatcher and Bobby Sale, a son of Sir Robert Sale, who was killed at Jallalabad in the first Afghan campaign. Poor young fellow, he was himself killed afterwards while shooting in the Himalayas. These two officers destroyed an incredible number of tigers during their stay in Chittagong. They had a small shooting box erected after the fashion of a bungalow, consisting of only one room with a verandah all round, on the top of a hillock, well surrounded with shrub jungle. Here on moonlit nights they used to take up their abode. A poor live goat or calf used to be tethered within gunshot, and no sooner was a tiger observed to spring on the unfortunate animal, than he had a bullet through his heart. It was taking rather a mean advantage of stripes, but no doubt the peasants didn't think so, since it lessened one enemy to their herds of cattle. I cannot say how many tigers these two officers killed during their stay in Chittagong, but it must have been hundreds. Years afterwards I heard of a colonel who had killed over 300 tigers in Lower Bengal in the same way. They certainly still exist in countless numbers in the Sunderbunds, where they live upon deer and other animals.

I have often wondered if tigers have any destroying enemies outside of the genus Homo. If they have, it can only be the dreadful snakes which exist in damp forests.

It was in Chittagong that I used to try and paint in my own way, and that was copying a picture out of a book, and then gathering flowers from the garden, to squeeze their colours for my picture. How far I succeeded I don't recollect, specially as I had no brush, but my father, seeing my poor attempts, said to my mother one day, 'Mary, this child must be taught, as she shows talent.' So immediately father set me to some sepia sketches, but I soon evinced no liking for these ugly brown pictures, as I called them, so he gave me up as a bad job. Thank God I have always had a good eye for both form and colour, and even now at the age of seventy-seven my eye for colour is perfect and I still paint and enjoy it, though I can't see without spectacles and I can't see really well with them, so it has become a matter of slow process. Still, I hope I am grateful for being able to paint at all under such difficulties.

Mother used to keep me up till past eleven o'clock at night, mending the little ones' stockings, while she mended her own and father's. It was hard on me considering I used to be dragged out of bed *nolens volens* at four o'clock in the morning during summer time, to be sent out for a walk and home again by five. So I naturally wished for more sleep. It was I presume for crying, screaming, and perhaps scratching too in an attempt to resist such hard measures that father gave me the soubriquet of the 'Junglee Billee' (wild cat). However, it was no use resisting, mother was inexorable when her sense of duty came in the way, and she would turn to me and say, 'See how good your dear little sister is? She never cries, but wakes up smiling so sweetly', to which I used to reply, 'Of course she is, she did not sit up till eleven o'clock mending stockings.' Mother was very strong and never took a siesta during the day, as other ladies in India used to do, and we children, the elder ones, were not allowed to either. I don't know whether the little sleep I had did me any harm or not, but I know that my long hair fell off so badly that the doctor advised mother to have my head shaved, which was done and repeated five times. It was dreadfully mortifying to be chaffed about it by the officers, for being nearly eleven at that time, I felt it very much.

Poor dear mother had a pet aversion all her long life, and that was a spider. She really was terrified of them, and that horrible little brother of mine knew it, so one day he thought he would give her a fright for the fun of the thing. So when he found the skin that spiders shed, he came into the room where she was dressing and put it on her.

'Mamma, look, there is a spider on you.'

My mother was not very strong at the time. She gave a piercing shriek, which brought my father to her side. Poor Edward never thought the mere shell of a spider could possibly hurt her. Now he fled for his life, and my father after him. Poor child, I really felt sorry for him, for I knew what he would get when my father caught up with him. He ran twice round that compound before father could catch him, but when he did he got that which made my mother very sorry for giving the scream she did.

My brother Edward was the plague of my life. Mother, being of a placid temperament, did not see the use of troubling about little things, but preferred letting them take care of themselves. So when my brother used to bully and tease me, and I used to get furious and beg her interference, she would only say calmly, 'Why do you mind him? If you took no notice, he would soon get tired of teasing you.' Hearing this so often, I thought at last I would put her advice to the test, for she might be right. Accordingly, I took up my work and began to sew, when up comes Edward and gives my long hair a good, hard pull, nearly wrenching my head off my neck. I said nothing, but went on working. Seeing it had no apparent effect, he came and gave me a severe blow on my bare neck. Now my wrath was rising. Seeing again that he had made no impression on me, he returned to the attack with another, more violent tug at my hair (this was of course before I had been shaved). I could stand it no longer, but threw down my work, flew after him, caught him, threw him down and sat upon him. 'Now,' I said, 'you don't go until you promise not to do it again, and beg my pardon.' He struggled and struggled until his fair face became crimson with exertion and rage, but I had the best of it and he had to apologize. Mother looked on placidly, correcting neither of us. When I had children of my own, I neither forced them to get up in the mornings to take walks, for it is the only time during the hot weather that one can get refreshing sleep, nor did I allow them to irritate each other's tempers or quarrel over anything. I think it is highly injurious to allow such things in a family, where all should grow up with strong affection for each other.

It had been decided that as I was now so old, nearly eleven, I was not to be sent home, but that my brother and younger sister were to leave for England about Christmastime. My dear father almost worried himself to death with the thought of the injustice of the case. All the other children were to have good English educations, but myself. 'This must not be!' he said, so in the end I was to go too. Mother now had more than ever to do in getting ready the necessary outfits for so long a voyage round the Cape for yet another child. I do thank my dear father's memory for his self-sacrifice. It was a great expense when he could so ill afford it. But God in his goodness sent him the glad tidings that he was to have command of a regiment —the 3rd NI. This was a great Godsend just at a time when the expense of bringing out a grown-up daughter and sending home three more children lay so heavily on his mind and added to his other burdens. My father had paid great sums of money for his various steps,[6] something like £3,000, to meet which he had borrowed money. This to a poor military man meant a halter round his neck for the rest of his days. Yet without buying steps, he, like other officers in those days, could never have hoped to rise to the command of a regiment, the precious goal to which all military men naturally aspire. At the time of his promotion, he had been over thirty years in the service and yet only a major. The last four years of this were spent in half batta[7] stations. An officer's income in India was made up of pay and allowance (or batta). By order of Lord Bentink, the then Governor-General, these allowances had been cut down to half for all those regiments which were stationed within a certain distance from Calcutta, on the ground that English supplies were so much cheaper there than they were up-country. To those who indulged in beer, liquors, hams, cheese and European goods generally, no doubt they were, but to the abstemious liver, contented with the produce of the country, Calcutta was no boon, so my father thought and felt.

Officers in former days used to be sent out as mere boys of fourteen or fifteen and kept in a place called Baraset, from whence they were despatched, in batches under the command of a senior officer, in boats as far as the nearest place to their respective stations. Reaching this, the officer in charge had to arrange for forwarding the boys by palkee dak to their destinations, the rest still continuing their journey by water till their own turn came—that is if their stations happened, as in most cases they did, to be inland. After a time, Government had to break up Baraset. These young boys, being congregated there in such numbers, became a terror to the native inhabitants round about, playing all sorts of pranks in the exuberance of their spirits and for want of something better to do, till at last Government had to listen to the many complaints.

The straw that broke the camel's back was the drowning of a poor native bill collector. The boys got hold of him and gave him what they meant to be a good ducking in a pond. Having fastened ropes round the poor fellow, they hauled him backwards and forwards from side to side until he was drowned. The boys were not only surprised, but terrified. None of them would peach on the real offenders, so they could not be punished, but Baraset was done away with and not too soon either, after which each officer, as he arrived, was sent up-country by himself, either by water or palkee dak. This last mode of travelling was by no means unpleasant. You could travel night and day if you chose, lying down or sitting up, reading a book or sleeping, just stopping at a dak bungalow for a bath and food and, if the time was your own, you could rest there during the heat of the day.

These dak bungalows were dotted along the Grand Trunk Road the whole way from Calcutta to the Upper Provinces, at a distance of ten miles apart, and were kept up at the expense of Government for the convenience of European travellers. All you paid for this great convenience was one rupee for a term of twenty-four hours or half that sum for three hours. Your food was extra, according to what you ordered. There was not much choice. A moorgee (fowl), or 'sudden death' as they were called, was cooked either as a curry, grilled or roasted. This, with rice kedgeree, dall, boiled eggs or an omelette, constituted a dak bungalow menu. By the by, an omelette is never cooked to such perfection anywhere as by an Indian cook, nor a grilled fowl either, better known to Europeans as Spatchcock, but even nowadays you cannot get the old-fashioned cookery done as well as it used to be. This primitive mode of cooking is nearly out of date.

Most assuredly, curries are no more the curries of former days either; there were at least a dozen different kinds then. It is no longer the fashion to eat curry at dinner in India, it is now purely a breakfast dish, and no Indian chef deigns to know of any variety. In my early days, curries were eaten three times a day, so cooks were necessarily good at variety. If any of my readers desire to taste a real, good Indian curry, get a Mohammedan woman to make one for you, only warn her not to make it too hot, for the English traveller does not consider it good manners to weep over his meals, especially just after giving thanks for what one is about to receive. I myself would not give much for a curry that was not cooked by a native woman, and I like it pretty hot too. There was a time when doctors put all ills connected with the liver down to hot curries, till one doctor with more sense than the rest discovered that red chillies, not black pepper, were very good for sluggish livers. As I am in a digressing mood, I may just as well tell you something of our thieves sixty years ago.

They were a somewhat unpleasant lot to meet alone anywhere. Thugs abounded through the length and breadth of the country. Though I am not aware of any Europeans having lost their lives through these highwaymen, they really were the terror of native travellers. In those days our sepoys[8] would never go to their homes in Oude singly, but generally in batches of fifty and sixty. Sepoys, like officers, were entitled to furlough of six months as their turn came round. When, as a boy of fourteen, fifteen, or sixteen, the Englishman left for India, he made up his mind not to see his home again for ten years at least, unless sent home on doctor's orders, on sick leave.

Furlough was only granted once in his lifetime after ten years' service. Then he was entitled to three years' leave from the time he left Calcutta, Bombay or Madras to his return to the port of embarkation, one year of which was spent on the sea, going and coming. Sepoys got their leave oftener, but only six months at a time. On these occasions they used to walk fifty or sixty in number, forty miles a night, never travelling by day, and so make the most of their leave with their relations and friends. Their leave commenced on 15th of April and lasted to 15th of October. Officers, too, could always have two months' privilege leave once a year during these months, and even six months on private urgent affairs, or without if their commanding officer considered they could be spared. Besides these privileges, they could often get also ten days' recreation leave all the year round.

To return to these Thugs, there were two species of this genus Homo.[9] One killed his victim for what he could get out of him, if only a few coppers, the other from religious motives. Thugs were all Hindus, and as such were full of superstitions. So the religious murderer considered, in taking the life of some lonely traveller, that he was pleasing his goddess Kali or Darree. She is the goddess of destruction, whether by sword or disease, and is blessed with six arms, each holding a weapon of destruction. Now the religious Thug, out of fear of her, had vowed to appease her wrath by taking the life of a certain number of persons every year, and this he did faithfully till Government took measures to catch and hang these good people. There used to be a highly respectable kuppra wallah (cloth merchant), who for nine months of the year used to go round from house to house amongst the Europeans showing off his goods, but was always absent the remaining three months. Naturally people believed he had gone to pay his family a visit, for the better class of native always keep their families in their village homes, and rarely if ever bring them into military stations. But one day he was caught carrying out his religious vow, and was tried and hanged.

The way these Thugs killed people was by means of a handkerchief with a coin about the size of a two shilling piece fastened in it. They looked out for a victim, probably some poor peasant going from one village to another some few miles away, who found himself suddenly waylaid by a neighbourly looking traveller who says, 'Brother, where are you going?' The poor man replies to such and such a village. 'Oh! I am going the same way, we will go together.' Upon which the unfortunate man knew his time had come. Nothing short of a bad omen could possibly save him. No sooner did the two reach a favourable spot for the crime than the poor man was garrotted and died without a struggle. The body was thrown into a thicket or well, and nobody ever heard anything more about it. Should a jackal, however, have appeared or howled on the right or left side of the road, I forget which, or an owl or a big bat fly out, then the man's life was spared, since all these were bad omens, and if ignored would have brought a curse on the Thug and his family.

By degrees these Thugs have been entirely exterminated. When caught, some of them would turn King or Queen's evidence and rope in a lot of their comrades. The one giving evidence would be sent to jail for life and end his days making jail carpets, the best in the world, whilst the rest were hanged.

There were also most expert thieves in former days, who would hover about a marching regiment, never showing themselves by day. These were closely shaved and oiled all over, so that if caught they could slip out of your grasp like eels. They always carried a deadly knife for self-defence, but their object was not so much murder as loot. On one occasion, I can't recollect on which especial march it was, the only other English lady in the regiment besides my mother was a Mrs Beckett. One dark night she awoke feeling very cold and found to her horror that she had no covering over her; not even her night garments were left, all had disappeared. In her confusion and distress she called out, 'Ayah, ayah! Bring a light, see what has happened.' The poor ayah discovered she also was without clothes. Thieves had entered the camp, in spite of the cordon of guards around it; but dark men on dark nights, without clothes, could easily creep in unobserved, which these rascals had done. There was always more than one man in this kind of thieving. One of the fellows would tickle the sleeper on the ear with a feather, who would then move and turn over to the other side, upon which they would draw out the clothes a little from under her. Then, giving her time to go off into a sound sleep again, they would repeat the trick until they had taken everything from her, leaving her without a scrap of clothes either about or on her person. When the ayah lit a light, judge of poor Mrs Beckett's feelings to find the thieves had deprived the children and herself of everything they possessed. The ayah took advantage of the dark night to creep into my mother's tent to wake up her ayah, telling her what had happened, and that her Memsahib had asked my mother to send her some clothes for herself and children, which of course she did at once, being most thankful no doubt that it had not happened to her. When Mrs Beckett appeared at the mess breakfast next morning, there was a shout of laughter. She was a great favourite, and joined in it, though at her own expense, for it was really too funny a sight for gravity and good manners. My mother's dress was too short by nearly a foot, for Mrs Beckett was an immensely tall woman and my mother the reverse.

Another time a thief got into my mother's tent and had packed up all our clothes into a bundle to carry off, but being alone had not attempted to do more. My mother awoke just in time and, fancying a dog was under the bed, called out to the ayah to turn it out. The man made his escape before he could be caught, leaving his knife under the bed, and all the clothes tied up ready to carry off the moment a favourable opportunity occurred.

Another set of thieves were cattle stealers, and these exist to this day. They would tie on to the fore hoofs of a horse or a cow a pair of native shoes, facing outwards, and another pair on the hind legs facing the opposite way, so that when they marched off with the stolen animal, it gave the appearance of travellers going both ways, which amongst hundreds of other shoe marks would have passed unobserved. As soon as they reached a ford, they would walk the animal across and, taking the shoes off, go on their way rejoicing.

River dacoits or pirates existed too in numbers, in those days, making a regular business of attacking boats moored alongside the banks. I believe these still exist, but as river traffic is greatly decreased, owing to railways, it cannot be so paying a trade as it used to be. My father's sister and a Miss Menzies were coming up by water some sixty years ago. They had no gentlemen with them. One night, just as they were going to bed, they heard a lot of music and tomtomming and asked the ayah what it meant. Neither could speak much Hindustani, but the ayah got them to understand it was a boatman's wedding. This quite put them off their guard. It was a beautiful moonlit night and my aunt was winding up her watch by it when the boat with the wedding party neared them and the robbers, for they were nothing less, jumped in. Miss Menzies, a very tall girl, put on her brother's hat, which she had brought out from England for him, thinking the presence of a gentleman would frighten the men, but there was no doubt the servants, with the exception of the ayah, were in league with the intruders. Finding she had failed in her attempt to intimidate them, she at once jumped overboard from the stern of the boat.

My poor little aunt, only four feet something tall, followed her example, and would have been drowned had it not been for the aid of Miss Menzies and the ayah, who were able to drag her out. These poor things passed the night in their wet night-clothes in an indigo field. At day-break the ayah was despatched to hunt up the indigo planter and his wife, who were most kind to them. The indigo planters of India are proverbially the most hospitable people to be found anywhere. A search was made afterwards for the boat, which had drifted down the river many miles. It was gutted of everything, with the exception of my aunt's watch, which she had put under her pillow. How it escaped their notice, no one knows, for they had even rolled up the mattresses to see if any valuables were concealed under them.

Before our regime in India, the native princes always punished thieves by cutting off one hand for the first offence and the remaining one if they were caught thieving a second time. I remember after I was married seeing a Hindu beggar with both hands cut off at the wrist. Upon asking him how it happened he said, 'Maharaja Ranjeet Singh (the last Punjabi emperor) ordered both my hands to be cut off, because I was caught stealing.' It was a summary way of punishing certainly, and no doubt was meant to be a deterrent in those lawless times; nevertheless it did not prevent thieving. My head carpenter, a Sikh, was telling me once what satisfaction the men of the Punjab enjoyed through our rule, since the conquest by the English of that vast country. His father, a handsome, long white-bearded old Sikh had told him how different it was in Ranjeet Singh's time, when no man's property was safe a day, not even his wife and daughters, 'whereas now', he said, 'you can walk about the length and breadth of the country, with your purse in one hand and only a stick in the other'.

This same man, in talking about the blessings of our rule, said he liked everything connected with it very much except one thing. I felt curious to hear what this one exception could be. He said, 'You teach our women to rebel against their husbands. If I find fault with my wife she says, "I will take you into court."' Does not this show that zenana teaching is sowing the seeds of women's rights even in India? Just imagine the audacity of a native woman in former days daring to threaten her lord and master to take him into court. Surely the world is moving.

But when this generation passes away, the next will know nothing of the days when their forefathers were under a very different rule, and then will be the time for wretched agitators, who are ever ready to poison the minds of contented people, to do their utmost by sowing the seeds of discontent, by their one-sided and distorted tales of our oppression compared to the happy times when they were ruled by their own people; indeed the last few months are proving this already. The poor Indian peasant can neither read nor write, but he can listen to and believe any amount of made-up lies, with the natural result of disaffection. I have lived long enough in India to know that the native character is not at present one to be governed by laws suited to the European, and therefore it is a mistake to make such laws for them. But the Englishman in England and the American in America who has not travelled abroad will not believe this; all I can say is let them go to India, stay there a year or so, and judge for themselves.

Having digressed already too long from the subject of Thugs, I will return to them. I said before there were two classes of this fraternity, one who killed for loot's sake and the other on religious principles, but both classes worshipped Kali or Darree. This goddess has a temple in Benares on the banks of the river Ganges, where you can see the idol with her six arms, and a European victim under her feet, showing that such are just as acceptable to her as one of her own race, if they only dared to kill them. But no Thug ever ventured to take the life of an European, for in the days when Thuggee was rampant in India, there were very few Europeans in the country, and these never had occasion to travel alone without some means of defence, such as a pistol or gun. Besides, killing an European in this sort of way would have been too hazardous; reward for the discovery of the murderer would soon have brought him to the gallows.

Until Oude, the King of Lucknow's territory, was annexed in '56, Thuggee existed in full force in this part of the North-West, but the English after the Mutiny soon dislodged them from their last remaining stronghold, and now there is not one single Thug left in the length and breadth of India, though there is still a Thuggee department, who are employed in looking after dacoits and other miscreants.

Towards the end of '39 my father left us by palkee dak to take up command of the 3rd NI, then in the Central Provinces.[10] I felt parting with him very much, but the excitement of going in a large ship (a great novelty to us children) made me forget the grief of parting with my parents sooner than I should otherwise have done.

I don't recollect much happening on that voyage till we reached Cape Town, when all the grown-up passengers went on shore, while we children remained on board. There was only one child older than myself, the others were all younger, many almost infants. These latter were being sent home with their ayahs in charge of the captain, on account of the deadly climate of Bengal.

Captain Hopkins of the old *Seringapatam*[11] was blessed with the soubriquet of the Bengal Ayah. He was so noted for his care of the little ones sent home in his charge that parents unable to accompany their children would entrust them entirely to him. My brother and sister and myself were placed under the care of Mrs Birch, an old friend of the family, who was taking home her own three children.

When we came to the Equator, Captain Hopkins called the older children to see the line through his telescope. We certainly did see a line distinctly but we did not know till afterwards how he had traded on our simplicity by fastening a hair across the lens. As usual in the evening, on crossing the line, there was great fun for all, both young and old, when Neptune came on board, trident in hand, tremendously got up, to tar and feather all who had not crossed the Equator before. We children were more or less frightened, till we found he only subjected the adults to this ordeal. The sailor lads who had not crossed before were all tarred and feathered, which caused great merriment. The passengers of course had already crossed the line on coming to India, so they got off, but were expected to do the generous thing and subscribe largely for extra grog for the crew, for which they were somewhat the worse the next morning, but as we were becalmed at the time and there was very little for them to do next day, it did not matter much. They danced and sang all night and had a really good time. Unfortunately the calm lasted so long that people's patience began to wear out, every day's delay making one less of their stay in England.

The Captain used to call us little ones and say, 'Now children, whistle for a wind.' We tried our best, but none of us knew how to whistle. So the long wished for cat's paw did not appear, but no sooner did the slightest breeze spring up than every sail was set in hopes of getting out of the becalmed latitude.

There was a man on board whom I disliked very much because he was always running after me to kiss me. I was getting to that age to feel shy at this kind of affection. He had a tremendous black beard, and how I used to hate that beard when it used to touch my face, and many a good pull did I give it in trying to extricate myself from his grip, but he didn't seem to mind it. At last one day Mrs Dampier, a very pretty woman on board, who was very kind to me, said, 'Next time you see him call out, "Whitelock, that beard of thine becometh thee not. It shall be shaved before thou are a day older."' The effect was perfect. I repeated the words with the same gestures as I had been taught. Everyone knew what was coming and applauded me and then screamed with laughter. No sooner had I repeated my lesson than I fled and hid myself behind Mrs Dampier's chair, after which he never looked at me unless with a withering scorn, much to my delight.

The vessel stopped at the Cape for three days to take in fresh provisions. Everybody went on shore, except the poor children, all the time longing to have a run on shore. It would have been a treat after being cooped up for so long, but children in those days had not much consideration shown to them for pleasures.

It is so long ago that I have quite forgotten what sort of a passage we had. Suffice it to say, it was a pretty long one.

We had on board a Colonel Colnett, who was very lame. He told us how he became so. Being one of the Baraset cadets, he was going up-country by water with a lot of young fellows, when as usual they all went out with their guns in search of sport, only expecting small game and thought themselves fortunate if they got that. Young Colnett began to linger behind, when suddenly an unlooked-for tiger pounced upon him and carried him off by his leg. Imagine the cool presence of mind of that young boy, not sixteen, to know that his only chance was to shoot the tiger through the heart, and this he had to do while being dragged on his back through the jungle. He took a long and steady aim, not daring to fire till sure of the result, and this with no revolver but a gun [rifle], a most difficult feat at such close quarters, as all sportsmen must acknowledge. He fired fortunately through the animal's heart, and there they both lay till search was made for him by all hands. When discovered, they found his poor knee so locked in the jaws of the dead brute that they had to break it before they could extricate him. It must have been a terrible wound, making him lame for life. Often did he say to us, 'Children, come and see the hole the tiger made in my knee', and our delight was to try and thrust our tiny fists into it.

The *Seringapatam* passed up the Channel in the beginning of April, and, as Mrs Birch's children were in Brighton, we left the old ship in a pilot boat and landed there. That night it blew pretty hard, at least so we imagined from the howling of the chimney up in the attic, where we were then sleeping. My brother was so frightened with the noise in the dark that I was obliged to get up and see where it came from. I groped my way to the fireplace and looked up the chimney, as it was evident the alarming sounds came from there. But how to stop them I did not know. At last, by what people call chance, I happened to touch something which made the damper fall, much to our comfort—I don't admit such a word as chance in anything.

After the necessary arrangements were made, we were sent off to London in the mail coach, all alone of course, the queerest lot of humanity one could wish to see. Our garments were of the time of Noah. My landing dress had been made out of a violet-coloured gown mother had brought out twenty-two years before, which I remember so well used to be shut up in a soldered tin box every year as soon as it got too warm for silks to be worn, and only brought out again the following October. This would not have been cut up for me, even then, but for my mother it was too antiquated to pass muster alongside of the latest fashions, brought out by my eldest sister. I had to get a smart dress to land in, so here was a grand opportunity to utilise the dear old gown.

It was not meant to have been opened on the voyage but I was so proud of my violet frock, a real silk one, that one unlucky day I could not resist the temptation of opening it to show it to Miss Forster, who thought it lovely too. When the time came, however, for dressing myself up in my finery, judge of my dismay when I opened the box to find the frock covered with sickly yellow patches right through. It resembled somewhat an unfortunate leper, but I had to wear it all the same. How I rued the day when I took it out in vanity, for vanity and exultation were at the bottom of the disaster. I do not recollect the bonnet I wore on that memorable day, for hats were not worn for many, many long years after that,[12] but my brother had a nondescript cloth coat, a cross between a tail coat and something else. I cannot well describe it, at this length of time, but his headgear capped everything. It was a tile-shaped one, with very elongated proportions and he was such a little fellow. My little sister's get-up I have quite forgotten. Well, we made our start in the world, as it were, with only one other passenger inside, a lady who asked us to change seats, as she did not like sitting with her back to the horses. Everything on the way was new and the journey, though a long one, passed pretty quickly to us.

At last we reached London Town, somewhere in the heart of the city, and we with our trunks were deposited in an open waiting room. It was quite dark when we arrived and we might as well have been three orphans as far as the world was concerned, so lonely did we feel. No one had come to meet us, so, as it was very cold, we crouched round the fire to keep ourselves warm. After a long time a portly lady, our family lawyer's wife, came waddling in, saying, 'Have any children come from Brighton by today's coach?' 'Yes, marm, there be three of 'em', pointing towards us. Mrs Pearce then came towards us, saying 'I suppose you are very tired my dears. We will soon be home now.' Then and there we were deposited in another vehicle and driven off to the old lawyer's house on St Swithin's Lane.[13] No sooner had we arrived than the whole family came to inspect us; my brother's hat and my dress caused a great sensation. Judging from their hilarity and pertinent remarks they certainly had much amusement at our expense.

We had not been in the house half an hour when we found my poor little brother was to be separated from us and packed off at once to Mr Beasley's school in Uxbridge near London, where my two elder brothers were. It was a moment of great consternation and grief, for though I used to say to him in his aggressive moods, 'I shall be so glad when you go to school and can't tease me any more', yet when the time came for him to go off so suddenly and unexpectedly we all wept in concert. Poor little fellow, I shall never forget his grief. It was hard upon the child, who had hitherto never been separated from us, to be torn away from those he loved, to go he knew not where. The reason for this apparently unkind treatment was that the Pearces had an entertainment the next day and there was no room in the house for him. I have learnt long since that English houses are not built so elastically as our own Indian homes, where we make room somehow or other for any amount of visitors, not only for friends but even for utter strangers, though, I am sorry to say, this kind of hospitality is dying out very fast, owing to so different a class of people coming out. But fifty or sixty years ago a perfect stranger could arrive in the night and the bearer would put him into the spare room, saying nothing about it till the morning, when his master was called for parade. Then, for the first time, the inmates of the house would be made aware that a strange Sahib had arrived by palkee dak and was sleeping soundly in the next room. At breakfast he would appear and introduce himself without much apology as Captain or Colonel so and so, on his way to join his regiment, probably some three or four hundred miles away. He was welcomed and made at home at once, being invited to stay as long as he liked.

I recollect, on one of these occasions, such a wayfarer, having run short of money, asked my father to lend him a hundred rupees. Without a word my father went and brought out a large brown canvas bag—such bags can hold a thousand rupees, but my poor father's own was never very full. He said, 'There, my dear fellow, take what you like.' And so he did. There was no thought of distrusting him, no counting out the money to see if he had taken any more than he had asked for and no note of hand or security taken. But in those palmy days there were no tramps wandering about the country; all were men who had nothing to gain by dishonesty, either officers in the army or covenanted civilians. The European community was a brotherhood of gentlemen, exiles in a foreign land. It is not so now when the country is full of globe-trotters and tramps of one kind or another, although a card of introduction will still open our doors to utter strangers, as in former days. To a bearer a white man is still a gentleman, unless in a private soldier's uniform. And even now, though to a lesser extent, a house meant to accommodate four people can be stretched in an emergency to accommodate double that number; beds will be improvised here and there at a moment's notice and all made welcome. I was very much struck in coming to the United States of America at the great want of this kind of hospitality. I thought it bad enough in England, but found it far worse in America.

After my little brother had been put into the train for Uxbridge, consideration was taken respecting my garments, for of course I could not appear in such a costume in the presence of their rich city friends. So Mary, the eldest daughter, was told off to take me to the shops and to fit me out in new clothes from head to foot. My delight was unbounded when Mary chose the daintiest pair of open-worked stockings and shoes for me. It was such a change for the better. Everything was lovely, being in keeping with the said stockings and shoes. My sister was not put into new garments that day, as she was too young to make her appearance before company. How well I remember that party. The aldermen's wives appeared in velvet turbans of all colours and were all more or less portly-looking dames. I was the centre of attraction as having just arrived from India. It was all so wonderfully strange to me. No animal in the zoo could have been more appreciated. I was asked a hundred questions about that far-off country, and had to speak Hindustani, which I did, though not satisfactorily to myself, for even in those few months I had forgotten many words.

At last it was time for me to retire, which I gladly did with the youngest daughter of the family, with whom I was to share a room. My sister Emily slept with an elder daughter at the very top of the house. I do not know if nowadays the City of London is still infested with as many cats as it was in 1840. All I know is that the caterwauling was something awful then. Poor little Emily used to relate her terrors to me every morning till she became more accustomed to these nightly family squabbles, for Indian jackals were nothing to it. I do not believe anyone who has not slept in an attic room in the heart of the City of London can imagine what it was like in those days.

Our first year in England was spent happily enough. We were not overburdened with study. My many years' savings of pocket money in India were all invested in a lovely baby wax doll and materials for clothing it. One day I was allowed to take it out wrapped up in a shawl. It looked very like a baby I must say, so it was not very surprising that several people thought it one. To my great delight I heard one old gentleman exclaim, 'What a shame to allow a child to carry an infant through these crowded streets', for in 1840 the city streets were not as they are now. It was almost impossible to wend one's way through them. In some places we had to wait half an hour before daring to cross over to the opposite side. On that occasion I came home perfectly elated with the thought that my doll had been mistaken for a real baby.

On account of the streets being so crowded we were generally sent out with a servant for a walk over the iron bridge and back, where we had to pay a toll per head of either a halfpenny or a penny, but sometimes as a great treat we were taken to the West End. In those days it meant either taking a cab or walking, so it was always the latter with us, and meant a day's outing, with buns for lunch. We thought it glorious fun looking into all the shops.

Then came the time for the family to go to Margate for six weeks or so. Mrs Pearce, her three daughters and our two little selves went by steamer. The father and two sons used to come down on the Saturday boat, returning on the Monday. It was all holiday there. The first thing to do was to go off sea bathing. I shall never forget that day of mental suffering. The girls hired a bathing machine and we all went joyfully into it and undressed ourselves. Mary took charge of me, but she gave me a good ducking and left me flounder-ing in the water. They who could swim thoroughly and were in water up to their necks enjoyed my discomfiture. In mortal fear I clung to the screen of the machine, with my whole body dangling beyond, till at last I could hold on no longer and promptly dis-appeared. Mary then got frightened and swam out after me, and just caught me in time as I was sinking, otherwise I certainly must have been drowned. It gave me such a shock that nothing would induce me to go in again. When they used to try to force me I used to cry my heart out with terror till Mrs Pearce, who was a kind old soul, took my part saying, 'If the child doesn't like sea bathing (she should have said sea drowning) it will do her no good, leave her alone.' From that time I was allowed to paddle about and enjoy myself in my own way, but never again could they entice me into a machine. To this day even I am afraid of going out in a boat.

While we were in Margate all kinds of German bands used to serenade us, and usually got rewarded if they were worth listening to. I recollect there was one singer dressed as a boy. They all vowed she was a girl from her figure. She used to go about with a man who played the piano and used, with a beautiful voice, to sing 'Long, long ago'. I can't forget the tune or singer, for she had a lovely young face. And then there was a man of the name of Scott who performed some wonderful feats. One was to throw himself off the yard-arms of a brig lying out in the harbour. An immense crowd used to collect to see his performance. He never seemed quite happy, judging from the time he took in making up his mind to give the leap.

On the 9th of November 1840, we were taken to see the Lord Mayor's Show and were delighted with the display of grand carriages, specially the gilt one, in which sat the Queen and the Prince Consort.

The Pearces being in touch with all the city magnates, we had a splendid view from one of the windows in an alderman's house. I thought the Queen very beautiful and was highly flattered when Mrs Pearce used to show me off to her friends as resembling her so wonderfully. I suppose I must have been so as a child, as so many people were agreed on the subject. Even Lord Nugent, brother of the Duke of Buckingham, a great friend of my aunt's, endorsed the opinion. And later on, when I was coming out in the P & O as a girl of seventeen, I recollect hearing two officers who had come on board at Madras saying, 'Hello, we have Queen Vic on board.' Whatever there might have been, certainly there was no resemblance later on.

While we were at Mrs Pearce's an awful murder took place in London, the thought of which haunted me for many months and filled my mind with unspeakable terror. Lord John Russell,[14] a very old man (ninety if I recollect rightly), had his throat cut by his Swiss valet of the name of Courvoisier. The valet tried to put it on to the housemaid but was convicted and hanged. The lawyer who took up his case had to quit England for having said, 'As God is my judge I believe my client to be innocent', when he knew all along that he was guilty, having made him confess the deed and show him the knife he had done it with. Of course being in a lawyer's house I heard of little else while the trial was going on, which made such an impression on my mind that I even look back upon it with horror.

St Swithin's Lane is a particularly narrow one, so much so that when a large cart passed through it we had to flatten ourselves against the wall of a house to prevent ourselves being crushed to death. The Pearces' house, a beautiful one for those days, was a common one. The back windows looked on to a large hall called the Salters' Hall, where we once went to see a grand banquet laid out.[15] All the plates and dishes were of gold, so they told us. There were some huge hothouse pineapples, real beauties, which brought back the memory of my home in India. These had cost twelve shillings a pound, and our Indian ones not more than a halfpenny, but things have changed since then, even the price of pineapples.

The Pearces' youngest son, sixteen years old and six foot high, fancied himself in love with me. I hated him so, for he always smelt of Gregory's mixture,[16] being apprenticed to a chemist, and used to

drink every evening sixteen cups of tea, which ended in his dying
some years later, not from strong tea, but strong liquor. I have
always maintained tea drinking is incipient drinking after all. I have a
daughter who declares she can't get out of bed without her cup of tea,
because without it she gets a headache for all the day. So says the
drunkard!!!

The Pearces used to dine on Sundays in the middle of the day, all
the family together, with Mary's fiancée, a Mr Woolley (with a very
woolly head of hair) as one of the party. This Sunday early dinner
always ended in a violent argument and a quarrel. The husband and
wife would not speak to each other for days after. Mary and her
young man quite dreaded these Sundays, after which every day you
would hear Mr Pearce say to his daughter Louisa, 'Ask your mamma
if she will have some of this.' In her turn Mrs Pearce would say to
Jane, 'Ask your papa if he will have some of this', till the quarrel was
made up. So that, child as I was, I used to say to myself, 'When I
grow up and get married, I will allow no arguing at my table.' It gave
me such a horror of it.

The first fall of snow, just before Christmas, was a novel sight to
us, born and brought up in the plains of India. We used to scream
with delight as one flake larger than another came slowly down.

They had a Christmas party on the 24th of December. Poor Mr
Pearce caught cold that night and died three days later from ery-
sipelas in the head, and Louisa, who was very fond of her father, got
typhus fever from kissing him when she had been forbidden to do so.
It was the first death I had ever seen and never can I forget it. Louisa
lay between life and death for a long time, but eventually recovered.
Poor Mrs Pearce was very cut up at her husband's death. How much
she must have regretted those silly Sunday quarrels. We should be
very careful how we say unkind things to those we love most, for to
have to think of them when the dear one is gone must be very
dreadful.

Early in the spring my aunt, Mrs Raine, came to see us. She and
my uncle, Captain Raine of HM's 96th, had just returned from the
Ionian Islands, where they had been quartered for some years. It
appears my father had asked the Pearces, whose firm of lawyers had
been my grandfather's legal advisers, to receive us until his sister had
returned from Greece, so this visit of hers was purely one of
inspection, to see what sort of children we were. She seemed a

charming woman with great conversational powers and rather attracted me, so when the time came for my sister and myself to go to Birmingham, we did not apprehend anything but a pleasant future. It was arranged that we should leave London in March for Birmingham, where my uncle, who had now retired on half pay from the service, held two military appointments.[17] It was the first time that we had seen a railroad. Everything was new, including the countryside, and we thoroughly enjoyed the journey, but alas it was about the last thing we did enjoy for years to come. My aunt, one of the old school, was some thirty years of age and had married at sixteen to spite another lover. They had had six children but all had died at birth. What would children of the present day, specially American ones, say to such hard bringing up?

The first twelve months we lived in lodgings, and I had to be down punctually at six o'clock summer and winter at the piano. I had no talent for music, though very fond of it. My aunt's theory was, 'You must learn what you don't like, for you will teach yourself what you do.' Oh, what a mistake. I had four hours a day at the piano, and the day I left Birmingham I made a vow I would never play any more, which vow I kept. After my turn at the piano came my little sister Emily's turn, whilst I learnt my lessons till breakfast time, which consisted of water and hunks of bread with a little butter.

As my uncle and aunt lived in lodgings in the town before they went into housekeeping, we children were sent for two hours every day, Sunday included, to the cemetery for our daily walk. It was a safe place for children, being in those days out in the country. There we played about till it was time to return home. This cemetery at that time was a new one, with comparatively new graves all kept in lovely order, full of flowers, so in that way it was a nice place for us to run about in, though at the same time a particularly trying one. Funeral after funeral used to come in, principally of children, parents weeping as they followed their darling ones to the grave. This was always too much for us. Seeing their grief, we wept bitterly too, so that our daily outing was not one of unalloyed pleasure. Probably it did some good, inasmuch as that both my sister and myself grew up with very sympathetic natures, and to this day I can honestly say that other people's troubles become my own, which I attribute greatly to that early training amongst the graves.

Harriet and Robert Tytler.

'Under the Tope'. Illustration by Mr Lundgren for W. H. Russell's *My Diary in India, in the year 1858–1859*. A regiment on the march halts for breakfast.

A houseboat on the Ganges at Benares. From a sketch by Prince Alexis Soltykoff in the *Illustrated Times*, 1858.

'Sick and Wounded in Doolies'. Illustration by Mr Lundgren for W. H. Russell's
My Diary in India. Harriet crossed most of the 900 miles from Calcutta to the Hills
by palkee dak (or doolie) on her return from England.

'My Gharree'. Illustration by Mr Lundgren for W. H. Russell's *My Diary in India*.
The Tytlers escaped from Delhi in their gharree.

The Residency, Lucknow, 1858. Photograph by Robert and Harriet Tytler.

The Chatter Mazil, Lucknow, one of the palaces of Wajid Ali Shah.

As soon as my uncle and aunt took a house of their own with a nice garden, it was no longer necessary to send us out into the country, as we could have enough exercise and fresh air within the garden walls. My aunt was horribly strict with us and really cruel in many ways. In the first place we were never allowed a fire through the whole winter. The piano was in the drawing room, which was never inhabited unless visitors were expected, and as my aunt was very exclusive, there were naturally very few of these in a manufacturing town. I had to be down summer and winter at six o'clock, clad in a low-necked, short-sleeved print dress all the year round. The only difference in the winter was that we were allowed to wear a small plaid shawl round our shoulders. This was all we had, whether out of doors or indoors, but after all both were about the same temperature. I was allowed no candle to practise by, although it is pitch dark at that hour nearly six months in the year as far north as Birmingham. This without a fire and every finger covered with chilblains. What torture I went through! My first hour at the piano was devoted to chords and scales. The first chord I struck always caused the chilblains at the root of the fingers to burst and bleed, when I had to bring out my handkerchief and wipe off the blood from the keys before continuing my practice.

At eight o'clock breakfast was on the table, and if it was not raining or snowing we had to take a plate full of bread and butter, such as I described before, with a glass of water, and go forth into the garden, place our plates under a favourite pear tree, and then begin our morning run round the garden, which we had to do for exercise, i.e. health's sake, fifty rounds three times a day, making four and a half miles of running daily. As soon as we finished one hunk of bread, we dived down whilst running, like an eagle on its prey, and picked up another. Sometimes I had the audacity to complain that the hunks were so large that I could not bite into them, but my aunt's invariable reply was, 'Well then, try the other side', but as they were square it did not mend matters much. In the bitter frosty weather, we would sometimes shrug up our shoulders under the plaid shawl, hoping to get a little extra warmth by so doing, when my aunt would tap from one of the windows, to signify that we had been caught in the very act of so heinous an offence, and down went our poor shoulders again. We were never allowed to speak to a servant except to say 'Good morning' and 'Thank you', though we had to pass through the kitchen to go to the schoolroom many times during the day, the said schoolroom being only a laundry over the coach-house at the end of a long yard. We used to learn our lessons there, of course without a fire, and do our drawing and mend our stockings, but we had to say our lessons in the dining-room with a roaring fire and our shawls off. As soon as that was through, back we went to the laundry, now honoured with the name of schoolroom.

During the winter months we spent our evenings in the dining-room, for economy's sake, the saving of a tallow candle being a consideration. As the clock struck eight, summer and winter, both of us went to bed. In the winter we had to break the ice in our jug to wash our faces with and our unfortunate chilblainy hands. Poor wretched children. I tell you there was no water wasted. But on Saturday nights we were allowed a hot bath, a real treat.

Though we were forbidden to speak to the servants, I often disobeyed orders, when I thought I was safe out of my aunt's hearing, saying, 'Tell me Charlotte, what sort of a humour is my aunt in this morning?' The reply usually was, 'Lar miss, she is in an awful bad temper.' This information used to fill my heart with terror, and bring me down to the dining-room trembling, where I would stand for several minutes, before I could summon sufficient courage to enter. Certainly my aunt had a most disagreeable way of showing it on all occasions. I recollect a new servant girl coming into her service, on a month's trial, but she took such a dislike to my aunt that she made a point of breaking a favourite piece of furniture every day, till my aunt was tired of replacing it and let her go in a fortnight.

Another time, I was passing through the kitchen, when my aunt was pitching into the cook. When I heard her say, 'Really mum, you are the greatest worrit I ever came across', of course I knew what she meant, but I thought I would give myself the pleasure of asking and said in a very innocent tone of voice, 'What did the cook mean by saying you were the greatest worrit?' She could see I knew perfectly well what she meant, and pitched into me most unmercifully for daring to ask such a question. She would usually upbraid us for nothing at all, but if we did commit the smallest offence, it brought forth, 'You bold little hussy', which I looked upon as the most revolting abuse. Her principle was never to give a word of praise. I believe she meant all for the best and thought praise might fill us with conceit. My poor little sister, having more of a timid nature than myself, was completely crushed by her. We often used to lock ourselves in each other's arms and sob ourselves to sleep.

My aunt never gave us a holiday as a rule, except the afternoons of Saturday, which after all was no holiday as it was spent in mending our clothes. On one of these said holidays she came up to the schoolroom only to find fault, and made my passionate temper so mad that as she went out of the room I banged the door after her with all my might. Of course back she came and said, 'Did you do that?' I replied in a very decided tone of voice, 'I did.' Upon which she caught me and thumped me down the stairs, each time nearly prostrating me on my nose. She continued this thumping till we reached the dining-room. There she sat me down on the stool of repentance and said, 'You shall not leave that seat until you beg my pardon on your knees!' Well I sat there for I can't say how long, determined never to say I was sorry, 'because', I argued with myself, 'it would be a lie, for I am not sorry'. She went on with her writing and I with my cogitations until I said to myself, 'Now Harriet, which is the best, tell a lie and get out of the sight of that hateful face, or stay here till I die', which I should have had to do with such an aunt. So at last I gave in and begged her pardon, all the time saying to myself, 'God knows I don't mean it', which at all events was true, and then left her to fly back to the schoolroom, where my sister met me with an exclamation of terror: 'Oh Harriet! How could you do such a thing? I have been so frightened. I thought aunt would have killed you!'

'Killed me?' I replied. 'No! But she made me tell a lie for I was not a bit sorry, though to get out of her hateful presence I did say so!'

Poor little Emily, we could not have been more unlike in our natures, I passionate, she gentle and sweet.

Once, my brother Edward was allowed to come on a visit for a fortnight, the only holiday we ever had, and the only time we even met. One day he went out and bought a quantity of cakes, tartlets —enough to have lasted us for ever so many days. Well, we ate a good lot before our dinner of cold mutton was due and naturally couldn't eat much of that detestable food, so my aunt suspected something and came up stealthily to the schoolroom and found our treasures. She never made a remark, but took the whole lot into her own room, and we never saw them again. My brother was furious with indignation, saying what right had she to take the cakes he had bought with his own money, not hers, for we certainly had none of our own; but she was a hard-hearted, cruel woman. Such treatment of us in America would have soon brought her to her senses, where children are not allowed by law to be cruelly treated.

When we went to have our music lesson in Edgbaston, one of the servants used to take us there and the other bring us back. On one occasion, as the cook had taken us, we naturally expected Ann the housemaid would have come for us as usual. Not so—the cook came again. On enquiring what was the reason for it, we found poor Ann had become very ill. It appears she was dusting the wardrobe in my aunt's bedroom when she suddenly fell in a kind of fit. My aunt, on hearing the thump on the floor, rushed up to see what had happened, and there she found the poor girl, almost unconscious, lying all of a heap on the floor. When we came home, as we passed her bedroom, which we had to do to go to our own to take off our things, I went up to her to wish her better, but she made no reply. My aunt never sent for a doctor but, seeing that she did not get better by the evening, put her in a cab and sent her home to her father and mother. Poor people, they got in a young surgeon, who at once saw what was the matter and said she must undergo a small operation. The poor girl was a modest young thing and wouldn't hear of it. Consequently she died the next morning.

The next day her old father, an Irishman by the name of Barry who had been a soldier in my uncle's regiment, interviewed my uncle and cursed my aunt up hill and down dale in the most awful manner, but my aunt never knew of it, as my uncle had forbidden my saying a word about it to her.[18]

I was so fond of happiness, and finding it in no other way used to get up in the lovely summer mornings at two o'clock sometimes, humming a tune while dressing with joy at the thought of the few hours' enjoyment I was going to have, either in drawing, doing fancy knitting or playing with my baby doll, which I did till I was seventeen. Just imagine girls of the present day doing such babyish things, but recollect that this was nearly sixty years ago. Since then the world has moved and girls of seventeen are women now. My dear little sister would on these occasions put her head out from under the bedclothes and say, 'Oh Harriet, don't sing before breakfast or you will be sure to cry before night.' The foreboding was so true that my spirits immediately fell below zero and did not rise again in a hurry.

My uncle was an invalid and lived upon chops principally. The servants were on bread, whilst my aunt had dainty little dishes cooked for herself, but we two children had cold mutton the whole week, finishing the Sunday's roast on the following Saturday. Never a soup, a pudding or fruit all the year round, though my uncle used quietly to give us some apples occasionally, but we were told not to tell my aunt. She used to insist upon our eating the cold mutton fat, which both of us abhorred. Poor Emily sat next to her on her right. I sat next to my uncle on his left, on the same side of the table as my sister. I used to get off eating the fat by watching my aunt. When I saw her busy eating, I would drop my fat into my handkerchief, which was laid out on my lap ready for such contributions, never caring whether my uncle saw me or not, for I knew he would never tell upon me. But Emily was too near my aunt and had to devour the fat as best she could, generally by trying to swallow too large a piece at a time and nearly choking on the spot, whereupon my aunt would fly at her and declare that her proper place was with the pigs and that she was not to do that again. However, poor Emily would try the same experiment over and over again in hopes of better success, each time failing just the same. Anyhow, it ended in my making a vow on leaving England in '45 that I would never touch a piece of cold mutton again as long as I lived, which vow has never yet been broken.

I recollect on one occasion bullying this dear little sister till I made her cry, when I felt very ashamed of myself and soliloquized again, 'Now Harriet, if Emily could have given you back as much as you gave her, you would have been too great a coward to have bullied her and made her cry as you did.' And, truly, I was ashamed of myself and went up to her and begged her pardon and kissed her many times over saying I would never do so again, and indeed I never did. I don't know to this day what devilry made me do it, for I was very fond of her and always have been.

My only happiness was looking forward the whole week for Tuesday to come round, that I might go to my drawing class for three hours. While there I left all my sorrows behind and was really in a small heaven for the time being. My master, Mr Everett, who kept an art shop in New Street and held his classes on the floor above, said, on one occasion, quite loud before the other girls who were all older than myself, 'Miss Earle is my best pupil.' That was a proud day for me.

When I came home I did not dare tell my aunt what he had said, but kept my joy to myself. Whether my face betrayed the exultation within I cannot say, but my aunt said, 'What did Mr Everett think of your drawing today?'

I hummed and hawed and, hanging my head down like a culprit, ventured to say in a very humble tone, 'Oh! Aunt, he said I was his best pupil', upon which she ordered me to bring down my drawing and show it to her.

On seeing it, she gave a grunt and threw it across the room, saying, 'Take it away, I never saw anything so badly done!'

I am afraid it had not the desired effect. However, I had received the praise and no words of hers could deprive me of it.

In spite of causing us so much misery, my aunt did have her good points. She brought us up on honour. We would have as soon thought of breaking our word as of flying. For instance, we were on our honour to run fifty rounds of the garden each time, and if it was raining to skip with a rope in the schoolroom one thousand times instead. This we did to the letter, always exceeding it for fear of any mistake in counting. Then she would sometimes, but very rarely, send us with a note to a friend in Edgbaston, saying, 'Now children, you promise on your honour that you will not turn your heads to the right or to the left, but go straight there and back.' This we did, though our eyes used to be everywhere, like a chameleon turning around as far as they would go, but never once did we turn our heads. She had instilled into our minds that a promise was a most sacred thing, once made, never to be broken. What a pity that the present generation have not a little of this training.

Once there was a likelihood of our being sent to a boarding school. I even went with my aunt to see it, and walked about the grounds from whence I could see the other boarders peeping out at me. But alas it was too good to come to pass and my aunt changed her mind. It was a great blow to my hopes for I longed for the companionship of girls of my own age (my sister being so much younger) and for freedom out of prison, for such was our home in Camden Hill. So miserable was my life that I determined twice on running away, both times when I was fifteen. Thank God for his mercies that I never got beyond the bottom of our lane. I begged of my sister to accompany me, but she was too frightened and began to cry, imploring of me not to go. My mind however was made up. My idea was to sell my trinkets to pay my railway fare to London, and then to go to the Pearces and beg of them to send me back to my parents in India. The idea was preposterous; my trinkets would not probably have brought in five shillings, and I would have found myself stranded in one of the most wicked cities at that time in England, and God only knows what my fate might have been. The thought of offending my dear old father and never receiving his pardon brought me back, however. Emily was overjoyed, but I cannot say I felt happy at doing so, for I longed to get away.

When I reached sixteen my spirits revived for I knew then that I should only have one more year to wait, so I tore up 365 pieces of paper and strung them together and hung them up on a nail in the schoolroom. Every day I pulled off one and counted the remainder to the very end. At last my seventeenth birthday arrived. I remember it was the most miserable one of my life. A little boy about eleven years old, by the name of Guest, sent me as a present Milton's *Paradise Lost*. He, and his elder brother who was about my own age, used to go to the same dancing school. I had only talked with them now and again in a quadrille or so, so that when the book arrived I firmly believed it had come from the old father, who was a stationer and knew my uncle and aunt slightly. Accordingly I wrote a letter by my aunt's dictation to thank him for it. Back came a reply from the old gentleman saying he had not sent it, but that his little boy had. That was enough! I was accused of duplicity and of having carried on a flirtation with him unknown to her, and that I knew perfectly well that he had sent it. All I could say to the contrary was of no use. At the time she was showing me how to pack my box and all the time she kept on nagging at me and lecturing me on the heinousness of my offence. I wept very bitterly; tears of indignation at being doubted flowed down my cheeks and many a one dropped into my clothes. Her nagging continued unabated till she heard my uncle's footsteps on the stairs (he having just returned from his office), and, knowing he would be terribly hurt at seeing me in tears on my last birthday, she ordered me to stop crying at once, and to go and wash my face and not let my uncle see I had been crying. But all the washing wouldn't bring down the swollen eyes to their natural condition. He said nothing before her, but asked me afterwards what it was all about. I know he was vexed at her unkindness in making my last birthday under their roof a very unhappy one. The sight of that book was hateful to me ever afterwards and I never would read it. *Paradise Lost* has been a sealed book to me ever since.

Two days later, my uncle, my aunt and myself went up to town to complete my wardrobe, and to show how hard my aunt's nature was, she wouldn't take my poor little sister along with us too, and give her the treat of seeing London Town, and going about with us shopping, but left her behind with the servants, with strict injunctions not to speak to them more than was actually necessary. I don't know how she could have done it, it quite marred my happiness at leaving that home for ever. Fortunately Emily was of a more placid nature and perhaps did not feel it so much as I did. She was glad no doubt in one respect to have a fortnight's respite from everlasting bullying. Had I know then that after all it would not be for years that she would be there, it would have somewhat comforted me.

I was to have come out to India under the charge of some responsible person, but no friend of mother's could be heard of just at that time, so I was to go out alone. From London we went down by train to Southampton. One of the officials of the P & O company was there to see the steamer off.[19] He was a great friend of my uncle's and told him that Captain Moresby's wife and daughter would be on board; they were going to join him at Suez.[20] My aunt thought this was a grand opportunity and proposed to put me under her care. Mrs Moresby had a very pretty daughter, a girl of sixteen, going out with her and was kind enough to say that she would take charge of me to Calcutta, so I was placed under her care. The time now came for the vessel to leave her moorings, the bell rang and all was ready. My uncle, who looked upon me as his daughter, for I was just the age his eldest girl would have been had she lived, was weeping bitterly. My aunt too was distressed, I don't for a moment suppose at parting with me, but probably for his sake. I tried hard to cry and would have given anything not to appear so heartless, but alas! not a tear would come. The joy within at going home to my father and mother was too great for hypocrisy, so that I could not even squeeze out a tear. My poor uncle was led away between my aunt and Mr Lovell in an agony of sorrow.

Soon, too soon, I myself was to shed bitter tears and know what real sorrow was. Tears flow from many causes and each cause has a grief of its own. None but those who have gone through the loss of a much loved parent, a child or a husband can know the difference of each grief. Tears from pain, anger or disappointment are also all different in depth of suffering, so that I maintain that even the most sympathetic nature, though it can grieve for other people's troubles, can never really know what each one is suffering, unless they themselves have gone through that very phase of the heart's agony. It is so with everything. Can the Queen of England or the Tsar of Russia know what the pangs of hunger are, or, still worse, those of thirst? They imagine they can. Can anyone feel the agony of being crucified or tortured, but the poor victim who has undergone it? Does the doctor know the suffering of his patients, when he has never had his own leg amputated or gone through the slow torture of cancer? Can those who have not highly strung natures understand the sufferings of those who have? Unless they know all this by personal experience, I maintain they cannot do so. Hence we are so often misjudged—our deeds, our actions, our motives, our very thoughts, are misunderstood by persons who are of a different temperament. Thank God He who made us will know, and judge us accordingly.

I suppose with the exception of Mrs Moresby, her daughter and myself, there was not another passenger amongst the 260 on board who had not someone to regret that they were leaving behind, but as soon as we had fairly started, the band struck up a lively tune, as it does after a soldier's funeral, to make each one forget the past. No doubt it had the desired effect on some, for I was asked by a young fellow—a perfect stranger of course—to give him the honour of a dance. Imagine my astonishment—I who had been snubbed on all occasions by my aunt and told, as I was not good-looking (in other words decidedly ugly), that I must try and make up for it by extra pleasant manners—finding myself not too ugly for a dance, and that I was asked for it as an honour! Believe me I accepted the offer gratefully and away we went, round and round the deck. After that I never wanted for a dance and was truly happy in every way, except when I thought of my little sister Emily; then a deep shadow would hang over me for a time.

The dancing stopped and we all went down to dinner. That too I enjoyed, after my aunt's cold mutton fare. I am afraid people must have wondered at my appetite. The P & O were remarkable for their princely tables in those days, but recollect they charged £150 and

£153 (2,250 rupees according to our present rate of exchange) respectively for a gentleman's and lady's first-class passage. Wine of the very best was provided ad lib. at meals. There was such waste in everything. I have seen the stewards pouring good whisky into blacking bottles to clean the boots with. Champagne flowed like water on Thursdays and Sundays at dinner. On these occasions I took especial care as to whom I danced with, for half the young fellows were much the worse for it. To see the airs these boys gave themselves, who had probably never even tasted champagne in their lives before. One, then another and then yet another, would call out, 'Steward, take this bottle away, it is corked.' The waste went on till competition came in the way and rates had to be reduced to £60—a good thing too for teetotallers, who always felt the hardship of paying for other people's liquor.

On one of these champagne occasions I was talking to a young fellow (he must be a general now, if still living) who I observed was rather queer. I longed to get away from him, but did not know how to do so without hurting his feelings, when Miss Moresby came up to us and I introduced him to her and left. Very mean I know! In due course of time the bell rang for tea and we all went down, but the two I had left together.

Later on, she dashed downstairs, and as she passed me she whispered that she was engaged to the handsomest man on board. On asking who that could be, she replied, 'Mr Traherne.'

'Why,' I exclaimed, 'you never knew him before!'

'No,' she answered, 'but he proposed to me and I have accepted him.'

Though I was only seventeen, it struck me as a rather strange proceeding. Next morning Miss Moresby got up very early to meet her young man, but no young man was there. All day long she looked for him in vain, and the next day too with similar disappointment. On the third day he met her on the stairs and passed on as if they had never met before. Poor girl, I can imagine her mortification. I found out afterwards that when he sobered down, he recollected what had happened and confided to one of his friends, saying, 'What am I to do? I don't want to marry the girl', and the other advised him to keep out of her way for two or three days and, when he did see her again, to simply ignore her. This he did, and so ended that little boardship episode.

Our principal amusements, I mean amongst the boys and girls, were dancing twice a day and playing cards—old maid and suchlike games—in the evening. Of course there was the usual amount of seasickness in the Bay of Biscay, while we were strangers to each other, but as soon as we reached Gibraltar[21] everybody forgot their sorrows and troubles, and all were ready to enjoy themselves. What a happy day that was for me. We went to the land and there I saw dear old friends, flowers that were so familiar to me in India, besides geraniums and roses growing in profusion. I gathered a large bouquet and no one stopped me. The pretty Spanish girls with their lace mantillas, high combs and fans pleased my fancy. I thought everything lovely. That day was a seventh heaven to me. We were introduced to some of the officers belonging to the garrison, who invited the Moresbys and myself to tea and to see the fortifications. Of course we accepted, and went and saw everything that could be seen, and returned quite late, after the gates were locked, the officers who had invited us accompanying us, and seeing us safely out and into our boats. I think one or two of them lost their hearts to Miss Moresby, she was really sweetly pretty. I too had my share of their gentlemanly attentions, and was quite sorry to part with such good company.

We only reached the steamer just as she was ready to start. I firmly believe we had kept her waiting. Mrs Moresby, being the wife of the senior captain in the line, had privileges the other passengers could not boast of, so nothing was said. The next morning I had a huge basket of the most lovely fruit sent to me by a Major Fraser, who went by the name of 'Long Fraser';[22] he was either six foot five or six foot seven and had lost the use of one of his hands whilst fighting back to back with two other officers in the first Afghan campaign. I believe they behaved most pluckily, the whole three, all more or less frightfully wounded. Major Fraser told me he lost the use of his hand through a sabre cut inflicted by a dead man, who in the act of falling back dead, sword in hand, happened to hit him on the wrist. As I said, this officer went by the name of Long Fraser. Of course the ordinary berth was not long enough for him, so they actually opened out a part of the partition into the berth of the next cabin for his long legs. I don't know if he had to pay for two berths, instead of one, but if he had, those legs of his cost him dearly. It was always surprising to me, why he sent me this lovely fruit, for he was rather a woman-hater than otherwise. Except that I was such a child compared to the other girls of my age, that probably he thought as a child I would appreciate them.

I don't recollect much of our stay in Malta[23] except that I bought a canary and three gold Maltese cross-pins, one each for my father, uncle and brother. I was sending off my uncle's one from Alexandria, when I found all three had been stolen as well as a black poplin gown of mine. I could have cried with vexation. We had an extra stewardess on board, who was going out to join another vessel. Some of the ladies knew this Mrs Henderson, having travelled with her before, and pointed her out as the thief as so many things had been missed before. The poplin gown and my letters, which were also missing, turned up, but the crosses were never seen again.

When we reached Alexandria, we went to Shepheard's Hotel[24] and from there went to see all the sights, Cleopatra's Needles (there were three of them), Pompey's Pillar and some of the palaces. The bazaars were very familiar to me, being so like our Indian ones, but I was disgusted with the amount of flies and surprised at the apathy of the Egyptians, who allowed dozens of them to cluster in the eyes of their children, even in those of little infants, without any attempt to dislodge them; the children too were utterly callous. Not surprising then that nearly every second person we met had lost one eye, even both sometimes, from opthalmia, a very catching disease, carried from one eye to another by these pests. All the plagues of Ancient Egypt are still to be found in the modern one.

In the early days of the Peninsular and Oriental Company's steamers, we had to travel from Alexandria to Cairo by boats up the Nile. A steamer, and another large boat towed by it, used to carry all the passengers to their destination. This was a very enjoyable trip. Here I met with another vexation. While sitting on the deck of the boat, I saw a little canary fly out and settle on the sandy bank. I called out, 'Do you see that? Can it be my bird?' I immediately ran down to see if it was. A young civilian out of pure mischief had let it go. I won't mention his name, for though he himself was killed at Cawnpore in the Mutiny of '57, yet some of his relatives, my dearest friends, are still alive. I know he was thoroughly ashamed of himself. Though he tried to laugh it off as a good joke, he could see however that I was of a very different opinion, and I was determined he should know it too, never having anything to do with him again. It was such an unmanly thing to do on his part, to let a poor girl's pet bird loose. True I had not had it very long, but I valued it, being my very own and the first I had ever had. It was cruel too to let it go in such a desert place.

I saw very little of Cairo. Those who had time to go on to the Pyramids of course did so, but Mrs Moresby, being most anxious to join her husband, managed somehow to be chosen for the first lot of carriages to cross the desert. Everyone else had to take their chance by lots. Six carriages holding six persons each were sent off to start with, then some hours later another batch of six went off and so on till the last set were provided with conveyances. These last ones had of course the worst time of all. Many of their horses died on the road from sheer exhaustion and ill treatment, adding more skeletons to the heaps already there. However, we were amongst the first lot, and reached Suez in due course. I do not now recollect whether it was eighteen or twenty hours that we took doing the eighty miles, all I do remember is that it was an awful journey. I sat next to a very nice young fellow, a tea taster going to China,[25] who, with Mrs Moresby and her daughter and Colonel and Mrs Bell, made up our carriage. I tried hard to keep awake but alas I was so overcome with fatigue that unconsciously I fell asleep and my head dropped on to Mr Wiltshire's shoulder. Fortunately for me I never knew it, nor that he cared for me (at least I didn't know it then), and being a pitch dark night no one could behold the spectacle, or I should have been chaffed out of my life. The only way I came afterwards to hear of it was through my sister Emily, who came out in the *Queen*, a sailing vessel, with the brother of this young man, who was the captain of it, and he told my sister how his brother had written home to his people to say what difficulty he had to restrain himself from kissing the girl he loved so much, as she lay on his shoulder.

I cannot say at this length of time whether our carriage had any springs or not, but I can say that the seats were so hard and so high, as well as so narrow, that it was only with difficulty that I could keep my seat as we went bumping over the skulls of camels, etc. Major Fraser with his long legs must have scored here, ordinary ones had to dangle in mid air. We were all bruised from head to foot with the fearful bumping we had received and my feet were so swollen that I was not able to walk for three days. Some of the married ladies became seriously ill and did not leave their cabins for several weeks.

As soon as we got to Suez we went to another of Shepheard's Hotels, where we waited until the last of the passengers arrived. They were if I remember rightly sixteen hours longer on the road than we had been, poor people! The skeletons on the road were our only land marks and over these the drivers used to go, heedless of the feelings of those within, and of how cruel they were to the poor ponies, simply lashing and driving them till they dropped down dead. None with the first batch of carriages died, but many did of those that came later.

In those days, the P & O steamers ran only once a month, carrying the mails. Freight in those days was I think £24 a ton and dividends were 12 per cent. How times have changed. Now they have a weekly steamer to Bombay and I believe the same to Calcutta, besides many others going here and there. When I went out, we were more than seven weeks reaching India; now, via Brindisi, you can get there in sixteen days, in one third of the time and nearly at one third of the price, indeed at one fifth, if you choose to go second class, which is exceedingly comfortable, though not so luxurious as the first.

Nothing particular happened till we reached Aden. The heat was unbearable in the Red Sea. It was far worse in those days than it is now, since the Suez Canal has been opened.[26] I do not know how to account for this, but it is so. When we reached Aden,[27] everyone with the exception of myself received letters from their friends. I was bitterly disappointed. It appears, however, there was a letter for me, and Mr Lamb the clergyman was to have delivered it in person, but when he came on board to do so, and saw such a happy, bright young girl full of spirits, his heart failed him. He went from one person to another begging of them to break the news of my darling father's death to me, but each one refused, till he got Mrs Moresby to say she would do it, but not until we returned from our visit to the Governor of Aden, as it would be cruelty to tell me before. So I went on shore quite happy and enjoyed myself thoroughly. The Governor and his brother-in-law, a young officer, were very kind to us. The latter tried to teach me how to play billiards, a new experience to me, and the Governor showed us his garden, a plot of ground about four feet by eight, the soil of which had all come from Bombay. The water that we drank was all brackish. Aden is, I am sure, naturally as God-forsaken a place as any on earth. Since those days, the town has greatly improved. Tanks have been built where the garrison is stationed to hold all the rain-water that may fall, but as it only rains once in every seven years or so, one cannot depend upon the rain-water. Now, however, they have a regular arrangement for making fresh water out of salt water. This water is sold in small leather bags. When I passed through Aden some thirty-five years ago, I stopped at Colonel Hailes' house. He was the Artillery Commandant of the place. I never thought of the scarcity of water and bathed my two little boys with plenty of soap as usual, when suddenly I heard Colonel Hailes call out, 'Oh! Mrs Tytler, I forgot to ask you not to use any soap in the washing water as I require it for the horses', but it was too late.

To return to my story, after the day's outing, we came back to the steamer and I noticed everybody looking very grave as if they had not enjoyed themselves at all, so I proposed that we should sing some songs, but they all replied, 'Not tonight, Miss Earle.' A little later I proposed some dancing, but again they said, 'Not tonight, Miss Earle.'

I could not understand this and said, 'What has come over you all, why are you all so dreadfully quiet?' My friend on whose shoulder I had fallen asleep looked at me so sadly.

It was getting dark then, when Mrs Moresby came up and said, 'I have a letter for you, Miss Earle. If you will come down to my cabin I will give it to you.'

I jumped up and clapped my hands with joy, saying, 'Oh! I have got a letter after all', and followed her.

As soon as I got down to her cabin, she commenced by saying, 'I am afraid some of your people are very ill.'

Instantly the thought came to me, it must be my sister's little girl, but she said, 'Oh! no, I don't think it can be her', and gave me the letter. Just as I was opening it, I repeated, 'It must be her, for it is my brother-in-law's handwriting.'

The first words I read were, and I recollect no more, 'I grieve to tell you of your dear father's death.' When I came to again, I found myself in my berth, just as I was, but alone. Oh what a night that was! I never closed my eyes, but wrung my hands in utter despair. I knew nothing about pensions, all I knew was that I must work to help my mother, but how that was to be done was the difficulty. No one knows the agony I went through. All my joy crushed out of me in one moment, and the hopes of years dashed to the ground.

Many of my friends came of course to comfort me, but I wanted no one and preferred being left to my sorrow and to my sad thoughts of the future. After three or four days, Mrs Moresby insisted on my going on deck, saying I would get very ill if I didn't. At last I agreed to go when it became dark, and I slunk upstairs as if I had been a culprit; the very thought of seeing those who had known me in my happiest days was almost more than I could bear. They were kind enough, however, not to intrude on me, and gradually I got more reconciled to my fate, but joy had left my heart, as it appeared then, for ever.

Time wore on, and as we neared Ceylon a severe storm overtook us. Part of one of the paddle wheels was carried away, as well as several boats, also the poor cow went overboard, and then one of the boats, instead of falling into the sea, flew up and stuck in the rigging, threatening to come down on to the top of the skylight over our cabins. So a couple of sailors were told off to get us out of our cabins as fast as possible. I was held up, as were all the others, by a sailor on each side of me, and deposited in the ladies' saloon. We were all in our nightgowns, and a sorry lot we looked. Many were very terrified and were praying most earnestly. I don't know how it was, but there was a ludicrousness in the whole scene, that which capped it all being the spectacle of Mrs Onslow, a very stout woman with an infant in her arms, who was squatting on the floor. Of course as the vessel lurched heavily from side to side she was bound to slide along backwards and forwards. This, in the midst of such woebegone faces, made it so absurd that I burst out laughing, a thing I had not done since the news of my dear father's death. I was immediately sat upon, everyone exclaiming in horror and disgust at my unheard-of conduct.

'How could you, Miss Earle, laugh at such a time when we may be going down at any moment to appear before our maker and answer for our sins?'

Of course I was very abashed and felt I deserved the reproof. Two days later, when we were all on deck, the Captain called us and said, 'Now ladies, you thought the other night that you were going down, didn't you! Well look ahead and see how good God has been to us, for, but for the sun coming out just now, we should have been on those rocks in another ten minutes!' He thought we had passed them in the night by fifty miles, but the current there was so misleading that instead of having done so, we were going straight on to them. I forget the name of this shoal, but at high tide all you see are the breakers. We had been making as straight as a die for them. Indeed God was good. The vessel changing its course, we soon left the rocks behind.

In due course of time, we reached Point de Galle in Ceylon, in those days a lovely spot full of tiny islands covered with coconut trees growing right down to the water's edge. Some friends of my uncle came and took me to their bungalow, where I spent the day, saw the cinnamon and nutmeg gardens, and then returned to the vessel. It was necessary to go on shore at all the places we stopped at, as the coaling was very disagreeable. I thought Ceylon a lovely spot, but oh! so hot and muggy. It is near the equator and full of tropical vegetation, with long and heavy rains, consequently very close. Here our Hong Kong passengers left us, amongst them my friend Mr Wiltshire, and were conveyed by another vessel to their destination.

After leaving Ceylon, our next landing took place in Madras. At first I thought I would stay on board, but I felt so sad all alone, and one of the passengers, whose home was in Madras and who had fallen in love with me at first sight, and who I did not care for though I did feel sorry for him, thought proper to propose before leaving the ship. So, as I had no intention of accepting him and finding it very difficult to make him give up trying to persuade me, I decided at last to go ashore with some of the passengers and had the pleasure of seeing what the surf was like, a remarkable feature of that coast. At times it was so bad that it was impossible to land. Many of the passengers got such a ducking as to be soaked to the skin, but I was more fortunate and only got a little wet.

At last we reached Calcutta on the 8th of December. Everybody at once went on shore, either to friends or to hotels. Of course I thought my dear mother would be there to meet me, but no one came. I did not know what to do. At last one of the stewards said, 'There is a lady come for you, miss.'

I asked, 'Is she in black?'

He replied in the affirmative.

'Is she slight?'

'No, very stout.'

My heart sank within me for I knew it could not be my mother. It turned out to be a Mrs Grant, a cousin of my brother-in-law, who had been asked to receive me till my mother's friend Mrs Birch, who had taken me to England, should arrive.[28] This she did after a fortnight, when I went to stay with her at Cossipore, a very quiet place, some four miles from the city, and where I remained till my mother came. It was a sad day for us both because dear father was not there. We wept bitterly, and the joy of meeting was so alloyed with sorrow. I learnt from her that I was to be left with the Birches, as she was going home to England with the younger children, till such time as my uncle and aunt could receive me in the North-West. My uncle and brother were in the same regiment and they were at that time in the Punjab campaign.[29]

When I heard of my mother's intention of leaving me, I implored of her on my knees not to do so but to take me with her, saying I would work for her and do anything if she would only take me to England with her. It was sad for her too to part with me so soon after we had met, but it had to be done. She explained to me that I would lose my pension if I went to England and that would be a serious matter, so I had to be left. My youngest sister, a little girl of nearly nine, and my youngest brother were to go with her for their education, but poor me, who had looked forward to the one happiness of my life all the miserable years I had spent with my aunt, was doomed to meet with disappointment akin to sorrow.

Owing to the shock of my dear father's death, I got the most awful neuralgia in my head called in those days *tic douloureux*, so my mother took me with her as far as the sand-heads. All the week I was with her in the ship my headaches disappeared, but the moment I returned to Calcutta they commenced again. I came back with some friends, who had been to see their children off. Mr and Mrs Sandys and myself were but poor company for each other, they had parted with four children and I with my mother, a sister and brother.

I felt myself an orphan now in the truest sense, and though my friends the Birches were so good to me, yet my spirit revolted against dependence. It is true I could have married over and over again, but the right man did not appear and I could not marry merely for a home. Fortunately the time came within a twelvemonth for me to leave Bengal and go up-country as my health was getting worse and worse from the old complaint brought on by the shock I had received. The doctors said I must either go back to England or up to

the Hills for a thorough change of air, so it was arranged I should be
sent up-country by palkee dak under the care of a Mr Neave, an old
civilian.[30]

Not knowing any better, and with none to advise to the contrary, I
packed my palkee heavily with underlinen, stowed under the mattress, by which means I thought I would save the expense of two or
three extra coolies. Each carrier bearer carried eighty pounds weight
in two bungalow-shaped tin boxes, one at each end of a pole
suspended across his shoulders. These carriers are called 'banghy
badars', whilst the men who carry the palkees are 'kahars', better
known by the newly imported English name 'palkee bearers'.

All being ready for a start, Major Birch was to see me as far as
Barrackpore, twelve miles from Cossipore, and there make me over
to Mr Neave. The bearers took me up with a groan, saying, *'Bhuya,
burra bhari'* ('brother, it is very heavy'). However, they proceeded
and we changed men at the next stage ten miles on without anything
happening. Major Birch, who had ridden so far by my side, now
returned home, and I went on with Mr Neave. We had not gone
more than a couple of miles when the pole of my palkee broke and
down came the whole thing with a crash. What was to be done now?
I am sure Mr Neave, a cranky old fellow, must have cursed the day
when he was so weak as to agree to take charge of a girl. Of course he
felt bound in civility to return with me, but what about his leave
which was up? Without much trouble I persuaded him to continue
his journey alone, and in my inmost heart was glad to get rid of him.
The men lifted me and my palkee on their shoulders, and we got
back in about five or six hours to the Birches' house, greatly to their
astonishment.

Now what was to be done? They knew of no one else to chaperon
me, but I wanted no one. I had had enough of Mr Neave and his
crankiness to wish to feel free to do as I liked, that is to stop and go on
when I pleased, so at last they gave in. A new pole replaced the
broken one, and no more clothes were packed away under the
mattress, but two additional banghy badars were engaged and added
to my escort, making the number up to twelve, eight for the palkee
and four for the baggage. I was delighted with such freedom, for I
was left entirely to my own devices, but knowing the world as I do
now, I have often wondered how my friends could have allowed me,

a girl of eighteen, to travel a journey of 900 miles alone. It was an awful risk, but in those days the peasants of India would no more have thought of harming an English woman than of flying, for they knew they could not have escaped punishment. But there were other dangers. I might have become ill, or been attacked by a band of dacoits.

However, through God's mercy, I reached my first destination, Patna, where I was to stay with the Sandys, with only one encounter which might have turned out very seriously for poor me. It took about a week to reach Patna, stopping every day at some dak bungalow for a bath, dinner and rest. Every night when there was no moon I had to pay for an extra man, and for oil for a torch. This was quite right as far as it went. Of course the bearers pocketed the money intended for the extra man, and shared it amongst themselves. Only four men at a time carried the palkee, the others being there to relieve them at short distances, so there was always an empty hand for the necessary torch. On the memorable occasion I am about to relate, we reached a place called the Dunwar Pass. A change of bearers took place, and the new men asked me for money for the usual torch business. I refused, there being a full moon to lighten the way.

'Oh!' said the men, 'we must have a torch to go through the pass with, for there is a man-eating tiger and we dare not go without one.'

Knowing that a native cannot tell the truth, especially when money is concerned, I did not believe a word of it and so would not give the money, but insisted on their going on. This just shows what a powerful influence the English had in those days. After a long deliberation, they took me up. I immediately nestled myself comfortably for a good sleep till I should be called up again in three hours' time to give the old bearers baksheesh (a tip), on taking on the new ones. This you must know is the custom in palkee travelling, a great nuisance, but at the same time a blessing, being an incentive to good behaviour. We could not have gone a mile when down came the palkee and with a yell every man was off. I woke up with dismay, fearing the man-eater was there. Could it be possible? Of course I did not dare to open the doors of my palkee to judge for myself, but waited in terrible suspense. The time seemed an eternity. At last I heard shouts and yells coming nearer and nearer, and the bearers arrived, armed with two torches. One man came up to me and said, 'Have you a gun, Memsahib?'

'No,' I replied.

'Had you been a sahib you would shoot the tiger.'

They then stealthily approached the brute, who was lying stretched across the road, with both their torches, expecting him to jump and pounce upon them, but still he never moved. 'Be careful,' cried some, 'he is shamming.' At last the bravest of the two got near enough to touch his whiskers with the torch, upon which the animal gave the most awful howl and sprang up the hillside and was out of sight in a second. No doubt he was terribly scared, for they say a tiger's whiskers are very sensitive, and by them they can gauge the space sufficient for their bodies to go through.

Evidently he was so gorged that he was dead asleep. Luckily for me, otherwise I should have stood a very small chance of escape, for in all probability he would have smelt me out, and with one pat of his huge paw would have broken through the frail panels of my palkee and dragged me out in a second. Though the animal was off, the bearers were still in a mortal fright, fearing he would pounce down upon them somewhere else and carry off one of their number, so they shouted and screamed all the way, till we got safely out of the pass, and only then did they breathe really freely once more. My one regret was that I never saw the tiger. His howl, however, was enough to convince me of his presence and of my wonderful escape. All the bearers stood between me and the sleeping brute, so of course I had no chance of seeing him unless I had been bold enough to get out of the palkee and make one of the group.

No wonder these poor men were afraid of entering the pass without torches, considering he carried off a human being every night. Not long after we reached Bankipore, the civil station of Patna, an officer and a company of native sepoys from Dinapore were ordered out by the general to shoot the voracious animal, which they did. Strange to say, that officer was a Lieutenant Tytler, who I afterwards knew to be my future husband's first cousin, who won a VC and died as a general after the Kabul campaign, from pneumonia caught by visiting his men in hospital.[31] This man-eater was a splendid specimen. I am afraid to say how long he measured, but it was an immense size.

My stay with the Sandys (who were amongst the most hospitable people in all India) was a most enjoyable one. I cannot speak enough of their kindness to me. A very sweet girl was staying with them at the time. She married a Dr Bowling later on and was to me all her life a bosom friend. She was killed, poor girl, in the Mutiny, while trying to escape with a little adopted infant. Her husband had been murdered by the sepoys, and she, with a Mrs Scott, her son Lieutenant Scott, and a young daughter, were all killed together while escaping on camels from Futtyphur, if I recollect rightly. I was so happy at the Sandys that it did not require much persuasion to make me extend my visit to two months. From Patna I was to have gone to the Mainwarings at Mirzapoor, but two days before my expected arrival poor Mr Mainwaring met with a dreadful accident. He was thrown from his horse close to the house and crushed his ankle, which, owing to his being a good liver and very stout, swelled up to such an extent that they could not take his boot off, and when the doctor arrived amputation was found necessary. Soon after this was done, they found it necessary to cut off the leg above the knee and yet again near the hip, all to no purpose. Mortification had set in so rapidly that he died the next day. His poor wife sent off a messenger to General Carpenter to waylay me at Benares and keep me there till I could go on again. There was but one road, the Grand Trunk, by which I could travel, so it was no difficult matter to intercept me.

The Carpenters were exceedingly kind and hospitable people. Mrs Carpenter, who was such a pretty woman, was a great invalid, so her niece Miss Dabine had to do the honours of the house. It was there I first met Lieutenant Donald Stewart (later knighted).[32] He was a young lieutenant who had joined my father's old regiment, the 9th, after we had left it in Chittagong. He was a tall, handsome young fellow and paid Miss Dabine, who was quite the belle of Benares, a great deal of attention. Eventually they were married, but I never saw them again until I met them in Simla several years after the Mutiny.

From Benares I went on by dak to Allahabad to pay a visit to Major and Mrs Wallace of my dear father's last regiment, the 3rd NI. All the officers did their utmost to show their love and respect for my father. Three of them gave a dance in honour of their dear commandant's daughter, so I had a very good time of it, with the exception of one occurrence which I always regretted. Unwittingly I caused one of the said three to fall in love with me. I say unwittingly because I was told he was already engaged to another girl who had gone on to

Simla. He certainly was very attentive to me, but in the innocence of my heart I attributed it all to the extraordinary love he bore for my father. I believe at the funeral his grief had been so great that he had actually thrown himself into the grave. Well, to make a long story short, on my departure, all the officers came to wish me goodbye except this young man. I thought it rather strange, but after starting never once gave it another thought. On the way out of the station I met a young fellow who was out for his ride, and who rode alongside of my palkee, chatting away, when up came the absentee. I didn't much like it, but went on talking just the same, till I thought it was time for both to go. Mr Grant took the hint, but my other friend had no intention of doing so. I now understood why he had not come with the rest to take leave of me. I saw there was nothing for it, as he would not leave me till I did, but to accept his offer of marriage. He denied being engaged to any other girl and vowed by all that was holy that I was his first and only love. All men do so, so my experience told me. Accordingly it did not affect me much, for I had no intention of really accepting him.

About midnight I heard clatter, clatter, the sound of horses' footsteps, and there was my friend back again. He had been late for a dinner party as it was, but no sooner was it over than back he came, I am afraid to say how many miles, to see me once more. I really was very angry. He ordered the men to put my palkee down so that he could the more conveniently have a quiet talk, but I cut the matter short by saying that if he did not go away at once, I would have nothing more to do with him. He knew he had vexed me, and not being at all sure of my love took his departure, much to my comfort. As soon as I reached Cawnpore, where I was to stay with Mrs Beckett[33] of my father's first regiment, I told her of my trouble and that I had no love for the poor fellow at all, having always believed him engaged to another girl, but that without accepting him I could not get rid of him, and that now I did not know what to do.

'Do?' she said. 'You must sit down and write at once and tell him that you cannot marry him.'

That letter cost me a great deal of pain, but I did it in as kind a way as I could. As soon as a reply could come back, I received one. It made my heart ache, yet it was better to ache for a while than to destroy the happiness of two people by consenting to give my hand without my heart.

From Cawnpore I went to Dadapore, near Seharampore, where the wife of Captain Henry Siddons of the Engineers[34] lived, and from thence to Landour in the Himalayas. Nothing in particular happened between Cawnpore and Dadapore, except that on one occasion the palkee had to be put on to a skeleton wagon and drawn by a pair of horses, to hasten on the journey, as it was getting fast into the hot weather and Mrs Siddons could not be kept waiting longer for me. We went on all right until we reached a bridge over a small river. Here the horses backed and backed until over we went, fortunately not into the deepest part of the stream. Nothing happened beyond getting a great fright and a slight ducking, but had the palkee slipped off the wagon, I certainly would have drowned, for I could not have extricated myself and no one could have pulled me out in time. All is well that ends well.

From Dadapore we went on by palkee dak to the Hills. What a glorious sight awaited me at Landour. Such a view of the snowy range! Far finer than anything I have ever seen since, either in Switzerland, the Rockies or at Simla, grand as the views from all these places are. I had not been there long when my friend from Allahabad arrived and renewed his proposals, all to no purpose. He then pursued another course, left Landour and went down to Mussoorie, where he began flirting with another girl, (hoping to bring me to my senses by making me jealous, but I am afraid it did not have the desired effect), till one fine day the uncle of the girl took him to task by asking his intentions. Of course he was obliged to say they were honourable.

Poor man, I met him at a ball the day before their marriage. He never went near her the whole evening, but begged to be allowed to sit out a dance with me, when he poured out his heart and cried like a child. I felt terribly unhappy and comforted him as well as I could and then asked him to introduce me to his fiancée. This he did with some reluctance. I congratulated her and tried to make her feel happy at the thought of so soon becoming the wife of such a good man, but when I met her again a fortnight later, as I was going down to the plains, I never saw a more unhappy-looking bride. He was riding on a mile ahead of her, and when he met me begged to have my conveyance put down that he might talk to me. Poor man, he cried again and told me how perfectly miserable he was. What could I do or say, but try my best again to comfort him? Some time afterwards his wife came up and passed us. He never looked at her or said a word to cheer her. Poor woman, what she must have felt. I thought it now high time to scold him and put his conduct before him in a proper light, which I did.

That was the last time I ever spoke to him, though I saw him again once or twice at a distance, after I was married. I am glad to say, his good wife, in spite of her trials, by unfailing duty and devotion to him, at last won his affections. They had four children, but one day he was found drowned in his bath like poor Bishop Heber.[35] Whether he had a fit or not I never heard. Probably it was heat apoplexy, or heart failure.

From Landour I went straight down to Rajpore with Mrs Siddons and a young man with whom I was so much in love. He was an Irishman of a very good family, his sister being married to an earl, but he himself was only a lieutenant in the Queen's army and without private means, which meant very slow promotion. In those days things were so different from what they are now.[36] It was a time when rich men could get poorer ones to take their places in the Queen's regiments going out to India by offering them a good bonus. So the poorer ones came out while the rich went into regiments at home, where they could rise quickly from lieutenant to colonel by the purchase system. Those officers who came out to India had little or no guaranteed pensions for their wives, whereas the widows and orphans of officers belonging to the East India Company's service were sure of a good pension, according to the rank of the husband at the time of his death. My mother understood this and therefore made me promise that I would not marry a Queen's officer. As luck would have it, the only man I did love then was this charming young Irishman, who was one. In spite of my promise I lived in a sort of fool's paradise, hoping against hope that something might turn up which would enable my mother to give her consent. Well, it was with this young man that I went down the hill, with Mrs Siddons and her little girl Sally. We stayed two days in Rajpore and then I had to leave for Lucknow to go and stay with my uncle and aunt. When the time came to say goodbye I felt very heart-broken, but was too proud to let anyone know it. But as soon as I had said goodbye and closed the doors of my palankeen I burst into bitter tears and cried as only babies can. He followed me on foot, to my great confusion. When he found I wouldn't open the palankeen doors, he begged of me to put out my hand once more, to hold it. I did so and he kissed it again and again, and no doubt wiped away a tear. I begged of him to go back, which he did, and then I burst out again into more tears. We corresponded for some time, and he used to send me presents, but as often I used to return them, not being engaged to him, nor ever likely to be. For, though I knew he was waiting for his captaincy to propose, yet even then my promise to my mother would have prevented anything coming of it.

In due course of time I reached Lucknow, which was a very favourite and gay station, only fifty miles from Cawnpore. In the cold weather of '47 it was particularly so, for Lord Hardinge, the Governor-General, as viceroys in those days were called, was expected and there were to be grand doings.

His visit to the King of Oude, of which Lucknow was the chief town, was entirely a political one, having been ordered by his masters, the East India Court of Directors in England,[37] to inform His Majesty that unless he governed his country better, they would take it from him and annex it. He knew this and was therefore most anxious to do all in his power to please the Governor-General.

He had only succeeded to the throne of his father the year before. While his father was dying, he made his band practise 'God Save the King' so as to be quite ready for his own coronation. A most extraordinary ceremony took place at the death of his father, the like of which I have never heard of being transacted elsewhere. I was not there at the time, but those who were told me about it. It appears that it had been a custom in Lucknow on the death of a king, or nawab, as the Kings of Oude were called, to have the body embalmed, taking out the entrails before doing so. These entrails were then washed in several waters, again with milk, and lastly in rose-water, after which a banquet was given, according to the Indian custom at funerals, to which all the nobles were invited, none daring to refuse, and each guest was made to drink a large thimble full of this delightful rose-water. How this custom arose, I never knew, but I conjecture it was by way of preventing the poisoning of their kings, for the longer they lived, the better for those who had to partake of this awful decoction. Anyhow, it was the custom, whatever its origin might have been.

After the Governor-General had arrived and the ceremonial visits had been exchanged, all the European officers, covenanted civilians and their families were invited to a grand breakfast. My uncle and aunt[38] would not go, but I was allowed to go with some friends. The breakfast was given in the King's palace and was a very grand affair. There were two long tables with chairs on one side of each. The King sat in the centre of one of these, with Lord Hardinge on his right, Colonel Richmond the Resident on his left, and the two little princes, his sons, close by on the right also, after which came all the native noblemen. The highest European officials and their families sat at the table opposite that of the King, whilst the others took whatever seats they could find at the second table. As I went with the family of the Assistant Resident,[39] I had a very good seat indeed, opposite the King's table, from whence I could observe all the proceedings. The King and his family were gorgeously attired in kincob (cloth of gold) and jewels. Such strings of pearls, emeralds and diamonds we had never before seen. Some of the emeralds were the size of large marbles, but so badly cut that they only looked like bits of glass. The diamonds too, though immense, were cut into thin, flat ones and made no more show than pieces of crystal would have done. Nevertheless, these jewels were very costly and gorgeous. The pearls were simply splendid, both in size and colour. The King had strings and strings of these from the neck to below the waist.

He never deigned to partake of a single particle of the food on the table. All he did was to chew pawn (the green pungent betel leaf, much appreciated by the natives of India). The pawn bearer stood behind him, as did a number of other attendants, two of whom drove off supposed flies from the royal head with chowries (whisks) made of peacocks' feathers with gold handles; others fanned His Majesty and so on. But the pawn bearer was a man of importance and a trusted friend, who stood ready to respond to a little click made by the King, which meant that he was ready for another pawn, the click being followed by a turn of the head and a gaping mouth, into which the pawn bearer popped the pawn, on which the King went on chewing as before. His lips and tongue were orange vermilion in colour, a great beauty in the eyes of these people.

Those who sat at a little distance down the table had their share of amusement in watching the native noblemen tucking into every-thing. When it came to dividing a fowl, they preferred tearing off the limbs themselves to having it carved. One would take a wing, his friend next to him another, and so would soon help themselves. Their great cry was for 'Belattee beef' (English beef), i.e. our ham. Had they called it by its legitimate name, horror of horrors! no faithful follower of Mahomet could have touched it, but as English beef it was quite another thing. I am sure they knew perfectly well what it was, and the Mohammedan servants who cooked it must have known also, but as long as it was 'Belattee beef' Mahomet could not object, so it was all right. As soon as breakfast was over, the King led the way, followed by Lord Hardinge and Colonel Richmond, to the place from where the great animal fights were to be witnessed. We amongst the lesser fry followed.

As soon as everyone was seated, the signal was given for the show to commence. A poor water buffalo (a species of cow) was brought in with its calf, and the doors of the tigers' dens were opened to let four out. These had been starved for a whole week, to make them all the more ferocious, but not one would venture out. The King getting angry, squibs and crackers were thrown into the dens, but in vain, no tiger responded. At last more squibs and burning sticks were thrown in, from a respectable distance outside the arena, and by force of such persuasion four tigers bounded out and then slunk into a corner. From this they were again dislodged in the same way with more crackers and at last came to the attack. The King and all his guests were in a balcony, well secured by thick iron bars. The poor buffalo fought well, keeping all four tigers at bay for what appeared to us as an endless time. Every time they charged, she was ready for them. Her poor little calf was crouching under her body, trembling with terror. At last one of the tigers got round to her hind legs and bit one of them right through. Just at that moment, when in her agony she could no longer defend her little one, he grabbed it and carried it off to the other end of the arena, where all four ate the poor little thing in less time than I can describe it. The whole affair was a dreadful sight. The poor mother, helpless, stood with her leg hanging by a thread, while the blood poured into a pool beneath her. On the King giving the order, the unfortunate creature was dragged out and doubtless had its throat cut to enable the King's employees to feast on her. No Mohammedan will eat any flesh, be it of beast or bird, whether shot or killed in any other way, but by first saying a prayer for the rest of its soul and then cutting its throat.

The next fight was now between the same tigers and the King's favourite brown bear. As soon as the door of his den was opened, the bear came out bravely on his hind legs and went straight for one of the tigers, got him in a corner and hugged him so tightly that in another moment it would have been all over for his opponent, had he not, in his dying desperation, managed to get the bear's jaw into his mouth and bite it, along with the tongue, clean in two. Not till then did he give up his hold, when the tiger slunk away. The brave old bear, in spite of his suffering, stood up again and made another but futile attempt to attack one of the other tigers, but he was powerless with suffering and gave it up. The King was furious at poor Bruin's defeat, for he had never been known before to fail in disposing of his enemy in a manner satisfactory to himself and to those around, so he arose and conducted his noble guest and Colonel Richmond to see other animal contests out in the open air. We were so thankful to escape from all this amount of cruel bloodshed. No one could have dared to leave their seats in the King's presence, such breach of etiquette would have been unpardonable, so there we had to remain till he arose. When he did, we needed neither invitation nor persuasion to follow his example.

The first fight outside was between two male elephants, which took place on the opposite side of the river Goomtee. At first the two animals did not appear to show much animosity, it looked more like playing than fighting. As soon however as they commenced locking their trunks in each other's, the mahouts thought it time to let them fight it out alone, and scrambled off their backs tailwards. Myriads of native spectators were on the same side of the stream. These two elephants kept pushing each other backwards, first one, then the other, till at last the stronger of the two succeeded in shoving his opponent right into the river. That finished the fight. The defeated elephant took to his heels and never stopped to look back, while the victor followed him as hard as he could go. The best part of this scene was the stampede amongst the natives, all terrified out of their lives lest the infuriated creatures should tread them down as grass under their feet, which they would have done too, had anyone been so unfortunate as to cross their path in this mad flight and pursuit.

As soon as the elephant fight was over, a most ludicrous one followed close to where we were all looking on. A donkey was brought to the front and then a hyena. We could not imagine how two such different animals were going to fight together, but the donkey thoroughly understood his business. He quietly took stock of his adversary and then, turning sharply round, let fly his hind legs as fast as they could go, killing the poor hyena on the spot. I cannot describe the scene properly, but it was so ludicrous and the very last thing one would have expected from a 'dhobee's' (washerman's) donkey that everyone went into fits of laughter, a comfort after the ghastly sights we had witnessed before. After this, ram fights and other minor exhibitions of the sort took place, winding up with hawking. The spectacle we witnessed that day will never be again seen in India. I have seen elephant and deer fights since in other native states, but that is all, very stupid and monotonous affairs.

In the evening we were invited to see the illuminations in the Chotah Imambarah.[40] A more lovely sight could not be imagined. It was perfect fairyland. The Imambarah itself was covered with little lights of various colours most artistically arranged and the whole garden was a mass of lights, also most beautifully arranged. Everyone thoroughly enjoyed that evening. A sight like that will never be seen again either, I am afraid. It is true the Nizam of Hyderabad in the Deccan did have grand illuminations both in his town and in his palace in honour of our late Duke of Clarence's visit to him. They were magnificent but lacked the fairyland appearance, resembling too much our European ones in that respect.

The next evening, the Resident gave a ball in the Residency. As we enjoyed ourselves that night, little did we think that in a little less than ten years it would witness within its walls such days of suffering and misery as it did during its memorable siege in '57. The festivities were over now, and Lord Hardinge with his staff returned to their other duties. The King of course promised to mend his ways, but did he? After revelations will prove whether he did so or not.

Later on, the 38th NI, a very crack regiment, arrived in Lucknow. It was then I first met my future husband, a captain in that regiment.[41] He proposed to me several times, but I could not forget my first love, though such a hopeless one. My feelings had so changed from knowing what it was to love and suffer that at last I accepted him out of sheer pity. Thank God I did, for he proved the dearest of husbands and my love for him grew day by day into earnest devotion.

The other poor fellow, when he heard of my engagement at mess, left the table, took leave, and went out shooting, no doubt to divert his mind and forget his sorrow. While out in the Hills he met with a terrible accident from the falling of a stone from the hill above, caused by the monkeys jumping from rock to rock. It fell on his head which caused a fracture in the skull and he had to be trepanned. About two years later he married an Irish widow whose husband had been killed in the first Punjab campaign. I was very glad of it because I felt that we were both happy now.

I must say it was a risky thing marrying a man with two little children out of pity for his sorrow. With some natures it might not have turned out happily, but I was always very fond of children and they were so very young and such dear little fellows, one only four and the other not three. The elder boy was his grandmother's shadow and did not take kindly to me, but the little fellow, having no one to care especially for him, except his old bearer Dabi, used to cry to be taken to his little mamma. It was very touching, because of course he couldn't remember his own dear mother, being such a baby when she died. So I took to him with my whole heart and felt the responsibility of such a charge very keenly.

After our marriage, I felt it was my duty to try to teach them lessons, but alas! I was too impatient and when I could not drive it into their heads as fast as I thought I ought to, I used to put them in the corner as a punishment. It was all well meant, but extremely stupid of me to expect wonders from such little mites, so my poor husband very kindly relieved me of this task by taking them in hand himself. I was only nineteen, and a child too at that age compared to girls of the same age of the present day. Outsiders, who knew I was so fond of amusement, especially dancing before I was married, laughed at my husband marrying such a giddy girl, but soon changed their minds when they saw how kindly I took to my new life.

I was told long after the Mutiny by my brother, who heard it from Mrs Peile, the wife of one of our officers, that I was called the angel of the regiment, as also the mother of it—I suppose the former from my love for the children and the latter because the young fellows used to come to me and beg of me to ask their young women to lunch, along with the boys, to give them a better opportunity of carrying on their little flirtations. Several of our young fellows did win their wives in this way, but oh! how many of those are dead and gone. Indeed I don't think there is one living now.

My husband was most kind and indulgent to me, and was very clever. Indeed, all I ever learnt was from him. His mother too was so good and always took my part against her son, which showed perfect wisdom, which answered so well that I carried out the same plan with my sons- and daughters-in-law. Consequently the proverbial mother-in-law difficulties never crossed our path.

A fortnight after I was married, my husband was ordered to go to Fyzabad in Oude with his company and a subaltern officer, to escort back some money from one of the treasuries (it was revenue I believe). To give you some idea of how the King governed his country, my husband on his way back was followed by a regiment of the King of Oude's soldiers, under the command of an European named Barlow.[42] My husband, knowing what they were after, put on double sentries and never went to bed at night, expecting an attack on the treasure at any moment. His knowledge of the character of the King's troops and his vigilance saved the money and his own credit.

Years afterwards we met Colonel Barlow up at Mussoorie and he told my husband that but for his precautions nothing would have prevented his men from looting the treasure. These soldiers of the King of Oude were never paid a day's wages, but were expected to pay themselves in any way they could. Consequently they would loot village after village, rob the poor inhabitants of their money, jewels and grain, and, if they offered any resistance, shoot them like dogs and carry off their wives and daughters if they desired to do so—and all this without the smallest hope of redress for the poor sufferers, the King of Oude and his courtiers lending a deaf ear to all appeals for justice. As long as the revenue came in for His Majesty's personal pleasures he was satisfied and would not spend a rupee on his country to improve it, or pay his soldiers and retainers; consequently they all paid themselves, taking good care not to allow any complaints to reach the King's ear. Almost every night whilst we were at our dinner we would hear the put, putting of muskets which meant that the soldiery were looting some village close to cantonments and, as we were only three miles from the city, the King too must have heard, but what of that, he did not suffer. It only meant more money to enjoy his licentious life with.

The King had 300 wives, real wives, besides their numerous

slaves. Three sides of the royal grounds were filled with small separate buildings, one for each begum and mahal; probably in that way he ensured peace amongst them. The high walls round the palace grounds had no outlet except through the five or seven, I forget which, highly walled-in squares, each with stupendous gates guarded by eunuchs, so that any unhappy woman who once got into the King's zenana or harem could never come out again. Of all these 300 queens, there were only four begums or queens by the first marriage, the others being mahals or queens by the Nicah marriage, legal marriages permitted by Mahomet as essential to the comfort of his followers. A Mohammedan man may marry as many of these as he likes, so long as he can provide them with food and clothes. He is not obliged to love them, they are wives of convenience, but their children are legitimate and the father can make the mother of any of them his favourite queen and raise the son to the throne by adoption. Mohammedans do not give their daughters in marriage till they are of a marriageable age,[43] and amongst their aristocracy are always espoused to their own cousins. Their relations, both men and women, can visit them after marriage, but no other male may do so. They are all called Purdah Nasheens, which means women behind screens, and are not visible to male outsiders. Even when they go out for an airing, they are accompanied by eunuchs and are strictly hidden behind cloth screens with tiny eye holes, through which they can see but not be seen.

In '49 my little boy was born and that summer we all went up to Mussoorie to our cottage there, an ideal spot.[44] The house was very tiny with a thatched roof, in the middle of a lovely garden, just after my own heart. I did not care how small the house was, as long as I had plenty of flowers and beautiful scenery around me. This was the second year of my married life. My mother-in-law was with us and had been all along; she was the dearest old lady possible and so kind to me, but with one great peculiarity. She considered pancakes the proper food for children. The two little boys loathed pancakes, but nevertheless had to eat a certain quantity of them every day. My husband had also been brought up in the same way and nothing would induce him even to look at one, though I of course might eat as many as I liked. I lived in constant dread of her making the baby eat one too, when perhaps I might not be by to help him. One day my husband and myself went out to lunch. The ayah had strict injunctions not to let the Burra Mem (big or senior lady) give baby the smallest particle of a pancake during my absence. Something told me she would do it. The moment I returned, the ayah rushed up and said, 'Oh! Memsahib, the Burra Mem insisted upon baby eating half a pancake.' I was really very angry, being sure the three months' child would die, but nothing happened, he was neither the better nor the worse for it.

I was very ill that year, so much so that when the time came for us to go down, the doctor insisted upon my going by water and not by carriage dak, so my husband ordered some country boats to be prepared as houseboats for our use at Gurmuktesar Ghat, the extreme navigable point of the Ganges. Dear old Mrs Tytler left us at Mussoorie to pay a year's visit to her eldest son at Kussoor in the Punjab. She always lived a year with each of her two sons, turn about, but this time she had been with my husband since the death of his first wife. We went down by palkee dak as far as Gurmuktesar, where we found both the boats ready for us, one for ourselves and the other as usual for the servants and kitchen. Both looked very comfortable indeed. While there we observed a European swimming backwards and forwards in the river, and wondered what he could be doing this for. The next time he approached the shore where we were standing we noticed he had a small packet in his mouth and asked him what his trouble was. He said, 'Sir, I am an old soldier who have taken my discharge, and have, with my wife, to be at Benares by a certain time, being engaged to go home to England with Colonel and Mrs Marshall, and I can't get these men to let me have a boat, though I have the money to pay for it. As soon as I go over to one shore to engage a boat, the men are told not to let me have one by order of the kotwal (a native magisterial officer) and when I swim back to try again the same thing happens. It is very hard sir, for I shall lose my service unless I get to Benares in time.'

He showed my husband his discharge papers, so the kotwal was interviewed and asked what he meant by his conduct. In reply he insisted that the man was a deserter and that he had a 'purwana' (a magistrate's order) to intercept him and send him back to his regiment. My husband said, 'Show me your purwana.' When he saw that my husband could read Hindustani he was rather taken aback.[45] Then my husband gave it to him hot, saying, 'How dare you stop this man, in what way does he answer to the description in your purwana? In it you have a young man of twenty-five, with blue eyes, light hair and of such and such a height. How does it tally with a man of forty-five with grey hair, etc, etc. You rascal, you deserve to lose your post, but rather than there should be any more trouble about it, I will take him in my own boat', so he offered the poor soldier and his wife a little dressing room and the palkee gharree (a palkee on wheels) to sleep in, for which the poor man was very grateful.

We then made a start for Cawnpore, giving ourselves plenty of time to reach it comfortably. On the third day of our journey, we stopped at a village and bought a milch goat for the children's use. Just as we had done this and left our moorings, a terrible white squall overtook us and sent the boat flying across the very swollen river to the opposite side. I was sitting on the floor inside with my baby in my arms at the time, quite unconscious of any danger, but my husband and the two elder boys were outside in the front of the boat looking on. In a second they became aware of the danger, as they saw the boatmen, who were rowing, had their eyes fixed upon the opposite bank, upon which the wind was driving us to our certain destruction. The men, who had lost all control over the boat, were panic-stricken. It was an agonizing moment for my husband, knowing that directly we struck those high limestone walls, every soul on board was doomed to immediate death. As we approached, the soldier, who was a marvellous swimmer, took a rope between his teeth and flung himself into the river, hoping to stop the progress of the boat by clinging to one of the buttresses of a submerged ghat which was visible far out in the river. The old soldier succeeded partly in his object, inasmuch as he was able to check the boat for an instant when the current swept him off, but this check, slight as it was, proved our salvation. The moment the boat struck the bank, they discovered to their joy that instead of it being the dreaded walls we had expected to strike, it was only one of sand at the mouth of a then dry nullah with a sandy beach of some two or three feet wide at the bottom. On this we struck sideways, the most miraculous part being that it only just fitted the length of the boat, for had our boat struck two or three feet further on either side, it must have foundered.

Fortunately for me, being inside of the cabin, I knew nothing of all this till it was over. The boatmen said, 'Sahib, make haste, if you wish to get out do so at once, for the moment the storm bursts, the

nullah will be a roaring torrent.' The servants promptly set to work
to scoop out little holes in the perpendicular sandbank to enable them
to climb up by. While enlarging a little one already there, out came a
karait (a snake as venomous as the cobra), but it fell and disappeared
without hurting anyone. The servants climbed up and then helped us
up, while the boatmen pushed from below. As soon as we reached
the top, we had to run for our lives and take shelter in a Brahmin's
house close by, only in time to be saved from a terrific drenching, the
boatmen first saying, 'Sahib, we cannot stay here longer for we shall
be swamped, but we will make our way to the first landing place and
moor our boat there.' A few minutes later the storm burst upon us in
all its fury; the thunder and lightning was very great, indeed it was an
equinoctial gale, which always announces the beginning and the
ending of the monsoons.

We remained in the good Hindu's house for hours, till the rain
abated, and then made the best of our way to the boats. We were all
bare-footed. It was indeed a journey to be remembered. Upon
reaching the nullah, we found it, as predicted, a roaring torrent,
above my husband's waist, and he was nearly six feet high. He took
me in his arms, the soldier did ditto with his wife, and the servants
each a child, whilst one carried the ayah. In this way we crossed the
nullah, wet and miserable, and by the time we reached the boat
footsore as well, from thorns. It was an awful experience! When we
entered the boat we found the thatch had been put on so badly that
everything inside was soaked, bedding and all. Indeed there was not
a dry inch to be found anywhere. I kept my baby in my arms all
night, and the servants held the other children. The next day a few of
the clothes were dried over a charcoal fire. The wind and rain
continued for three days, all of which time we could not leave our
moorings.

Meanwhile my husband went on in such a strange way. I could not
account for it, little knowing then how the shock had affected his
brain. He talked all night and day at random about the water coming
into the boat and wetting his feet, and every now and then would
jump up and order the men to add more fastenings to the boat,
harping perpetually on the dangers that were now past. I could not
make him believe that we were safe and that we would stay where we
were until the storm was over. At last the wind somewhat abated and
he became conscious of the necessity to go on, so as to reach

Lucknow by the 15th of October, when his leave would be up.

The poor soldier, who had behaved so bravely and done us such a good turn for the little kindness we had shown him, was anxious to reach his destination too, as his wife, who was not very strong, was now really far from well, so that it was incumbent to move, come what might. My husband fortunately became calmer and more like himself.

On reaching Cawnpore, we left the boats and continued on our respective ways by land. The following day we reached Lucknow and my husband, who by this time was very feverish, sent for the regimental doctor. In the evening I drove out with a friend to look for a house, as I was not satisfied with the one we were in, and which had been engaged for us prior to our arrival.

On my return I found the doctor waiting for me. Calling me aside he said, 'You don't seem to be aware, Mrs Tytler, that Captain Tytler is very ill; you cannot possibly move him into another house at present.'

Judge of my astonishment and terror, for I had no idea his case was a serious one. From that moment he grew rapidly worse. The next day a second doctor was called in and then even a third one. It was a severe case of brain fever. The children were all sent out of the house for the day, returning only in the evening, in time to go to bed. Two officers of the regiment were asked by the doctors to sit up and watch all night to see that his medicine was given regularly every two hours. There was no necessity for this, for I never slept and often had given the doses twice, before they came to remind me. During the ten days when he was expected to die momentarily, I never changed my clothes, but watched him night and day. He took 500 grains of calomel[46] before they could salinate him. At last they succeeded, and then came some little hope, though even then he was not out of danger. The doctors said it was his abstemious habits that pulled him through, for had he been in the habit of drinking, even to the extent of one glass of beer a day, nothing could have saved him.

As soon as my husband was sufficiently strong to be moved, he was ordered to England, and we once more started in boats and went down to Barrackpore, the station our regiment had just been ordered to. He was so wonderfully well by the time we reached Calcutta that he begged of the doctors not to send him home. After some persuasion that consented, saying, 'As Barrackpore is so near

Calcutta, you could be sent home at a moment's notice if necessary, so we will let you try it.' And thus we remained, my husband God be praised improving day by day.

Our regiment also came to Barrackpore by water, arriving there some weeks after us. On seeing some of the officers on the day they arrived, we heard of the sad death of young Dunsford, such a nice boy. He had been a foundling and was adopted by a lady who had brought him up as her own son. It appears on one occasion when the boats were coming down the river as usual Dunsford said to his bearer he would have a plunge in the river. That was the last seen of the poor fellow. The supposition was that either an alligator had carried him off or an under-current had swept him away. No one ever knew what was his real fate. A search was made for his body for three days, but to no purpose. Some even thought he took his plunge on purpose for they said in the regiment that he felt being a foundling, though he never breathed a word of it to me. Three or four days after the regiment reached Barrackpore, Lieutenant Williams of our regiment shot himself just before going to parade—nobody could account for this either. Two more ensigns were added to our regiment[47] and things went on as usual.

My husband bought me a most beautiful carriage and pair of horses. Being a very large one, we used to take out for a drive every evening four other ladies who had no conveyances of their own, chiefly young people. In those days, the band of one or another regiment used to play every evening in the park.

Calcutta being only sixteen miles from Barrackpore we often used to go down there on visits to our friends. On one of these occasions I met with a very serious accident: while driving in a palkee gharree through the China Bazaar, the bottom of the carriage fell out and I disappeared in a minute. My husband made a dash to save me from falling under the wheels by grabbing me by the arm, dragging me along, and calling out to the driver to stop. But instead of stopping, he drove all the faster. I kept saying, 'For God's sake let me go.' It was extreme agony that made me call out thus, for I felt my arm was coming out of its socket. As soon as the driver found what was happening, he left us and ran away. Just then a passerby offered me his palankeen to take me home, for which kindness I was truly thankful for I was terribly hurt and had to keep to my bed for three or four days.

The next day we saw an article in the papers describing the scene. We could attribute it to no one else but the kind Eurasian gentleman who gave me his palankeen, for he talked of the gallant captain who had saved his wife's life so marvellously. It was altogether a unique production and quite worthy of an Eurasian.

That first year of our stay in Barrackpore was a very sad one altogether. First my brother-in-law Captain Siddons died. Then my dear little baby was born and died, and later on my husband's only brother also died. My dear baby's death was a great blow to me for I had looked forward to the birth of that child with such pleasure, a pleasure I never felt at the birth of my first child because I was so afraid of giving my heart's love to him, lest my husband and mother-in-law might think I loved him more than the other little ones. So I used to go against nature and keep him at a certain distance. But when the second was born I felt that I could love him with all my heart and cause no ill-feeling to anyone, but God thought it best to take him from me to teach me not to idolize any earthly thing.

He was such a fine, bonny baby, till my husband in the pride of his heart took him out too late on a November evening to show him to a friend. He caught cold and got lockjaw and died the next day. We had a terrible old doctor who hated women and children. The baby cried all night, but knowing him so well, we were afraid to send for him till morning. When we did, he certainly came, but on hearing that the child was quieting for a few minutes he went away. Immediately after, the poor child began screaming again. We sent off the bearer to call him back, but he wouldn't come, saying he would do so after he had visited his hospital. When he did come, I told him that baby had had convulsions.

He replied in a rude way, 'Have you ever seen a child in convulsions?'

I said no, I had not.

'Then what do you know about it?'

Unfortunately it so happened every time he got a convulsion both the nurse and my husband were out of the room. Of course we did not know he had lockjaw, so that when he could not suck each time he tried, he went off into a fit. The doctor persisted there was nothing the matter with the child and ordered him out of the warm room and into the cold drawing room, and said to me, 'If you wish to

see me you must come into another room', and though hardly a
week confined, he made me walk out and lie on the couch in the next
room.

At last baby had a very violent fit when both my husband and
nurse were present. Servants were sent in all directions to fetch the
first doctor they could find—this was about six o'clock in the
evening. Dr Christie was the first to come and then Dr Griffiths, our
doctor. The child was in a hot bath, when I said, 'Can he open his
mouth, doctor?' Upon which he thrust his big thumb down the little
thing's throat, saying, 'Of course he can.' During the time the baby
was in the hot bath he broke out in an eruption all over his stomach
but this disappeared in a few minutes and he was brought in a blanket
and put into my arms. So little did I know myself that I wouldn't ask
God for his life, as I said He knew best. Soon after this the doctor
went away, in spite of my beseeching him not to do so, and then
came back to see my poor baby die. My husband noticed a very
slight twinge in his little face and said, 'He is gone doctor, is he not?'
Griffith then and there rose and said, 'Yes. Thank God I have no wife
or children to bother me. Good night.' And away he went. He little
thought when he said that, on the 5th of November 1850, that he
would die himself out at sea with no wife or children to bother him,
and that too on the 5th of November two years later.

I never cried when my baby died, though my poor husband did. I
undressed and laid him out on the table. He looked in perfect health
and as if he was only asleep. I stood watching him and trying to
comfort my husband till two in the morning, when he implored of
me to come to bed, saying, 'You will be very ill if you don't!'

The next morning early I went to my baby and realized for the first
time the truth. I gave one piercing shriek of agony, saying, 'My baby
is dead, my baby is dead!' I would take no comfort. My husband
brought me my Bible, knowing I loved it, but my heart was too
rebellious. I threw it from one end of the room to the other, saying,
'Take it away. God has taken my darling baby from me, the baby I
loved so dearly. Why did He not take someone else's baby?' But I
found comfort a week later in my Bible and then I was truly ashamed
of myself. Ever after, if I felt I was getting too fond of a baby child, I
used to tell the nurse to take it away. But I mourned over my loss
terribly. Every evening I used to go to the grave and throw myself on
it. I just felt each time as if my heart would break. My poor husband

always let me have my cry out, for nothing else comforted me. Of course I was very ill after my baby died, as might have been expected.

Before baby was born, there was a grand tamasha (fête) going on in the lines. Our regiment was one of the very few who ever indulged in so expensive a fête. It was called the Ram Lila and lasted a fortnight. This was a fête in commemoration of Ram and his wife Seeta, who the giants of 'Lanka' (Ceylon) had carried away into the mountains of Nevaraglia. The monkeys in the forests at the foot of these inaccessible haunts found their god Ram in great distress at the loss of his wife Seeta. On finding out the cause of his grief, they vowed they would not rest till they had rescued her, so goes the legend. They thought of a plan of setting fire to the forests and then to make a dash through the flames and rescue Seeta, leaving the giants to be burnt to death. The ingenious way they set fire to the forest was by tying torches to their tails. Whatever they did had the desired effect, for they brought Seeta out, but their faces became blackened by the smoke. This is the great grey monkey with a black face known as Hanuman that the Hindus worship, though they reverence all monkeys, and in Hindu towns like Muttra you dare not shoot them. At this Ram Lila they always have two Brahmin children, little things between four and six, to represent their god and goddess. These poor children have a fairly good time of it in so far as they are given plenty of sweets and garlands of flowers, presented to them by the soldiers, but strange to say they never survive the fête very long, being sent to the Village of the Dead, where they stay till they die, I presume by slow poison.[48] Once there, they lose all caste, and a sweeperess by birth can live with and marry a Brahmin. I am told there are two such villages now, up the river Hooghly some miles from Calcutta, and that the missionaries are doing good work amongst these castaways. Good comes out of evil. Sometimes. The whole fortnight there is tom-tomming and squibs being fired at the fortifications, which are supposed to represent the homes of these ogres or giants, till the last day, when the whole place is attacked and blown up. Of course I was not well enough to go and see it, but I could hear the row and imagine the rest.

Soon after this scene, my brother Edward and my sister Emily came out in the *Queen*, a sailing vessel. It was a great joy to me. My brother, being in the artillery, had to go to Dum-Dum, a few miles from Calcutta, and Emily stayed with us. Then old Mrs Tytler and poor George's widow came, the former to stay with us, and the latter to go home with her only boy.

After my baby's death, my husband thought if only he could think of something for me to occupy my mind, it would divert my thoughts from my great grief. So he went to Calcutta and brought home a little stereotyped painting of the 'Infant Samuel', with paints and brushes and a little book of directions to guide me, and persuaded me to try and copy it. Being so passionately fond of drawing, it had the desired effect. I worked away very hard at 'Samuel', though without success. I very nearly gave up the fine arts in sheer disgust, when a great friend of ours, Mrs Pattle, our general's wife, came to see me.[49] When she saw me struggling over my 'Samuel' she said, 'What are you doing, Mrs Tytler?' I told her of my vain efforts to copy it. She advised me to drop 'Samuel' and begin with something worth copying, promising to send over a large portrait of her husband painted by Sir George Hayter.[50] When I saw the picture I felt dismayed at the thought of trying anything so difficult, but my husband encouraged me so greatly and ordered a canvas and stretcher from Calcutta. I knelt down before the picture and asked God to guide my fingers and then I began. Well, to make a long story short, I took a month to finish the picture, which turned out a facsimile of the original. When General Pattle saw it he was so pleased that he called out 'Bravo, Mrs Tytler' and told me to order the finest frame I could find in Calcutta and tell them to put it down to his account, which I never did. Then Mrs Pattle lent me one of the General's mother painted by Zoffany,[51] a Spaniard who visited India nearly a century and a half ago. This was a more difficult one to copy for there were two halves to it, but in due course of time I got through that too and was now considered quite an artist by my friends. Of course I painted a number of other pictures but none so large.

While we were in Barrackpore, a letter was sent to all the officers by the head sweeper of the burning ghat of Calcutta offering his daughter in marriage to any officer, promising to give her a dowry of £10,000. It was great fun amongst the young men who were delighted to chaff. I believe some of them sent for her photo out of that pure mischief the Bengalis[52] have.

Now came March and the Burmese campaign.[53] Lord Dalhousie[54] had remarked our fine men when they were doing their turn of duty in Fort William, Calcutta, and gave an order for the 38th specially to be chosen for Burma. Now our regiment was not what used to be called in those days a general service one, and therefore could not be sent on service anywhere by sea.[55] They were all very high caste men from Oude, and to make them go by sea to Burma would have caused a mutiny. What they should have done was to ask for volunteers, which would have meant that the colours and some of the elder men would have stayed behind, showing the regiment wasn't going, only such sepoys as wished to do so. This very regiment had on a former occasion volunteered and crossed bayonets with the French in Egypt. Consequently they were designated the Volunteer regiment and had a skull and crossbones on their caps. It certainly was a very fine-looking regiment—all the men in the Grenadier company were from six foot to six foot four in height and great athletes.

As soon as Lord Dalhousie selected the 38th for Burma he was told by old generals that they couldn't be made to cross the seas, as they were not a general service regiment. Lord Dalhousie, who was a very obstinate Scotchman, exclaimed, 'What soldiers won't go where they are ordered to go? They shall go!' When we came to hear of his determination, my husband said, 'I know my men will never go if ordered, but if the Government would only ask them to volunteer they would go to a man.' But he was only a captain, therefore what was his opinion worth? Our colonel, to please Lord Dalhousie, said he was sure the regiment would go. So, as they could not make them, they compromised the matter by saying they would ask them—another great mistake.

A parade was ordered for the next day and all the subahdars and jemadars came the evening before to assure the colonel that the regiment would go. My husband said, 'Harrie, mark my words, the men will never go!' Well, the parade came off and Colonel Burney harangued the men and told them what an honour the Governor-General had conferred on them by selecting them out of so many other regiments to be the favoured one to go to Burma and would they go? All the subahdars and jemadars came forward with their swords down and said, 'Sahib, the men refuse to go.[56] They are quite willing to walk to Burma, but they won't go by sea.'

This was wired off to the authorities in Calcutta and Lord

Dalhousie, on hearing of it, said, 'Oh! so they are fond of walking, are they? They shall walk to Dacca then, and die there like dogs.' It was Christianlike to wish these poor men, who had only upheld their religious rights, to tell them to go where they were to die like dogs. Then and there as a punishment we were ordered to walk to Dacca and relieve the 74th, who had been nearly decimated by its terrible fever, dysentery, diarrhoea, and cholera. We had to obey, but such a thing had never been heard of as to go by marches to Dacca.

Within four days we were off. The heat in Bengal at that time was intense, but I set to it with a good will and packed up everything, sent all our heavy baggage by water and went by land in heavy marching order ourselves. No one can conceive the difficulty of that march of fourteen days. We had to cross sometimes three huge rivers like seas in one day. The inhabitants of the villages, who had never seen a soldier still less a white man, all ran away, leaving their villages deserted and empty, so that we had the greatest difficulty getting food en route.

The outgoing regiment gave us a ball to welcome us to the gates of death. We chafed terribly at the injustice of being sent there as a punishment, but we were determined to put a good face upon it and appear as if we really liked the change. So soon as we reached cantonments, our first thought was to secure a good home. There was a very nice roomy house with a very large garden which my husband decided to take for his mother and ourselves. It had the credit of being haunted, and also that all who went there died. So a body of our sepoys went to my mother-in-law, who was a very old lady, and begged of her on no account to let the Sahib take the house. She became nervous on hearing this and persuaded my husband not to take it at any price. So we took another without a vestige of a shrub even, and four of our officers, Major Knyvett, Captain Shelton, Lieutenant Castle, our adjutant, and Dr Scott took the haunted house between them. Very soon Major Knyvett became ill and left the station.

The other three jogged on and for a time nothing happened. At last one day Dr Scott said to Castle, 'Let us shoot some of these owls', and ordered his servant to bring out their guns. An owl was shot and all the sepoys said, 'Now the fate of these gentlemen is sealed.' I must say I don't like killing owls, for the day in which my baby was taken ill, an owl flew into the drawing-room in broad daylight and my husband immediately shot it as a specimen for his collection, and my little stepson brought it in alive to my bedroom for me to see. I observed that he fixed his eyes on the little one, who was quite well then. And I exclaimed, 'Oh Robbie, take it away, take it away!' As the boy was taking it out, the bird turned his head round and kept gazing at the baby till he was fairly out of the room. I thought nothing more about it then, but when baby died I felt his flying in in the middle of the day was an ill omen and have ever since disliked owls.

After Dr Scott had shot the owl, which lay at his feet apparently dead, he said to Castle, 'Let us cut his throat to make sure he won't come to life again and give these fellows occasion for more forebodings.' A carving knife was sent for, but no sooner did the knife touch the creature's neck than he gave a flutter and off he flew. This circumstance strengthened the belief in the minds of the sepoys that these two were now doomed. The natives of India have a strong belief that there are certain spots in their country inhabited by spirits of souls not at rest. One of these places is Dacca.

Young Castle had only just returned from England where he had been on sick furlough. One day, while in Dacca, he came in from parade and said to Shelton, who was sitting near the entrance of their public room, reading, 'Shelton, I am very tired and will lie down for a little. Don't let anyone disturb me.' Saying this he threw himself on the couch and fell asleep. Presently Shelton looked up from his book and saw a tall gentleman dressed in mufti sitting at Castle's office table writing a note. He remarked to himself, how strange that he should have brought in a friend without introducing him to me. Somehow he couldn't take his eyes off him and presently noticed that after writing for some time, he dabbed the note on blotting paper, put it into an envelope and addressed it. Rising, he went up to where Castle was lying with his face towards Shelton and gazed steadfastly at the sleeping man; then, passing by him, he went out of the door. Immediately Captain Shelton flew to the desk to see the note, but there was no note. He then rushed down the stairs and questioned the sepoy on duty as to where the officer had gone. The sentry replied, 'No officer came this way, Sahib.'

Shelton said, 'But there was a gentleman who came out of our room and went downstairs.'

The sepoy insisted upon it that he had seen no gentleman pass that way.

Shelton, in relating this incident to us, said, 'Thank God I never saw that man's eyes.' But he was so disturbed about what he had seen that he spoke to Dr Scott about it and said, 'Do you think I should tell Castle?'

He replied, 'I think you had better not.'

However, some months later, as these two were sitting out on the chabutra (terrace) in the evening, Shelton said, 'Do you believe in ghosts?'

'No indeed I don't! What makes you ask me such a question?'

'Well,' he said, 'as you don't believe in them, I will tell you', and then related the facts as he had done to us.

Poor Castle made no remark for some time, but seemed to be in deep thought, and then said very sadly, 'That was for me.' Poor young fellow, he was engaged to be married, and his fiancée was to have come out very shortly, but before she could, he died from severe pains in his head. He said to me when he came to say goodbye before we left Dacca for England, 'Oh! Mrs Tytler, I do not know how much longer I can bear this agony in my head', and a few days afterwards he became so violent that they had to put him in a straitjacket. He lived three days and then died.

Now one of the doomed had gone and Major Knyvett had left for the Hills, sick. There was only Dr Scott and Shelton left in the haunted house. I will tell you of their fate later on.

Dacca was a place remarkable for its gauze-like muslins and embroideries in silver and gold, as well as silks. The former used to sell for £1.10s. a yard and had to be made under ground for so fine was its texture that the slightest breath of air would have destroyed it while being woven. When we were there, in '52, they made no more of this lovely quality as there was no market for it. The best then made was sold at 2s. 8d. a yard. The reason there was no market for it was the nawabs and rajahs began to wear English clothes and went up to the Hills in the hot weather. There were only two old men then alive who in their younger days used to make the beautiful kind. In this way so many of our former exquisite manufactures have died out.

The deadly climate of Dacca had told upon us terribly. On the 1st of October, less than five months after we were sent to Dacca by

Lord Dalhousie, there was only Colonel Finnis, Lieutenant Castle and one of our fine men,[57] who stood at muster. The rest of the 600 men who were stationed there, for 300 had been sent to Sylhet, were either dead or dying in hospital. I was one of the first to take the fever and had it for over five months. It was sad to see the poor little children suffer, for none escaped. My poor husband's mother, being so old, died on our way down to Calcutta. My husband used to get no fever but always an attack of cholera with every new moon, and each time nearly died. So Lord Dalhousie's curse came too true in fulfilment. He wouldn't believe we were all dying and thought so many officers being away on sick leave was a subterfuge to get out of Dacca, so he ordered a little steamer and went off to see for himself. But take my word for it, he didn't walk to Dacca.

I forgot to mention, when he uttered that curse, he also added that no officer of the 38th should ever get an appointment while he was Governor-General. Well, when he arrived we had left on our way to England. He must have felt some pangs of remorse when he saw the few poor men in the hospital who had survived up to that time. Seeing was believing, for he then and there struck out the name of Dacca—never to be a military station again. I believe the present one is in a healthier locality, some fifteen miles from the old station.

My little Frank was born on the 5th of September and has always been delicate. Naturally I attributed his delicacy to my wretched health. We left Dacca when he was about three weeks old and left all our things to be sold by auction. They were sold for nothing—a palkee gharree for five shillings, a child's pony for a shilling; my mother-in-law's antiquated carriage and a pair of horses also went for almost nothing. When she heard of it she never got over the shock and from that day failed fast and died in the boat on the same day as the Duke of Wellington.[58] They were about the same age too.

We had a terrible scene with the boatmen who had been engaged to take her body down to Barrackpore. When they found what they were conveying, they nearly threw the corpse overboard. My poor husband was in a dreadful state of mind, not knowing what to do, and cried to think that they were treating his darling mother's body so. It was in the Sunderbunds, nothing but water and jungle on both sides. However, at last they quietened down and went. Our old bearer Dabi, very ill himself, went in charge of her body. The weather was very hot and she arrived in a terrible state of decomposition. All the officers in Barrackpore, who had seen her only six months before a handsome old lady, went to her funeral, and she was buried at the foot of my baby's grave.

The day before she died we noticed how bright and happy she looked, sitting by the window of our boat. I was so pleased, thinking she was better, and said, 'Mamma darling, you are looking so much better today and we hope now that you are going to get well.'

She replied, 'Oh no my dear child, I am no better! The fever is devouring me just the same, but I am so happy I don't wish to live another day.'

We asked her to tell us why she was so happy, but couldn't get her to divulge what she had seen. All she would say was, 'I have seen that which makes me so happy I don't wish to live another day.' Sometimes she would say on being questioned over and over again, 'I am not allowed to tell you more than I have seen that which makes me so happy I don't wish to live another day.'

She died during the night some thirty-six hours afterwards. My sister Emily, though herself ill, was so good to her through all her illness and I know she was very grateful to her for it.

As soon as we reached Calcutta, my husband went to Barrackpore to see his dear mother's grave and to know all had been done according to her last wishes. She had always expressed a wish to be buried in the graveyard where her only and beloved daughter had found a resting place, and she had her wish granted.

Dacca, in our day, in the rains, was an awful place, a deadly climate to the European and the North-west sepoy. The fungus that grew up every night on our mats was over an eighth of an inch high and quite green. Even oil paintings suffered. As for the river, it became a roaring torrent and overflowed on the opposite side till every tree was submerged and the natives had to take to their boats till it subsided; you could realize what the flood meant in the days of Noah. As soon as the land was again visible the inhabitants sowed their fields with rice and lived again on terra firma till the next rains, when they would again resort to their boats.

While we were in Dacca, the Revd Mr Shepherd showed me a little box full of the seeds of a sacred tamarind tree, one of the acacia family, which he had with great difficulty obtained from an old Hindu priest, they being considered very valuable on account of their scarcity. Every bean was the size of ordinary tamarind ones, the only difference being that each of them had a perfect human face and each was different from the others, as if carved out by human hands. There was some tradition about the sanctity of this tree, but I cannot recollect what it is just now. I wanted very much to get a few, but could not persuade the priest to part with any to a European barring a Padre Sahib, who was to him in the place of God, and could not be refused.

Our regiment was now ordered to go by water to Cawnpore, for the few men out of the 600 who were alive were too weak to march. On the way up Dr Scott and two other officers went out for a stroll in the evening when the boats were moored for the night. While out they observed a large tree covered with beautiful red berries. They knocked some down and Dr Scott and Captain Nepean tasted one each, when they gave a cry of anguish and spat them out, but not before the mischief was done. The third officer had only just tasted his and spat it out in time. He escaped very narrowly with his life, but the other two unfortunate men died very shortly from an agonizing excoriation of the throat. A native, observing these officers knocking down the berries, called out, 'Sahib, Sahib! Don't touch that tree, the berries are poisonous!' but his warning came too late. (That such trees are allowed to exist is astonishing, except for the apathy of native natures.) Now both Castle and the doctor were dead, Knyvett had become ill, and only Shelton remained so far unhurt out of the four who took that haunted house. But it was not for long. His wife, who had returned from England, proved unfaithful and the unfortunate man left the regiment never to return to it.

We had taken our passage in the *Camperdown*, a sailing vessel, so as to have a long sea voyage in hopes of shaking off this deadly fever. Nothing particular happened till we reached the Cape, except some usual bad weather. At the Cape we stayed ten days and took in fresh passengers, among them a Miss Solomon, a naval officer, his wife, an English servant and four children. Captain B was quite out of his mind and wished to shoot himself the moment he came on board, so his son, a lieutenant in the navy, brought a pair of pistols and laid them on the table saying, 'There father, you can do it.' But seeing his father had changed his mind, he withdrew the pistols at once, fearing he might want them again.

Now we leave Cape Town and proceed on our journey, taking in

St Helena on our way. From the first day, Captain B took it into his head that the people on board wanted to rob him and nothing would make him leave his cabin door, but there he stood with his double-barrel gun to shoot the first man who approached him. Needless to say, nobody cared to do so. After some time he gave up this idea for a new one, which was that everyone on board wanted to poison him. Nothing would induce him to touch a morsel of food for the rest of the voyage.

Seeing his poor wife so distressed, for he was getting visibly thinner every day, my husband offered to try and make him eat, so went up to the poor mad man and said, 'Look here B, do you know that they are trying to poison you and me.'

'Ah,' he replied, 'I know it too well.'

'But look here,' said my husband, 'I know where the steward keeps all the stores, and if you like I will go quietly, unknown to anyone, and get some nice things out, which you and I can eat in your cabin quietly.'

'All right, Tytler.'

My husband, who had arranged everything beforehand, got a whole lot of things from the steward and took them into Captain B's cabin. They then commenced to eat, when all of a sudden B took up a knife, jumped up, and tried to stab my husband with it, saying, 'You are the one trying to poison me.'

My husband then and there snatched the knife out of his hand and left his cabin, going up to his poor unhappy wife and saying, 'It is no use, Mrs B, I can do nothing with him.'

Miss Solomon, one of our new passengers, confided to some of us a burden on her mind, which was that unknown to everybody she had brought her father's corpse on the ship to have it buried on his beloved St Helena. The burden was a terrible one for fear that if the sailors found it out, they would chuck her father overboard. Of course we were all under vow not to disclose the terrible fact of a corpse on board, so that when we reached St Helena and the contents of that case were safely landed, her brother Nathaniel came on board and said to those his sister had confided in that she had told him how kind we had all been to her. Therefore he invited us to his hotel as guests. It was really very good of him and his sister because I can answer for myself that I had done nothing so wonderfully kind as to merit so much goodness from them. Nathaniel also placed a carriage and pair at our disposal, for which we were not asked to pay, which enabled us to go and see Napoleon's tomb.

Though his body had been removed and taken to Paris, where it now lies in L'Hospice des Invalides,[59] we saw the empty grave and the willows that had wept over him all those years. Napoleon had suffered terribly before he died of cancer in the stomach, but he was so proud he would not let his enemies know of his suffering. Only Madame Bertrand, his one friend who attended him night and day, knew and kept the secret. I was told on St Helena that the poor prisoner (for though I have no sympathy with him, whose ambition caused him to put away his wife Josephine and marry another for the sake of a son and heir, and whose same ambition caused so much bloodshed in Europe), yet one cannot help pitying the once great man, now so humbled as to be a life prisoner in this isolated island, from the highest point of which he could be seen every day with his telescope, watching for a boat on the horizon coming to rescue him. He firmly believed to the last that France would rescue him, so what must have been his disappointment when day after day no boat made its appearance. They told me on the island that thunder is never heard owing to its great distance from land, but the day Napoleon died distant thunder was heard. I was also told that when the body was exhumed it was found in perfect tact, showing no decay beyond the crumbling of one little finger and that only on being touched. So lived and died the dreaded scourge of Europe.

Through him, my grandfather, grandmother and their four children, amongst them my mother, were kept prisoners for fifteen years in France. Of course the womenkind were not prisoners, but my grandmother would not leave her husband and son, and used to make artificial flowers to sustain herself and the family and to give a few creature comforts to my poor grandfather. They were kept a part of the time in Bordeaux and a part of the time in Verdun. My uncle Tom, as a boy, was apprenticed to a cabinet-maker and was the inventor of the French polish of today. After the Battle of Waterloo, they were released and returned to England, staying with my grandfather's brother, Dr Lempriere, author of the Latin dictionary.[60] It was there that my father, on furlough from India, met my mother and married her. My grandfather, who before his capture was a rich man, was through poverty forced to leave England and try his fortunes in Tasmania. There my uncle Tom became commissary general, and afterwards died in Aden on his way to England to see his sister (my mother). The Lemprieres are well known in Australia to this day, many of them holding high positions out there.

To return to the *Camperdown*, we met with terrible weather and had to eat sea pie for a whole month (sea pie is a dish composed of meat, potatoes and lumps of pasta all cooked in a large cauldron, when it is too rough to cook other food). We used to eat this on the floor, holding on with one arm round the cleated leg of a table. During this time we had as we thought to save the lives of our two large cages full of little birds, which my husband was taking home for the zoo. The cages were placed on the floor for fear that they would be thrown off the walls of the cabin from the terrible rolling of the vessel. But the noise overhead was so great that though the cages were between my husband and myself, we could not hear the fluttering of the poor birds as they were being devoured by the rats. When daylight appeared, judge of our horror on finding that three-quarters of the birds had been eaten up by these wretched rats. Some of the living ones had their legs bitten off and died later on. My poor husband was so mad over it that as soon as this terrible weather had abated he got a rat trap and caught four, which jumped out of the stern window into the sea as soon as he opened the door of the trap. We could see them trying to swim for their lives, but of course in a minute they were out of sight and met the fate they deserved. These dear pretty little birds had cost us a lot of money, for it was only the rare ones that my husband had purchased for the zoo.

All the whole month we saw nothing of the other passengers for everyone had to keep to their cabins. How Captain B fared I don't know, but when we met again he was but a shadow of himself. We had sighted land (Cornwall) and then had been blown out to sea again, knocking about in adverse winds – all this time we were living off sea pie. As soon as the wind changed we set sail for London, expecting with such a fair wind to be there quickly. When the pilot came on board my husband told me to prepare to go on shore off Portsmouth. I begged of him to let us go to London, for the Captain said we would be there the next day. 'No, no,' said my husband, 'I have had enough of this.' So when the pilot left the vessel we were put on board his little boat and sent down to the cabin below, expecting to reach Portsmouth in a couple of hours, instead of which another fearful storm overtook us and we did not get in for some eight hours.

As soon as we left the *Camperdown* we saw a small Danish vessel come up; a man, their only passenger, stood up on the deck and offered the pilot a sovereign, which he held up between his thumb and forefinger. The pilot called out no, saying he could only take him for double that amount. The poor fellow said he had no more. That little Danish vessel was lost off the Goodwin Sands and all perished. We heard about it afterwards from our passengers. The *Camperdown* was supposed to have been lost in that awful weather in the Channel, for she was not heard of for a whole fortnight. Our Captain called out to the Danish vessel when so close as to be heard, 'Do you know you are drifting on the sands.' They replied, 'My God, we know it too well!' Our vessel was saved by a perfect miracle and came in to docks in an awful condition. How thankful I was that my husband did not listen to me. She was five months and a week at sea and they had nothing to eat at last, so they had broken into our cabin and taken everything in the way of food out of it, for we had brought with us a supply of biscuits, rusks, and water in bottles.

As soon as the vessel anchored, what did Captain B do but drag his poor wife round the deck thrashing her with a horsewhip most unmercifully. Poor woman, she was soon rescued by the crew and he was taken and put into an asylum at once, where fortunately for the whole family he soon died. Not long after, his eldest son, the young lieutenant, shot himself, and still later one of the two hand-some younger boys shot the other by accident, and Mrs B's eldest daughter, who had married a civilian in Chittagong and to whose care the poor mother had sent her two grown-up daughters, died of cholera. Now the poor woman was left with two little girls, one a baby, a little boy and the remaining elder boy. Could anyone imagine so much sorrow and trouble to fall to the lot of one poor woman in so short a time? She had been a very handsome girl when Captain B married her.

After staying till we got all our things out of the ship and putting our two elder boys to school, we went to Scotland to visit some of my husband's relations, having first exchanged our native ayah, who went back to Calcutta, for an English girl. We had not been long in lodgings in Aberdeen when the girl and the two little children developed whooping cough. It was a great trial, though my husband's people did not mind it, as they had all gone through the same thing. From there we went to Glasgow to some dear Indian friends, saw Loch Lomond, and then went across to Ireland. We stayed a few days in Dublin in Greshams Hotel, saw all we could, even the exhibitions, and from there went to Cork, which we enjoyed very much. It is a lovely place. Before leaving for England, we visited Killarney by excursion train, but were most unfortunate in having a very rainy day and saw nothing except Blarney Castle on the way and Macroom Abbey in ruins. We returned in the evening with a lot of young college boys, many of whom had their valets with them. They had evidently had a good time of it, though it was such a bad day, and were in the jolliest of moods. I don't think we ever enjoyed anything like that return journey. These Irish boys with their wit and pranks were too much for the railway officials. A railway director, unknown to them, was sitting next to my husband and said, 'The boys must have their fun.' So the inspector got the worst of it and left them with his policemen baffled on every side, and the boys triumphant. So ended our excursion to Killarney.

After staying several weeks in Cork, we went across to Weston-super-Mare to see my dear old mother and my widowed sister with her four lovely children, but they were all so terrified of the whooping cough that they would not come near for fear of carrying the infection on their clothes. We soon got so sick of this nonsense that we took our departure back to London, and made our way to Southsea, where we had Indian friends.

Southsea used to be a great place for tea parties and cards afterwards. We were often invited out and my husband asked to play, till they found out he would not play for money, when they had no further use for us. The first time this discovery was made was at the house of an Indian friend who was living with her mother and brother, a celebrated doctor. One of the guests that evening was a portly dame, who set her heart upon having my husband as her partner at whist. He was asked to play but refused, saying he never played. They persisted and persisted till at last he gave in, to the delight of the said dame. The other two players were a poor Indian captain like my husband and a poor oldish maid. No mention was made about money so the playing went on until the game was over, when my husband's partner joyfully took account of how much they had won. £20!!

It was then that my husband, who was a first-rate player, gave her to understand that they had not mentioned that the game was for money, or he would not have played at all, being contrary to his principles, and refused to take his share. Of course had he lost he would have had to pay, but he knew what he was about and had no fear of losing the game, with his wide-awake partner and their opponents, so he had some pleasure in drawing the old gamester out. She was furious and said that it was an understood thing in Southsea to play for such and such points. My husband said he was sorry they had not informed him, but he couldn't touch the money, that they could arrange it between themselves if they liked. Consequently she had not the face to take her share, so the poor captain and the old maid got off from losing £10 each. How glad they must have been, for just before they had very woebegone faces. Needless to say, Captain Tytler was never asked again to play, being such a muff, but he was no muff, only extremely clever in all points and enjoyed a game at cards for love's sake as much as anybody. That did not suit the Southseaers.

I found out a good portrait painter in Portsmouth and took some lessons from him, watching him paint his own pictures. It has always been my way of learning anything, for one gets into the way they handle their tools better than by being told how to do it. Not only that but there are so many tricks in the trade which are never shown to pupils, but which painters use when painting their own pictures.

As soon as the children got well of their whooping cough, we went to Felpham, a little village near Bognor, on the south coast of England, to stay with Mrs George Tytler and her father Colonel Squire.

It was our intention to have stayed there as paying guests until time for us to return to India, but Colonel Squire's son-in-law made himself so disagreeable and used to beat his wife, so that we did not know what would happen next. One day, as we were at dinner, he tried his best to provoke my husband to say something so that he might call him out to fight a duel, but fortunately for me, my husband was a man with such control over his temper that he could not succeed. I put up as long as I could but he was so insulting that I thought it was time to stop him, so I took up a knife lying on the table and was on the point of throwing it at him, when my husband caught my arm and stopped me. Then and there I left the table, vowing I would not stay another day in the house, and immediately started packing up our things.

Next day we were ready to return to London when Colonel Holcombe came forward to shake hands and begged to let bygones be bygones. I put both my hands behind my back and said, 'I will never shake hands with a murderer', for he had fought many duels. My husband said, 'We are going now, Harrie, just to say goodbye', but I could not forgive a man who could beat his wife and kill men in cold blood. His poor wife, though a strong woman and one who could have taken him by the scruff of his neck and thrown him out of the window, was so crushed by his constant cruel conduct that she had no spirit left in her and died soon after. This was the man she once loved so desperately and would have no other, but love was gone and hate and fear had taken its place.

After we left Felpham we went to London to make arrangements to store our furniture and then go to Paris, where we stayed for some months. We placed our two elder boys in a school near L'Arc de Triomphe and took a little house outside the Barrière de L'Etoile, where we had a Breton for a cook and a Scotch girl for a nurse. A sad tragedy took place not far from where we lived. A young French girl, who had been engaged to a man whose marriage to another she saw in the papers that morning, was so stricken with grief that death appeared preferable. Both our servants were out for a walk with the children and saw a very well-dressed young woman with her little dog go up the steps of the Triumphal Arch and, very soon after, witnessed the terrible scene. She had tied up her dog at the top, evidently fearing he would jump after her, and then took the fatal leap. Marie the cook described the scene most graphically. Poor girl, she was perfectly unrecognizable except by her clothes. It made an awful impression on us all.

One of my greater enjoyments in Paris was to visit the Madeleine. We used often to go there to hear the requiems held for the rich, on account of the glorious music, and then buy lovely, lovely flowers in the flower market just by the church, and return home through the Champs Elysées. One evening, as I was walking home arm in arm with Marie in the Champs—a common custom in France but never to be heard of in England—Marie stopped for a moment. Throwing her arms round my neck, she cried and said, 'I never get a mistress I love, but she leaves me. Oh madame, take me with you to India!'

I replied, 'Marie, how can we do so? You know Marjory has been engaged to go and we could not afford to take two servants.'

'Madame, I want no wages, only my food and clothes, if you will but take me.'

I was so touched with her tears and devotion that I promised to speak to my husband on her behalf, which ended in his consenting to take her also. All our acquaintances, both French and English, laughed at our softness, saying, 'You'll see, she won't stay long with you, for she will die with "*mal de pays*" and you will be glad to send her back.' I told Marie this and her reply was, '*Bien, nous verrons Madame.*'

Towards the end of May, when Paris was commencing to be very hot, we returned to London, leaving the two elder boys at school, and came away with the two younger. Marie had gone home to Bretagne to take leave of her people. My dear mother came to stay with us till it was time for us to go to India. It was a great pleasure to me, for I may say I had not seen anything of my mother, except for those six weeks after my father's death, since I was a little girl of eleven, and now I was five and twenty.

In June 1854 my little Edith was born within the sounds of Bow bells, which I believe constitutes a cockney.

We left England early in the following August in the *Collingwood*, which had been chartered to take out European troops for the East India Company. Our sick leave was for three years but my husband felt we could not afford to live another year on English pay without going into debt, so we gave up a whole year of it. Colonel Whish was the officer commanding, Captain Tytler second in command, Captain Symons of the artillery the adjutant, and Dr Brown our doctor. We had 262 recruits with also some of their wives and children on board, all going out to join the European regiments, the 1st, 2nd and 3rd Bengal Fusiliers. Some of the men belonged to the artillery and some to the sappers and miners.

When my husband found out the name of the vessel chartered by Government for this service he came home greatly excited and asked me to guess the name of the captain who was to command the *Collingwood*. On my failing to do so he mentioned a Captain Tanner.

'Surely not the *Camperdown* captain?' said I.

'Yes,' he said, 'the same!'

'Well then, I won't go in that vessel, for we will never reach India.'

My husband soon made me understand that there was no choice in the matter, he had elected to go with the troops and could not now draw back. It was a great shock to me and proved no saving of expense after all, for the owners of the vessel made up for the cost of his free passage by adding it on to ours, knowing we had to go.

There were no other passengers besides Mrs Whish, Mrs Symons, Miss Whish and her little sister Kitty. In our party we had besides ourselves our five children, my sister, the two servants and Mr Schilling, the boys' tutor. We sailed from Gravesend in August 1854 and had fair weather for the first few weeks. Poor Mrs Whish took a chill before she came on board, which developed, and she went into rapid decline. Our food was very bad from the beginning, so much so that she gave up coming to the table and had her meals in her cabin. On one occasion she sent her plate back with her compliments to the Captain saying she was not accustomed to eating nails for her dinner. Sure enough there were actually three nails quite an inch long on her plate. Often I used to have my meals also in my cabin and force myself to eat, holding my nose tight so as to get down some of the very objectionable food as best I could, for the sake of my infant. Before we had gone six weeks on our journey, there was no more white sugar, only very coarse brown, and the children were without fresh meat for more than half the time. Even my little boy, barely two, was fed on salt beef, except what I could give him, when dining in my cabin.

The soldiers fared much better, for simply they would not have stood it. If any of their provisions were not good, they just threw it overboard and demanded more, and got it too. I firmly believe if Colonel Whish had refused to eat the food we had, they would have given us better, but he was a very easy-going man and spent the greatest part of the time in bed from seasickness, so he allowed everything to slide and no one else had a voice in the matter.

At last we came in for very bad weather. Captain Tanner took us too far south in hopes of not losing time by being becalmed, but unfortunately he gained nothing by it but otherwise, for we had contrary winds and heavy gales the whole way—no less than eight heavy gales, a cyclone, and, not having had enough, a hurricane. The gales blew every Sunday for eight consecutive weeks till our course was turned northwards. While we were far south and amongst the whalers, we saw, after one of these severe storms had somewhat abated, a sailor's straw hat floating on the sea and soon after the body of the poor fellow to whom it belonged, lying calmly in death. We could see his features so clearly, he looked a lad of some twenty years of age.

In fine weather the soldiers and sailors used to sing on deck every evening; some of them had splendid voices. While my husband and sister used to enjoy themselves on the poop above, I had to content myself by staying in my hot cabin looking after the children. My husband would not allow them to be left to the tender mercies of the two servants. I felt it was hard for me and told him so, and that we should take it by turns, but I fear the best of men are selfish and he would not see the justice of my proposition. Both Marjory and Marie liked flirting with the men and therefore could not be trusted with the care of the two very little ones. Marie's great friend was a young private who spoke French well. He said he was the son of a General Repton and had had a quarrel with his father over some love affair and enlisted to spite him. Of course Marie couldn't speak English at that time.

One evening she came very excitedly into the cabin saying, 'Madame, Repton tells me the soldiers are going to throw Captain Symons overboard with his wife and child (this little child, a girl, was born on board), and if any of the officers try to prevent it they will be thrown over too.' I immediately called my eldest stepson and told him to run up and tell his father I wanted to see him. The moment he came down I related the alarming facts. Of course he lost no time in reporting the matter to the colonel, when the roll-call brought all the men on deck. The ring leader, an old soldier of some fifty years of age and a well-known bad character, was put into irons and sent down into the hold, where he remained in the enjoyment of his own society until we reached Calcutta. The remainder of the soldiers, mostly boys, were told the same fate awaited them on the first sign of insubordination. Fortunately nothing of the kind occurred again, because a mutiny at sea is a very terrible thing.

Poor Symons was not at all liked, being somewhat of a martinet, and too severe with such raw boy recruits, who had not learnt discipline yet. Poor man, he was killed afterwards in '57, in the Battle of Chinhut in Lucknow, where he was wounded and then had his throat cut by the mutineers in that first unfortunate engagement.

If any of my readers have ever been at sea in the centre of a cyclone, they would understand it better than I can describe it. The sea was as smooth as a mill pond and the air very close, with the barometer falling rapidly. The Captain knew at once what to expect and prepared for the coming storm. And it did come, with a vengeance, throwing the vessel on her beam ends. When it had passed in its full, we had reason to be thankful to God for having brought us out of it safely.

For some weeks the weather was less stormy and the men resumed their concerts. Poor Mrs Whish grew worse every day and said to me, 'I know I can't hold out much longer and must lay my death at Captain Tanner's door.' Our food was getting worse and worse every day and often did Marie fetch me some edible food from the soldiers' table that I might eat something for my baby's sake. Her petit François would also get something better to eat than salt beef, poor child.

We had a very exciting time during this voyage being followed by a very suspicious-looking craft for days, but not close enough to make her out properly. At last she began to get nearer and nearer. Our men were ordered to keep down on the under deck till ordered to come up. When she did come up alongside of us, she had apparently only two men on board. There was no doubt in the minds of everybody that she was a pirate and the rest of the men were hidden away. She couldn't give a good account of herself so all our men were called up. Seeing we were well prepared for her, she slunk away and we saw no more of her.

Another time we had a very narrow escape. The vessel was going at fourteen knots an hour and constantly tacking. There was another vessel doing the same but going in exactly the opposite direction. We saw this vessel in the morning at a distance and then lost sight of her altogether. In the evening she passed us like a meteor and was out of sight again. In passing, she was so close that we could see into her saloon distinctly and they must have seen us in the same way in ours. Had we collided, both vessels must have gone to the bottom in a few seconds. We hadn't time to think of our danger before it had through God's mercy passed and we were safe.

A few days later I was sitting in my cabin with my baby in my arms looking out of the storm windows, which were on a level with the platform and usually used as seats, but in the *Collingwood* had been converted into beds for my husband and myself, when all of a

sudden I noticed what looked like an extraordinary phenomenon, a
dust storm at sea. This proved to be sea spray flying miles ahead of
the hurricane. My husband was on the poop talking to the sailor at
the wheel. He said to him, 'I fear we are going to have dirty weather
again.'

'Yes,' said the man, 'probably a hurricane!'

It came on so rapidly that my husband had barely time to get down
to the saloon. The Captain came down and, looking at the barometer, he tore his hair and said, 'My God. It is all over! There is
nothing more I can do to save her!'

The little children were in the passage leading into our cabin. My
husband, with one foot on the floor and the other on the side of the
walls of the cabin, struggled in with the two youngest, calling out to
my sister, the servants and the two elder children to come into the
cabin. Before this happened, a sailor had been in and closed all the
windows so that nothing could be seen through them. I knew from
this that another storm was brewing, but didn't know it was to be a
hurricane. Everything happened in such quick succession that one
had hardly time to think when my husband came in with the
children, followed by all the rest, and said, 'My Harrie, the Captain
has given up the vessel as lost!' It was a terrible moment. He went to
the cabin door and, closing it, said, 'Let us die all together.' Marjory
was crying bitterly and my poor sister too, but Marie was as brave as
a lion, calm and cheery, holding her petit François, only just two, in
her arms. My husband was close to me on his knees, offering up a
silent prayer, when the two elder boys, who were old enough to
understand the danger we were in, cried bitterly and said, 'Oh
mamma! If God will only save us, we will say our prayers three times
a day.'

'Hush children, hush!' I said, for it was a moment for everyone to
hold communion with their God, pleading for forgiveness ere we
entered into His presence. At this critical moment the vessel took a
lurch which brought her to the verge of capsizing. I clasped my baby
girl to my heart and said to myself, 'Now, now, in another moment
we shall feel the cold water as she goes down.' As she lay on her side
she trembled violently and then lurched over to the opposite side,
where she again lay and trembled, as if her very life were going. We
again thought it would all be over in a few seconds. The timber
creaked as if she was going to pieces. The noise above and all around

was so deafening that no cries of anguish even in the cabin could be heard—anguish of the soul was there, knowing that every minute was bringing us nearer to eternity and to face our God. No one can realize such a moment except those who have gone through it. The vessel again took her third lurch in the same dreadful way, only this time, after trembling violently as before, she righted herself and then flew before the storm. By this short time the waves were mountains high and any one of them falling on the vessel would have swamped her at once, but fortunately for us closeted in our cabin we did not know of our imminent danger. My husband tried to get out to learn what news he could, but he came back only to tell us we were still in great danger.

The ship was flying before the storm, but no one could say whether it was possible for her to weather it. But thank God for bringing us safely through that awful day. The poor soldier boys were most of them down on their knees praying as possibly they had never prayed before, praying to God to save them from a watery grave, and I am sure the prayers of the many mothers for the safety of their dear ones were had in remembrance before God on that memorable day. Life is so dear to us all, specially when we are young and have none of the sorrows and troubles all humanity has to go through during a protracted life. The boys all behaved nobly in doing their duty manfully, even the youngest of them.

The ship had not her full complement of able-bodied seamen. The stingy owners had trusted to the many hands on board being able to do what should have been done by trained sailors alone. Yet, in spite of all this and God's mercies to us, imagine our disgust when, a few days afterwards, the Captain at the dinner table called out to the chief mate, 'I say Allen, do you recollect when we had that cat's paw (the hurricane) the other day and those fellows from their mothers' apron strings were down on their marrow bones, what fun it was!' He evidently had forgotten he did not think it fun when he tore his hair and cried that it was all over. If only he knew how we despised the man who is a blasphemer in the hours of safety and a coward in the hours of danger; and had he seen or been conscious of the withering curl on my husband's lips he might have guessed the utter contempt he felt for him. God did not permit him to see many such storms, for we heard he died not long after.

Thank God this worst of all was our last before reaching Calcutta.

We could not have held out much longer for we had been nearly five months on board and were reduced to one salt pig's cheek at our table. No one knows the delight of tasting fresh bread and butter after all that time! In those days of over fifty years ago, hermetically preserved fresh butter was not known. What we had to put up with was very salty and rancid. Even poor Mrs Whish, who was dying, her voice not being audible, enjoyed the fresh bread and butter brought on board to us as we were coming up the river. And when my husband took up the papers to Colonel Whish for his signature, refusing to pay the owners for our board, which he should have done in justice to all the passengers, he said, 'Oh! Tytler, let it go. I am in too much trouble and grief to fight it out.' So they got off scot-free and probably tried it on again with the next trooper.

The moment we dropped anchor, Marjory came, my baby in her arms, and said, 'There, take the child, ma'am. I am going to be married today.'

We had tried hard to stop that flirtation on the voyage, because she was so superior to the man she was going to marry, and we believed she had really given him up.

'Now who has left you first, Madame,' Marie said triumphantly.

We heard soon after that the saloon steward had deserted his vessel and firmly believe that he never married the poor girl, but deserted her too, though she showed Marie a wedding ring on her finger when she came for her wages. We tried our best to find out what had become of her, intending, if the scoundrel had deserted her, to take her back into our service, but could never get any tidings of her, poor girl.

We had now to wait on board till orders came to my husband where to escort his men. The artillery men and sappers were landed at once in Calcutta and sent off with Captain Symons in charge to Dum-Dum, about seven miles from Calcutta. My husband's men, for the infantry, were put in light boats called dinghies while he had a heavy green boat, in honour of his position. The consequence was that the dinghies got well ahead and hugged the shore of the river Hooghly all the way to the Howsah station. Native dealers, knowing the weakness of European soldiers, filled them well with liquor all the way to Howsah. The result was when we reached the station the men were disgracefully drunk. I myself saw one young fellow, about sixteen, waft off a half-pint bottle of Aruck, a native liquor worse than any rum or whisky, and drop down instantly as if he had been shot. The men were in many instances so riotous, with the exception of Repton, and Roberts his cousin, that the passengers who were to have gone by that mail train fled and left the platform. When the time came for the train to leave, the railway guards, aided by Repton and Roberts, bundled the dead drunk soldiers in. My husband, not accustomed to European troops, was in an awful state of mind, sure that nothing short of a court martial awaited him.

For a time everything seemed quiet in the third-class carriages, but as soon as the soldiers began to regain consciousness with the fresh air, the uproar commenced until it became a perfect bedlam. Repton and his cousin had as much as they could do to keep some of the men from chucking each other out of the windows. My husband had previously promoted them to a higher rank for being the only ones who were not drunk. When we reached Chinsura some hours afterwards, the men were all got out. My husband spoke to them very seriously, saying, 'See, my men, what trouble you have brought me into by your disgraceful and unsoldier-like conduct.'

Their reply was, 'We are not drunk sir, and wouldn't cause trouble on no account', all the time trying their utmost to stand straight. It really was too laughable to watch them.

The officer on duty soon turned up and my husband, in full uniform, went up and explained matters to him. 'Oh Captain Tytler,' he said, 'I don't suppose you are accustomed to European soldiers. I think the lads are pretty all right, considering their long voyage. My sergeants will soon be up and take charge of them.'

What a relief to his highly indignant state of mind. True enough, the sergeants arrived with carts. Those who could walk were marched off, those who couldn't were thrown into the carts like sheep and off they all went, while we went off in palkee gharrees and drove to the barracks, where we had to stay for some weeks before being allowed to leave.

A few days later some of the young soldiers came to my husband and, touching their hats very respectfully, complained to him that they had not enlisted for such work. The work they objected to was doing the goose step. My husband told them he had nothing whatever to do with them now, and that they had to complain to the adjutant. Poor boys, they soon had to learn that strict obedience was the first law of the army and no doubt many of these boys had to taste

General View of Delhi, with the Jumma Musjid mosque in the centre. From a sketch by Prince Alexis Soltykoff in the *Illustrated Times*, 1857.

The Bridge of Boats, photographed by the Tytlers from the Red Fort, Delhi, 1858.

The Magazine and Cemetry inside the city, photographed by the Tytlers.

Bahadur Shah, the 82-year-old King of Delhi. From a miniature by the portrait painter to the King, in Charles Ball's *The History of the Indian Mutiny*.

Zinat Mahal, the King's favourite wife.

Brigadier-General Archdale Wilson, commander of the Field Force at Delhi when the city was assaulted.

Major-General Sir Henry Barnard, who assumed command of the Delhi Field Force on the death of General Anson on 27 May and who in turn died of cholera on 5 July 1857. From the *Illustrated Times*, 1857.

The Flag Staff Tower on the ridge at Delhi, from a sketch made during the siege by Brevet Major J. R. Turnbull, late ADC to Brigadier-General Wilson. To the left of the picture are the Mosque and Observatory.

'Delhi, from the Flagstaff Tower', showing the minarets of the great mosque, the Jumma Musjid, as sketched by Major Turnbull during the siege.

the pleasures of bread and water and solitary confinement till they had learnt not to complain about the goose step or any other thing.

We heard afterwards that poor Repton and Roberts had tried deserting from Burma soon after their arrival in that country, which act deprived them of the chance of taking their discharge after two years of service, and that poor Repton had died. But Roberts went through the siege of Delhi to die later in Kussowlee, from where he got a comrade to write to my husband, thanking him with his dying breath for all the kindness he had ever shown him and his cousin.

As soon as we could get away, we went to Calcutta and stayed with my husband's brother-in-law, Mr Milson, manager of the Agra Bank, after which we went up-country to join our regiment at Cawnpore. Having given up a year's furlough, my husband was allowed six months' privilege leave and so we went up to Mussoorie to his little cottage there, called Rock Cottage. Schilling, the tutor we brought out, had behaved very badly towards us, for no sooner did we reach Calcutta than he asked for permission to go on shore and while there he saw some of the heads of the educational department and secured a good situation for himself. He never even apologized, made any excuse, or offered to pay for his passage out, and we never saw him again till after the siege. It appears he had obtained the headmastership of the Martiniere School in Lucknow, and during their very troubled times in '57 he and his boys kept the Baillie Guard and did so so valiantly that Government gave him property worth over £10,000.[61] He then married and came with his wife to see us in '59 when we were in Mussoorie. The poor young wife died very soon after. I don't suppose any woman could have been happy with him, because of his restless habits at night. He seemed possessed in some way and couldn't sleep, so he used to wander about on deck almost the whole night.

At the close of the season, at the end of '55, we left Mussoorie and returned to Cawnpore and took with us two young girls, the daughters of two retired officers whose wives had been very kind to my husband after his first wife's death. We meant to give them a good time, but had not been long in Cawnpore when Captain Tytler received orders to go with young Glubb, his subaltern, to Orai, where every three months a detachment of a company was sent from Cawnpore. It was a great disappointment to us and a great expense when we could so ill afford to buy tents.[62] Orai not being a military station (it could hardly even be called a civil one, there being no one there but an Eurasian uncovenanted collector), the girls had a very stupid time of it. I used to amuse myself all day painting in the circuit house[63] till evening and then go out with our whole party for a drive. Marie had left us in Cawnpore to return to her home and see her little baby. She never told us that she had left her child with her people in Bretagne and now her mother's heart longed to see the child again, so we got a situation for her for the voyage and let her go.

I missed the good old soul terribly. Poor woman, when she got home she found her baby had died and at once wrote to my mother to get her a return situation. She came out with a Captain and Mrs Evans, poor people, who were murdered in Cawnpore so soon after. She joined us in Delhi only a few months before the Mutiny.

The annexation of Oude had taken place a year before this, but the country was not settled, so our regiment was ordered on service to subdue such of the Rajput Thakoors in Oude who did not like to acknowledge our rule or submit quietly to the new regime.[64] So after staying with some friends, the Homfreys, in Lucknow for a fortnight, during which time one of the girls got engaged to young Homfrey, we went up to Mussoorie with the girls and our two little children, while my husband with his regiment went to the scene of war under the command of General Sir Frank Wheler, my old Mussoorie friend. The two elder boys were at the Revd Mr Maddox's school as boarders and Fred as a day boarder.

In Oude there was really no fighting to speak of, just settling some little squabbles and taking the Thakoors' forts and so on, till at last our regiment was settled for a time in Gonda, where there were no houses or any appearance of civilization. The only occupants of the land where the regiment was located were cobras and scorpions innumerable.

As soon as the monsoon set in in Mussoorie, Edith began to get ill. The young station doctor (we could have no other) insisted it was only teething, but as she began to show symptoms of convulsions I got very alarmed and begged for another doctor to be brought in for consultation. The young doctor saw no necessity for it. I said, 'My husband is away on service and I cannot take the responsibility of this child's illness without being satisfied it is nothing but teething', so he had to consent and I wrote Dr Bruce a very beseeching letter begging him to come and see her, which the dear old man did. Edith was lying in my arms when he saw her and said, 'Is this the child you are so frightened about?'

I replied, 'Yes doctor, but you must not judge her by her face, all my children are round-faced, but her body is frightfully reduced and she has not attempted to walk for weeks.'

'Oh no!' he said, 'Of course I must examine her, so undress her and lay her down', which I did. He then gave her three taps on her liver and, turning round to me with a very grave face, he said, 'I grieve to tell you Mrs Tytler, your child is in a most precarious state. She has an abscess on the liver, but her life is in God's hands. We can and will do our best!'

I thought my heart would burst. Our only girl! Dr Bruce went on to the verandah and pitched into the young doctor most unmercifully for nearly an hour as he walked up and down. I heard him say, 'She must have twelve blisters[65] if she can only stand it.' He then told me what I was to do. One was to be put on one day on this lobe and another on the third day on the other lobe. I had never seen a blister put on, so dear Mrs Weyness came to show me how to do it. The poor child said nothing but 'Nai mamma', trying to pull it off. She never uttered another word, though she must have suffered intensely. The third day the second one was put on and Dr Bruce came to see her. He cried out, 'No more blisters! The child can't stand them! She is sinking fast. We must try something else', which was acid baths, showing me how this was to be done. Meanwhile they had telegraphed to my husband to say, 'If you want to see your daughter alive, come at once.' This message he took to Sir Frank and begged him for leave, which the kind old man gave him at once.

Poor little Edie used to get these baths three times a day. I was giving her one when the door opened and I saw my husband look in and turn away. Our old faithful bearer Dabi would hold her while I sponged her and all the babe would say was 'Nai mamma, nai mamma'. She had a huge abscess which protruded several inches on her right side. My husband said it sickened him that the child he had left so bonny only a few months before was such an ashy colour.

The dear little thing remained in this condition, neither better nor worse, for months, never uttering one word, except 'Ahloo (potatoes) mamma', which of course she was not allowed to have. From later experience I believe it would have been good for her, knowing as I do of the curative powers of the skin of potatoes in cases of severe spleen.

One morning when I was out with her, in September, the sun, which had not been seen for some weeks, came out. She was in my lap, utterly oblivious to everything. Suddenly she turned her head and said 'Mamma', as if that sunlight meant life to her.

Now the 15th of October was at hand, when all military men and doctors must be back with their regiments. It was time for Dr Bruce to return also. The child, though alive, was neither better nor worse and he said, 'As she is no worse, I can only hope she may live by outgrowing it.'

Our regiment had been ordered from Gonda to Delhi. We wished to go down in November, but the young doctor would not hear of our taking Edith down, saying, 'It would be her certain death.' So my husband, thinking he had had enough of this doctor's opinion, called in another who said, 'Take her down at once. The cold up here would certainly kill her!' So much for doctors and their opinions. So we went down and Marie, who had returned from France, joined us in Delhi. Dear old body, she brought something for myself and all the children.

As soon as we got down to warmer regions little Edith began to mend and this terrible abscess worked its way out in time through her eyes and lips. She lost her beautiful long eyelashes, which never came back again either so long or so curly as before, but she quite regained her health, thank God, and at the time of the outbreak there was no trace of the abscess left, though she suffered from sties for several years and the lids to this day are very weak. In after years, Dr Bruce met us in a dak bungalow, when she was about ten years old, and said to me, 'Is it possible that is the same child I was instrumental in curing? I thank God for it for she is indeed a lovely child!'

In November we came down from Mussoorie, and just six months afterwards the Sepoy Mutiny broke out. We would not take Edith up to the Hills that hot weather as they seemed to have disagreed with her, and lent our house to our colonel's wife and children, but we could not foresee what she was to go through in Delhi and yet with God's mercy live through it. I think the prickly heat from which the poor child suffered terribly was probably her salvation, helping to draw out all that remained of the abscess in her system.

PART TWO

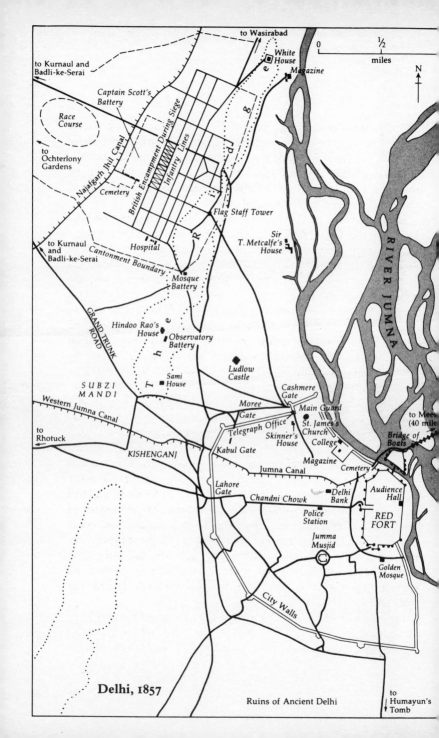

Delhi, 1857

to Wasirabad
White House
Magazine
to Kurnaul and Badli-ke-Serai
Race Course
Captain Scott's Battery
British Encampment During Siege
Infantry Lines
Najafgarh Jhil Canal
to Ochterlony Gardens
Cemetery
Flag Staff Tower
Sir T. Metcalfe's House
to Kurnaul and Badli-ke-Serai
Cantonment Boundary
Hospital
Mosque Battery
GRAND TRUNK ROAD
Hindoo Rao's House
Observatory Battery
The Ridge
Sami House
Ludlow Castle
SUBZI MANDI
Western Jumna Canal
to Rhotuck
KISHENGANJ
Cashmere Gate
Moree Gate
Main Guard
St. James's Church
Telegraph Office
Skinner's House
College
Kabul Gate
Magazine
Cemetery
Jumna Canal
Lahore Gate
Chandni Chowk
Delhi Bank
Audience Hall
Police Station
RED FORT
Jumma Musjid
Golden Mosque
City Walls
Ruins of Ancient Delhi

RIVER JUMNA

to Meer (40 miles)
Bridge of Boats

to Humayun's Tomb

0   ½
miles

N

HALF a century has passed since the events I would now record took place, and abler pens than mine have written of the Great Sepoy Mutiny. Still, as a survivor of the memorable 11th of May 1857 at Delhi, and as the only lady at the siege of that city, I am led to think a simple narrative by an eyewitness of those thrilling events may interest others.

In the cold weather of 1856 my husband's regiment the 38th NI,[1] known as the 'Balanteer Titteelee Ka Paltan', reached Delhi, its new cantonments. The 54th and 74th, the latter the regiment we had once relieved at Dacca, were also stationed there; besides these regiments a bullock battery was in the cantonments, completing the garrison, composed entirely of natives without any English troops at all.[2] This garrison of native troops was meant as a corps of observation on, and safeguard against trouble in the strongly fortified, thickly populated city of Delhi. The military cantonments lay at a distance of about three miles north-west from the Great City, which was built on the left bank of the river Jumna and surrounded by a high fortified stone wall and deep broad ditch.

At the time of the Indian Mutiny, the reigning emperor was Bahadur Shah, an old man quite in his dotage, who lived, surrounded by the remembrance of past glory and vast power, on a generous pension provided by the East India Company.[3] His two sons,[4] along with the old man, had evidently but one idea and that was of regaining their power as soon as an opportunity should occur and for which opportunity they had waited over fifty years[5] and had never shown their teeth, until '57. But when the order for the use of the Enfield rifles was issued, they at once set to work to poison the minds of the Hindu soldiery, who thoroughly believed them and nothing could convince them that we had no desire to destroy their caste. They would have it even that the paper supplied to them by Government was also polluted, with bullock's fat for the Hindus and pig's fat for the Mohammedans.

I must here mention that the Indian army consisted of two-thirds Hindus and one-third Mohammedans, as our great safeguard. In signing the treaty with the conquered but very wily Mohammedan emperors of Delhi, and later on of Oude, we were only to have three regiments of native infantry and a battery of six guns, officered by a few Europeans, these to be stationed not nearer the city than three miles. So all the Mohammedans had to do to drive us out of the country was to poison the minds of the gullible Hindus. Now the time had come to do this and they succeeded to their hearts' content.

Two companies from every regiment in the Indian army were to march to their respective headquarters to learn under proper instruction how to handle the new rifles. Our headquarters being Umballa,* our men marched to that station and, though before leaving Delhi they evinced some insubordination, still the officers hoped it would all pass off as soon as they saw we had no desire to destroy their caste and turn them into Christians.

But the Mohammedans had worked so stealthily and brought so much to bear on this prejudiced point, which, added to other grievances the soldiery felt they were suffering under, made it soon visible that Government could not stem this disaffection in the Indian army. Yet they kept hoping to the contrary.

At this time we had in Cawnpore the first flour mill in the Upper Provinces, which gave so much satisfaction to the natives, the flour being ground better and at a cheaper rate than could be done by hand. But the instigators of the rebellion took the first opportunity to poison the minds of the Hindus, who are for the most part a very ignorant and gullible race, by telling them that we were mixing dead men's bones, picked up on the banks of the Ganges, with this flour, just for the purpose of destroying their caste, taking good care to distribute pure flour to the Christians.

The Hindu soldiery were already dissatisfied with the annexation of Oude, for the following reasons. Our finest men had been recruited for several generations from the districts of Oude and were specially favoured in their homes since their families were not subjected to the looting and molestations of the King of Oude's officials or soldiers, as the other poor peasants were. For, if by chance they were so molested, all they had to do was to write to their relatives in the East India Company's army and make a formal complaint. This complaint was immediately brought to the notice of

* Modern spelling is Ambala.

the captain commanding the aggrieved sepoy's company and reported to the colonel, who had to report it to the Government. An order would then be sent from them to the King of Oude to see the family's losses were made good. Consequently the native soldiers' families held an enviable position amongst their less-favoured neighbours. But now that Oude had come under the rule of the English, every native was treated on equal terms. No one was allowed to loot or ill treat another without being punished for the same. This was a grievance to the soldiers.

Another cause of dissatisfaction was the issuing of the postage stamps, which, causing a pecuniary loss to the soldiery, was a real grievance.[6] Before this a soldier could write as many letters as he liked, the same being franked by his officer. A native loves scribbling if it costs him nothing, but now that he had to pay two pice (a halfpenny) on each letter, his pet occupation was gone. With these grievances, imaginary or not, the Mohammedan conspirators had it all their own way.

Before the Mutiny broke out at Meerut and Delhi, broken pieces of chupattee (unleavened whole flour bread) had been known to be sent from village to village,[7] but the officials took no notice of it, not understanding this proceeding and probably thinking it had something to do with their religious rites, till after it was too late, when it was discovered to mean 'Be prepared for a revolution'.

Bulletins kept coming in from Umballa to the Brigadier stating the great dissatisfaction the men were showing to the use of the Enfield rifle and its greased cartridge, and my husband often said to me, 'If our natives were to rebel against us, India is lost.' He really became very anxious as days went on and symptoms of disaffection were showing themselves everywhere, till at last one soldier called Mungal Pandee (from which came the word Pandee for every mutinous native) was tried for insubordination, or in other words mutiny, was convicted and, being the ringleader of his regiment, the 34th, was hanged in Barrackpore, our military station near Calcutta, and the regiment disbanded as a warning to all the men of other regiments.

About the same time the 3rd Bengal Cavalry at Meerut, all Mohammedans, showed such serious insubordination that they were tried by a court martial of native soldiery, the president of which was Munsoorally, a subahdar-major in my husband's regiment, a man unusually respected by all. He called upon my husband (who was on very friendly terms with him[8]) the day before he left for Meerut, saying, 'Sir, if I find these men guilty, I will give them the severest punishment in my power', and certainly he meant what he said, for he gave the ringleaders, some eighty Mohammedans, ten years' penal servitude with hard labour.

The officers of the whole army now considered the unrest was over as the rest of the 3rd Cavalry showed no inclination to rescue their comrades, but allowed them to be put into irons and marched off to prison. Besides, the men of different regiments who were sent to their headquarters to learn how to use the new rifles were on their way back without showing any further outward signs of rebellion. But we little knew what they were waiting for. The fact was, as we learnt afterwards, that the day fixed for the general rising all over India was to have been in July, whereas through God's infinite mercy it broke out some two months earlier among the 3rd Cavalry men, who showed their teeth too soon, when all the regiments were as it were unprepared.

It is wonderful to think how unanimous they were, Hindus and Mohammedans, in the one object of exterminating the hateful Christian in India. On this occasion the Mohammedans and Hindus were one, their bitter antagonism to each other, which had always been our safeguard so far, was for the time overcome. The gullible Hindus, two to one in each regiment, firmly believed Pirthee Rai's raj would return and then they would be masters of India. The wily Mohammedans, who were using these poor deluded men as a cat's paw, encouraged the belief, knowing all along that they would soon find their mistake, for the Mohammedan meant to reign by the edge of his sword, which would also be used to proselytize the poor idol worshippers.

On the 10th of May 1857 (Sunday) the eighty imprisoned men were released by the remainder of their comrades, who had their irons removed, taking a very necessary precaution to cut all the telegraph wires at both sides of the station before doing so. They had arranged a well-conceived plan, which was to release these men just in time to reach the church for the evening service where they expected to find most of the European soldiers and Christian inhabitants of the station, then seize the arms piled outside the church and slaughter all within.[9] But it so happened, through God's mercy, the chaplain had at the morning service issued a notice that the evening service for the future would be held half an hour later. Consequently, when the rebels arrived, there was not a Christian to be seen within the sacred walls. Observing this, they turned their thoughts to cantonments and there began their dreadful deeds.

The ayah of the chaplain's family, on seeing the 3rd Cavalry men, warned her master of something being wrong, and soon all the officers in the station were out with their men, to coerce the mutineers. No officer of a native regiment for a moment thought that at such a time their men would prove disloyal. Colonel Finnis of the 28th was the first man to fall. He was shot by his own men. A general scrimmage followed and, but for having English troops, both infantry and cavalry, the Christians of Meerut would have shared the fate of those later on in Delhi. As it was, many officers were killed and some of the poor unprotected women too, amongst whom was a beautiful young girl, the wife of an officer of the 11th. When the husband returned to his bungalow, what did he behold but his poor young wife lying dead in the compound, perfectly nude, with her unborn babe lying on her chest. Three days later the butcher, who had killed her, was caught and hanged. The only offence this poor girl had committed was to tell this butcher that if he brought such bad meat again she would tell the other ladies not to buy from him again. The man was caught making his escape in a hackery, a country bullock cart, covered over with a dirty chuddar (a native woman's wrap). The poor husband begged to be allowed to go at him, but his brother officers held him back with main force. His one cry was, while struggling to loose himself from their hold, 'For God's sake let me go at him.'

I can't help thinking it would have been a mercy if they had let him have some personal revenge. It might have saved his mind from becoming deranged. I knew the poor young fellow well, when his regiment and ours were stationed together in Barrackpore. At the siege, he used to sometimes, when off duty, come and sit with us of an evening, but he seldom uttered a word, only sat brooding over his sorrow with his head on his hand, a picture of despair. I don't know what became of him after the siege was over beyond hearing that he had gone out of his mind, poor fellow!!!

This is only one instance of similar brutality which the Moham-medans enacted under similar circumstances. I don't believe a Hindu would have been guilty of such cold-blooded atrocities, with the exception of the 'Nana Sahib' at Cawnpore.[10]

I had a cousin in the 20th at Meerut.[11] He had been staying with us in Delhi at Christmas time. Poor fellow, he was in a terrible state of mind knowing what our fate would be the next day and went to the general to beg of him to give him four troopers from the Carabineers that he might gallop over to warn us of our danger. But the general refused, saying, 'We have not enough men to protect ourselves'!!!

That same Sunday morning, while we were driving to an early service at St James's Church in the city, the only church the Christians possessed, we met a dak gharree and in it was young Burrowes of the 54th, returning from Umballa where he had been with his men to be instructed in the much-detested rifle. My husband called out, 'Well Burrowes, what about the men?'

His reply was, 'Oh, they are all right now Tytler and are on their way back.'

That evening[12] we heard the tootooing of a dak gharree bugle in the lines, a very unusual thing, for native soldiers never travel in a dak gharree. So my husband came to the conclusion it must be old Munsoorally, our subahdar-major, returning from the court martial at Meerut. Presently the bearer came back to say Munsoorally had not returned, but some men from Meerut had come to see their friends in the lines. My husband thought it was a strange thing but never gave the matter any serious consideration. Now what were these friends of the sepoys, but emissaries sent over from Meerut to warn the soldiers to be prepared for the next day's proceedings, which up to that time nobody knew anything about. We were utterly ignorant of any mutiny in our neighbouring station only forty miles away.

Mr Fraser our commissioner received a letter like an ordinary native petition just as he was going to church in the evening. He never opened it, thinking it was only a petition, but thrust it hurriedly into his pocket. The next morning, when the dreadful news came that the mutineers of the 3rd Bengal Cavalry were in the city, he tore open the envelope and there he found a timely warning sent by some unknown friend, telling him of what was to happen the next day. But it was too late. He ordered his buggy and drove off from Ludlow Castle (now the Delhi Club) to give his friends Captain Douglas, commanding the Lahore Gate of the palace, and the Revd Mr Jennings our chaplain and his daughter, warning of their danger, but he had not got above the third step of the stone stairs leading up to their apartments when he was cut down by the King's nujeebs. On our entering Delhi we saw the bloody traces of that tragedy.

On the evening of the 10th the order book came round containing an order by the Brigadier, from instructions received from the commander-in-chief, to say each of the regiments in Delhi were to have a parade at day-break, where the quartermaster of the regiment was to read out to the men the punishment accorded to Mungal Pandee as the ringleader of the mutinous conduct of his regiment in Barrackpore. Later on our quartermaster Lieutenant Holland wrote to my husband and asked him to perform this duty for him as he was not well. My husband, being a passed officer,[13] was only too glad to oblige him and sent a reply 'certainly'. Little did we expect what the 11th of May would mean to every Christian, man, woman and child, in Delhi.

At day-break every officer was on parade and to each regiment this order was read out, a sort of proclamation, telling the men what they might expect if they chose to follow their brother soldier, Mungal Pandee's example.

As soon as my husband came home he said to me, 'Harrie, my men behaved infamously today. They hissed and they shuffled with their feet while I was reading out the order, showing by their actions their sympathy with the executed sepoy. But I will give every one of my men drill to their hearts' content.' Little did he dream that before evening came, he would not have one man to drill.

The early morning passed as usual, every door being one may say hermetically sealed to keep out the raging hot wind. Tattees were fixed to the outer doors and watered.[14] We had all had our baths and Marie and the children had had their breakfast, when my husband and myself sat down to ours. This was about eight o'clock. The tailor was sitting at his vocation in the enclosed verandah and all seemed quiet and peaceful. Just as we were getting through our last course (melons), the door flew open and the tailor rushed in with his hands clasped and in a most excited manner said, 'Sahib, Sahib, the fauj (army) has come.'

My husband jumped up saying, 'Give me my boots, my hat, I must go and see the Brigadier at once.'

I did not know what 'fauj' meant and, seeing him so excited, said, 'What is the matter?'

He replied, 'Oh! nothing. Only those fellows from Meerut have come over and I suppose are kicking up a row in the city. There is nothing to be frightened about, our men will be sent to coerce them and all will very soon be over.'

Consequently I was not frightened. Very shortly after this my husband returned and told me that it was just as he expected. 'The Brigadier has ordered Colonel Ripley to take his regiment to the city to quell the disturbance', adding, 'Graves has ordered me to go with Gardner and two companies to the White House and guard the ferry there to prevent the mutineers from coming round into cantonments and blowing up our small magazine.' He said, 'Now don't be frightened, there is nothing to fear, and don't leave the house unless I send for you.' Making so light of it, I did not anticipate anything more serious, for of course we had no idea of what had taken place in Meerut the previous day.

Captain Gardner and my husband then went to the lines and got their men together. In serving out the prescribed number of rounds of ammunition to each man, they noticed the sepoys, especially the young recruits, were most insubordinate and tried to get as much as they could, but, not being quite out of control, they were made to put it all back, just taking their allowance of 200 rounds each man.

On their way to the White House my husband looked in and told me all this, assuring me there was nothing to fear, but soon after he left I could see there was something very wrong. Servants running about in a wild way, guns tearing down the main street as fast as the oxen could be made to go, and Mrs Hutchinson the judge's wife, without a hat on her head and her hair flowing down loosely on her shoulders, with a child in her arms and the bearer carrying another, walking hastily in an opposite direction to the guns. What could it all mean? My two little children left to themselves were getting trouble-some, which made me call out to Marie, 'Oh! Marie, do look after the children.'

She replied, 'Madame, this is a *revolution*, I know what a revol-ution is.'

And there she was shutting up under lock and key everything she could lay her hands upon—even the clean clothes the washerman had brought in that morning were all locked up. Now came a note from Mrs Holland saying, 'Come over to our house.' I wrote back that I could not do so as my husband had told me not to leave the house unless he sent for me.

A little later came another letter from the Hollands, this time sending their phaeton, saying the Brigadier had ordered all the ladies to go to a place of rendezvous and that I must not stay any longer. Things began to look very serious and I knew I must, as a camp follower, obey the Brigadier's orders, so in spite of my husband's admonition we left the house, never to see it again. I noticed Marie had her little wooden box with her and this, it appeared afterwards, contained some of my trinkets which I had worn the week before, such as a gold chain and watch and one or two other things, and the silver on the table amongst which was a valuable old teapot—also the money she had received through the sale of some of the presents she had brought from Paris for me and which I would not accept, telling her I could not let her spend all her savings upon me. Poor woman, I think she was disappointed, but she did as I bid her and thank God she did, as the sequel to the occurrence proved. In the hurry and scurry of leaving the house it never occurred to me to order my own carriage to follow me, which was very thoughtless on my part.

When we reached the place of rendezvous I found we were in the bungalow of the sergeant-major of the artillery. His wife seemed pleased to have us, which was very kind of her, for we filled it to overflowing. Soon after, a counter order came from the Brigadier, saying we were all to go to the Flag Staff Tower on the ridge. Of course everybody got into their carriages. Mrs Holland's one was full with two other friends staying with her at the time, so there was naturally no place for us. Very foolishly I began to cry, not knowing how we were to reach the Flag Staff Tower in the burning sun and at that distance with bare heads and no umbrellas. Mrs de Tessier was the last to leave the house. On seeing my distress, she very kindly offered to take us all in her carriage. How thankful I felt for her kindness. She was alone in her very roomy carriage with her baby and ayah so we managed very well and eventually reached the Flag Staff Tower. We had to go very slowly, picking up carriages as we went along. The long cavalcade resembled more a funeral cortège than the living flying for their lives, but to some it was indeed a funeral march as they never saw the light of another day.

At last we reached our destination. There we found the Brigadier and his staff awaiting us and four guns, with the soldiers of the 74th and the remainder of our own regiment, less those 200 at the White House with my husband, and also our Christian Band boys. A motley group it was and oh! *how* hot,[15] but we bore it all, believing as we did that it could not be for long. Even the Brigadier did not know what was taking place in the city till Dr Stewart of the 74th came in. It was he who brought the terrible news of the massacring that had been going on from early morning of that accursed day. He came near me and said, 'Oh! Mrs Tytler, God only knows how this day will end, for they are massacring everybody in the city.'

He then told me he had gone down out of curiosity to see what was going on in the city and, as soon as he entered through the Cashmere Gate, he saw the ghastly sight of all the officers of the 54th lying dead, with the exception of the colonel, who was virtually a dead man, though still alive. He had been bayoneted in nine places by his own men, but some say by the men of our regiment who were there on guard duty at the Cashmere Gate. Dr Stewart took him into his buggy and drove him to his own hospital and there attended to his wounds. Later on, on hearing from his men that we were all taking refuge in the Flag Staff Tower, he came on to be with the rest, just as we were leaving it. My little boy Frank, only four years old, who evidently had heard the servants on the other side of the Tower talking of how the rebels had killed the little children—showing they all knew what was going on while we in the Tower were perfectly ignorant of it—came to me crying bitterly, saying, 'Mamma, will these naughty sepoys kill my papa and will they kill me too?'

He was a very blue-eyed, fair child. I gazed at his little white throat and said to myself, 'My poor child, that little throat will be cut ere long, without any power on my part to save you.' It was a dreadful moment, but I pulled myself together and said, 'No darling, don't be frightened. No one will harm you. Stay close to your mother.'

Edith, my little girl of two, said to me while I was holding her in my arms, 'Mamma do home, me no like this place. Do home.'

I thought to myself again, 'My poor child, what home have you now, with cruel death awaiting us every moment?'

Lieutenant Thomason of the Bengal Engineers was engaged to be married to the chaplain's daughter. He had been very ill, but when he came to hear they were murdering everybody in the city, he was bent at all costs on getting to the palace gate to rescue his fiancée. Some of the other officers dissuaded him and would not let him go, saying, 'You can never save her. She must have been killed long ago.' Poor girl, and so she had been, along with her friend Miss Clifford, who had come in with her brother from Goorgaon to take sacrament that morning and stay with her for a few days. The brother had returned to his civil duties that morning and so escaped that day, but I believe was himself killed later on, Goorgaon not being far from Delhi.

Many stories were current after we returned with the force to the siege of Delhi as to the way these poor girls met their death. The one generally believed was that when Captain Douglas and Mr Jennings had been murdered, the two poor girls in their terror hid themselves under their beds and were dragged out and thrown out of the window on to the pavement below, a merciful death compared to what might have been their fate. Some of the natives said a friend of Captain Douglas's, 'a Colonel Sahib', had arrived that night, a very tall man, and was killed trying to make his escape while running along the parapet of the high battlements within the palace walls. No one ever knew if such was the case or who that officer was. A young ensign of ours who was at the city dak bungalow that morning, waiting till after breakfast to dress himself and go into cantonments and report his arrival to our colonel, was murdered, as also all those resting there for the day.

Here I must go back to the early morning of that memorable day to tell you how and when the rebels from Meerut came into Delhi. As soon as they found they could not cope with our European troops in Meerut they decided to gallop off to Delhi and begin their inhuman work there. They rode hard over the forty miles and reached the city about six in the morning and went to the river gate of the Emperor's palace, calling out from below who they were and what their mission was. The royal family immediately gave them permission to enter, which of course they did. Anybody who has ever been to Delhi and seen the palace walls from the side of the river will have noticed the gate, which leads by a flight of steps to the beautiful apartments of the Emperor. There they parleyed with him and his wicked sons and got their permission to go and slaughter every 'kafir' (unbeliever) and 'sāf kurrow' (clean out) the city of them. The two elder sons of the Emperor, whom Hodson shot, were the real instigators of the rebellion, not that the old Emperor did not desire to do his best to turn out the white invaders, forgetting that his forefathers had also been invaders, but he was in his dotage and not altogether responsible for much. History can tell what cruel masters these Mohammedan conquerors, from their first conquest in the eleventh century, were to the poor Hindus of Hindustan, who knew little respite from their injustice and misrule until the English became masters of the country.

To return to the doings of the 11th of May, the sowars, after receiving the King's blessing, rode out of the Lahore Gate of the palace, cut all the telegraph wires, killing the operators, and made for the only English bank in the Upper Provinces of India, where poor Mr Beresford and his family were living. All this time we in cantonments knew nothing of their doings. Mrs Beresford behaved most pluckily. As she ran down the stairs to the ground floor, she took up a spear on the landing and with it speared three of the sowars before she herself was killed. Two of their little daughters were at Mrs White's school at the time their parents and three sisters were being killed, two of whom were grown-up young girls just out from England, while the youngest was a baby in arms. After the wretched troopers had killed the family, they looted the bank, and it was not till they had their fill that they galloped down to the Cashmere Gate to face the 54th.

Colonel Ripley had, on receiving orders from the Brigadier, taken his men down to the city to coerce the enemy. On entering the Cashmere Gate he drew up his men between the gate and the church to await the arrival of the rebels. Poor man, little did he realize the disloyalty of his men, so as soon as the sowars galloped up he gave the order 'Fire'. At once the regiment turned round and fired at their own officers, killing, as I said before, all but one officer and the colonel. The other officer was Lieutenant Osborne, who though badly wounded did escape death by dragging himself into a culvert and hiding under it. As soon as the men of the 54th and the guard of the 38th had fraternized with their comrades in arms, the troopers began the general massacre in the city, a few only escaping, only to be murdered later on. A great many, I believe 250, took shelter in the magazine, others in tykhanas in the large European residences in the city, hoping they would escape from the vengeance of the cavalry till a favourable opportunity for escape turned up, but out of all none escaped but one woman, of whom I shall speak later on, and a family named Forrest.

The Forrests were living in a house close to the Cashmere Gate. Their two daughters had just arrived from England. Two of our officers, who were on duty in the city and were the admirers of the girls, helped to save them, along with Mrs Fuller's daughters, by throwing themselves into the moat and scrambling up the high perpendicular wall on the other side in a most miraculous manner. The poor old people, Mrs Forster and her sister Mrs Fuller, who were very stout, could not do this feat and begged to be left to their fate. This party escaped to Meerut after wandering about at night[16] and hiding themselves by day, until discovered by a party of brave officers from Meerut, young Gough of the 3rd Bengal Cavalry amongst them, who escorted them back to Meerut in safety.

My readers must now go back with me to the Flag Staff Tower where, after hours of agonizing suspense, expecting every moment to be killed, no attempt was made by the Brigadier or the other officers to form a retreat while there was time to do so—every moment's delay made it more difficult—but no doubt the poor Brigadier and all the officers present expected European troops would have been sent from Meerut, only forty miles away, to help us in our imminent danger, but none came. Probably he had not the moral pluck to leave his post at such a critical time. Colonel Keith Young, in his letters to his wife up at Simla, wrote the following, 'Of the extreme unfitness, however, of Brigadier Graves for command there can be no question, and I hope to hear of his being superseded.'[17] Again on page 88 Keith Young says, alluding to another officer first as being superseded, 'as has been Brigadier Graves, who has, I hear, decided to apply for four months' leave. Quite right! This is no time to stand on ceremony, and keep inefficient men in important posts.' On page 90 Keith Young says, 'Longfield being appointed a Brigadier in the place of Graves, who as I told you, had got a hint to apply for sick leave, which he has done'. Still, I do think Brigadier Graves would have done better had it not been that he was expecting troops, which he had a right to expect. Had a large body of them come over *at once*, such as even half of the Carabineers, that day's slaughtering would have been prevented. I don't think anything would have prevented a mutiny altogether, but every station would have been better prepared to cope with it. And

Brigadier Graves should have taken the responsibility of forming a retreat even if it had cost him his commission. By doing so he would have saved many a life that was lost, even of those in the Flag Staff Tower.

For hours I never saw Marie. She knew the children were with me, so she amused herself talking to the officers in French, probably anxious to know more than we women could tell her. An order came for all our Christian Band boys to go to the top of the Tower and, with muskets and arms which some of the other ladies as well as myself helped to send up to them, to be ready for the expected attack. For want of seated accommodation we ladies had to share a charpoy and two chairs by turns. At last dear Mrs Peile of our regiment gave me her own chair to sit upon. A great comfort it was, after hours of either standing or sitting on the floor.[18] But now that we had to help in handing up arms and ammunition, I seated myself on one of the stone steps leading up to the top of the Tower, with little Frank clinging to me on one side and Edith the little girl in my arms. As I said before, Marie was nowhere to be seen.

While helping to pass up the arms we heard a most sudden and awful explosion, when everyone jumping up ran to the door facing the city and called out, 'My God, what was that?' It soon spoke for itself, for we could see a white cloud extend itself across the city, looking like a very long sheet, which gradually turned into a thick brown mass. It was indeed the magazine, and everyone believed till we knew to the contrary that the mutineers had done it. As you may imagine our hearts were filled more than ever with hopeless dismay and, at the smallest noise, my little children would clasp me all the tighter and I myself felt, as I am sure everyone else did, that our last moment had come; God only knows the misery of that heart-rending day, borne so heroically by all with silent resignation. I thought several times I would try and run over to tell my husband what was occurring in the city, but then the thought of leaving my children to their fate held me back, and the fear that going across those three miles of the ridge to the White House in the burning sun of May with a furnace-like wind would be too much and I might drop down dead with a stroke of the sun, so I had to give up the idea of ever expecting to see my darling husband again and prepare myself for death. I thought they would have shot me or cut me down, but thank God I never supposed that I could have met a worse death, which I afterwards learnt was meted out to so many poor women.

I must now take you to the White House. As soon as the two officers reached it, the men were ordered to pile arms and go into the house. The latter they would not do, showing a very strong spirit of insubordination. They would say, 'No sir, we like the sun.' It was no such thing. They were simply defying his authority. One of the young recruits, a Brahmin, was haranguing the men, saying, according to their prophecy after the Battle of Plassy, the English were to be turned out 100 years from that date.[19] The hundred were just over and this was the time to complete the prophecy. My husband again ordered the men to go inside and with difficulty got them to obey. They sat about in clusters, grumbling and looking very dissatisfied, till the explosion took place when, with one accord, they flew to their arms, picked up the muskets, and with a shout, crying out '*Pirthee Rai ka raj*',[20] they fled down the road to the city and, as they passed the Flag Staff Tower, fired at Captain de Tessier who was on the point of starting off with another two guns to relieve those in the city. His poor horse had six bullets fired into him, all of which were meant for the rider, but fortunately, though covered with his charger's blood, he himself had not been wounded. He had just time to turn his horse's head and reach the Tower, when the poor thing dropped dead. The two guns which were to have gone with him were carried off by the native gunners to the city.

When my husband saw his men depart, he flew after them and called out, 'For God's sake men, be true to your salt.' His pleading had the effect of getting back some forty of the older soldiers, and with these he turned his back on the post he had been ordered to guard, knowing he could not do so with so very few men.

On his way to the Flag Staff Tower, he met a young officer of the 74th, Brigadier Graves' adjutant,[21] telling him to bring on his men to the Tower, upon which my husband turned round and said, 'These are all I have left.' From that young officer he first heard of the dreadful doings of that day, and then and there no doubt formulated his plans to get the Brigadier to form a retreat.

When at last I saw my husband enter the open door of the Tower, I called to him. He replied, 'I can't speak to you. Where is the Brigadier? I *must* see him at once.'

I answered, 'He is somewhere in the crowd.'

Then I heard my husband say in a very clear, audible voice, 'Excuse me sir, but what are you going to do?'

He replied, 'Stay here Tytler and protect the women and children.'

My husband said in a most emphatic manner, 'It's madness sir, have you any food?'

'No, Tytler.'

'Have you any water?'

'No, Tytler.'

'Then how do you propose protecting the women and children with the two remaining guns ready to blow us up?'

'I know it,' he said, 'but what can we do? If we put out our heads they will shoot us down.'

My husband said, 'My men will never shoot us.'

Then and there came a shout from all the other officers, 'For God's sake don't listen to Tytler. He has been talked over by his men.'

My husband said, 'Look here gentlemen, it is not for you to say listen or don't listen to Tytler. We cannot hold our post, therefore it is our duty to form a retreat.'

The Brigadier then said, 'Go and ask your men, Tytler.'

My husband went out bare-headed and empty-handed and said to the men, 'Listen to me my men, if you intend to do any harm to those within, let me be the first to fall, that they may know their fate. But if you will be true to your salt, and will go with us wherever we tell you, then say so.'

Some of the men came forward and touched the hair of his head, which is with the natives an oath. 'We will not harm any of you and will go where you tell us, provided you guarantee to us three things: one is that you command us and not the colonel, another that you give us water to drink, for we are dying with thirst, and lastly that these two remaining guns go with us, or we will not go.'

My husband came and repeated what the men had said to the Brigadier, upon which all the officers called out again, 'For God's sake don't listen to Tytler.'

My husband then said, 'Very well gentlemen, do just as you like, stay here and be butchered, but I will go with my family and stand my court martial. I will not stay to see my wife and children butchered.'

The Brigadier then said, 'Go Tytler and ask the men again.'

My husband did so, whereupon the soldiers said, 'Are you playing with us sir? As you know the troopers are now in the Ochterlony Gardens refreshing their horses, and as you have stayed here all day they expect you to stay here all night and will come on and kill you at their leisure. If you don't go at once we won't go with you.'

Just a little before this, a bullock cart arrived from the city, bringing all the dead bodies of our poor officers of the 54th, young Burrowes amongst them. We never knew whether these bodies were brought to the Tower out of kindness or to intimidate us. I am of the opinion it was for the latter purpose. The cart with the bodies remained on that spot until our return in June, by which time they were only skeletons, and were buried behind the Tower, where there was a tomb erected to their memory, poor fellows, but it has since been removed. Why I don't know.

As soon as the Brigadier and officers heard of the fate awaiting them, they realized how near their end had come and then there was indeed a stampede, everyone rushing to their carriages to see who could get off the first. Fortunately my husband had had the presence of mind to order his palkee gharree, a vehicle he used to go out shooting in, to be brought up to the Tower. It had just arrived and we were put in. Captain Gardner had never thought of ordering his buggy, so my husband put Mrs Gardner and her little boy in with us. It was a terrible crush, for a carriage only meant for two persons inside to have six. How we all got in I don't know. Marie and myself sat with our backs to the horses with little Edith on my lap and Frank crouching with terror at my feet, hiding himself in our petticoats, while Mrs Gardner and her boy sat opposite. I never could have believed so small a child could have realized the awfulness of our situation.

Poor Colonel Ripley, on hearing we were all taking refuge, ordered his doolie (litter) bearers to carry him in his bed to where we were. He had only that moment arrived, as we were leaving the place. I can never forget his poor death-stricken face, and could realize his feelings of despair at coming to be with his comrades and then being left by them to his sad fate. It was nobody's fault. There were not enough conveyances as it was to save the lives of all those in the Flag Staff Tower. Those who could get away on horseback or in carriages had a chance of escape. Those who had not almost to a man met their deaths on the way.

The plan of retreat had been formed by my husband. It was to take the two guns to a place called Baghput where there was a ford, there to spike them and leave them in the sand and go on to Meerut, the nearest military station to Delhi. My husband gave our servants instructions which way to go and told me to follow the guns; this being done he went back to take command of his men, according to his promise. The officers of the other regiment, the 74th, followed but kept aloof from ours, saying, 'You may have as much confidence in your men as you like, but we have none.' Nevertheless they were glad to have their protection, as long as it lasted.

When we got down to the bottom of the road, where we should have by rights turned off to go to Baghput, the servants came to me and said, 'Sahib told us to go this way', pointing out a direction.

I replied, 'Sahib told me to follow the guns.'

They persisted we were to go their way. I would not hear of it as his instructions to me had been to follow the guns. Thank God I did not go into cantonments, as the servants had wished me to, for had I done so we would surely have met our deaths, as we learnt afterwards from Munsoorally's son, who went into our bungalow thinking he would try and save some of my husband's pet chemical things, for his father and Captain Tytler were very busy before the Mutiny experimenting with making gold. The preparations were nearly completed at the time the Mutiny broke out for a final test and it was this the son wanted to save. When he got to the bungalow he saw our two Mohammedan table servants, the khansamah (house steward) and the khitmutgar, sitting at the gate, each with one of my husband's double-barrel guns. On asking them what they were doing sitting there, they replied, 'It is not likely the sahib will escape the soldiers, but, if he does, he won't escape us.' From this we knew how disloyal some of our domestics were, with the exception of Thakoor Singh, our orderly.

We afterwards learnt from our washerman, who had been in our service ever since our marriage, that our tailor and the bhistee (water carrier), both Mohammedans, had gone to their homes in Cawnpore in our buggy and that both the table servants had become sowars and had been killed fighting against us. I think I could at that time have gone some miles out of my way to have seen them hung for their base and treacherous ingratitude. We had raised that khansamah from a musolchee (washer of plates) to his then exalted position and he had brought us our lunch and iced water to the Tower, which none of us touched except the water, not even the children, and then he took it to my husband, with the same results, pretending to be loyal, and yet in his inner heart he was arranging to kill us all that evening.

When my husband got down to the bottom of the Flag Staff Tower road, just where I had my discussion with our servants, he saw an awful sight. It was two of our sepoys, who had been blown up while doing duty at the gate of the magazine. My husband said they were skinned from head to foot. Immediately the soldiers, on recognizing their comrades, said, 'What is the meaning of this?'

'The meaning of this,' they replied, 'is that we were doing our duty in the magazine and Sircar blew us up.'

It appears young Willoughby, a young gunner of the artillery who had just joined us at Delhi, saw the necessity of not letting our small arms and powder fall into the hands of the mutineers, so he decided to blow up the magazine. He ordered his subordinates to lay a train of gunpowder, and at a given signal, which was the taking off of his hat, to light the fuse. Those five or six brave men never flinched from their duty, while he stood watching for the first head which should appear above the walls which they were scaling. As soon as one native's head appeared, off went his hat. That moment the fuse was lit and that terrible explosion was the result.

Poor young Willoughby was not killed in the explosion—nor was Mr Forrest, the father of the two young girls who escaped from the Cashmere Gate, though badly wounded—but he and another officer, in trying to save Captain Osborn of the 54th, who was so badly wounded that he could not walk, lost their own lives while in the jungle foraging for food. Thus one of our pluckiest men lost his valuable life. There were two Willoughby brothers, only sons of a widow. The other brother too was killed during the mutiny at Saugor. The 250 poor refugees who were taking shelter in the magazine were also killed at once, or wounded and killed later by the inhabitants of Delhi.

Some forty poor women and children who had hidden themselves on that day were caught afterwards trying to make their escape. And, though promised their lives by the King's soldiers who had captured them and taken them to the palace known as Lall Killah

(Red Fort), they were a week later brought out, by order of the eldest son of the old King, to be slaughtered at a given signal, viz. the firing of a musket. This fiend, who was one of those shot by Hodson, sat in the Nobid Khana Gate, which you can still see in the centre of the fort, and there gave the signal for the cold-blooded murder of those poor helpless creatures, one of whom had only been confined the previous night and who begged to be allowed to speak.

The Nawab said, 'Let her speak.'

Poor thing, with her baby in her arms, she implored for all their lives saying, 'Oh! Nawab Sahib, such a thing as killing poor helpless women and children was never heard of as being done by brave men.'

Upon hearing these words, the Nawab said, 'Is that all she has to say?' and gave the signal. One of his soldiers then and there speared the poor new-born baby and threw it up in the air before the unhappy mother's eyes, and then all were ruthlessly slaughtered in the large courtyard, next to that of the Diwan-i-am,[22] where stood a tree hanging over a little pukka tank (stone reservoir).[23] Strange to say no horse would pass that tank without shying. The natives firmly believed that the spirits of the murdered women and children haunted that spot.

When the two sepoys said 'Sircar' blew us up, my husband, believing as every European did that it was the work of the natives, said, 'Never, never.'

'Yes Sahib, we were doing our duty at the gate of the magazine and Willoughby Sahib blew us up.'

'Very well,' said all his men, who had been faithful up to this time, 'from this moment we will take the blood of the English', and at once began to scatter.

My husband implored of them to be true to their salt, but all they said was, 'Go sir, save your wife and children, we won't hurt you, but we cannot answer for the other soldiers', meaning of the other regiments. 'Where is the water you promised us? Where are the guns you promised us? They have gone to the city and will turn round and blow us up. No, we won't go with you another step.'

Seeing it was no use, the men being so determined, he went off to the Brigadier and said, 'Sir, what shall we do? The guns have taken a wrong road.'

'Go after them Tytler and bring them back.'

'I have no horse sir', upon which Major Nicholl said, 'Take mine Tytler.'

He was a fine charger. Captain Tytler jumped upon his back and was out of sight in a minute, galloping at full speed to catch up the guns and bring them back. As he neared where we and they were, he met the Gujars coming out on a looting expedition with their iron-bound 'lahthes' sticks. These Gujars are a set of Mohammedan peasants,[24] the very opposite of the Hindu Jats, who live by thieving and blackmailing. If we wished to have our property taken care of at nights in Delhi, we were bound to have a 'chowkedah' (watchman) from the Gujar village. A chowkedah from any other village would have been incapable of protecting our property, for do what either you or he might, you would be sure to be robbed. These men with one accord made a dash at my husband's horse and tried to knock him off, but thank God they did not succeed. The noble creature just flew over them and was out of sight in no time.

As soon as he got to where the guns were my husband called out, 'De Tessier come back, you have taken the guns on the wrong road.'

Upon which he replied, 'It is no use Tytler, they are quite out of hand. You had better look after your wife and children and save them.'

Captain Tytler, supposing we had gone to Baghput, said, 'But where are they?'

De Tessier said, 'They are somewhere in the crowd. I saw them a little while ago.'

Just then I saw my husband on a strange horse and beckoned to him to come to us. He then and there jumped off, while Thakoor Singh held the horse, and was for coming with us, when poor Mrs Gardner gave a most piercing cry of 'Oh! Captain Tytler, where is my husband, where is he?'

At once my darling husband, in the generous impulse of his heart, said, 'I will go back Mrs Gardner and bring news of him dead or alive.' I covered my eyes with both my hands so as not to see him go and said, 'My God, I shall never see him again.' Surely it was God's goodness to the poor wife which prevented me from crying out 'Oh don't leave us'. Thank God I did not, for surely Captain Gardner would have been killed by the Gujars and I would never have forgiven myself.

Captain Tytler again flew over those bandits, who again tried to knock him off and again failed. He met poor Gardner close to cantonments, running three steps, walking three steps and then running again, holding a revolver in his hand. My husband called out, 'Jump up behind me Gardner, there is no disgrace now, we must fly for our lives.' So the poor fellow (who was by no means a very strong man) jumped up and held on to my husband, when for a third time they had to encounter the Gujars and with the same successful result. When he joined us he mounted the coach box and put Gardner on to a seat behind, and the syce (groom) with Marie's box on the roof. In this way we drove for our lives.

Poor Thakoor Singh, our orderly, begged so hard to be allowed to accompany us, but there was no room in the carriage. I only wish we could have been able to take him, for the fellow deserved a better fate than awaited him, which was to be killed on the 8th of June, the day of our first battle. My husband saw his body lying side by side with his uncle, our kot havildar, who we found out afterwards to be a terrible rebel. His nephew evidently knew this when he begged so hard for leave of absence on urgent private affairs, but he was only a recruit and was not entitled to leave. No doubt his one reason for wishing for it was because he was very fond of the children and did not wish to stay and witness their murder when the Mutiny broke out as planned for July. All my jewellery was kept in the quarter guard for safe custody in his uncle's hands, which, we were told afterwards, he possessed himself of, as also our last month's pay, which came in so late on Saturday night that my husband told him to keep it till Monday morning. Thereby we lost that too.

There can be no doubt every native knew there was something up and that we were to be chased out of the country, but had not the pluck to warn their masters, whether as a matter of honour to their own cause or for any other reason, I cannot say. But I know poor old Dabi, one of the most faithful servants, who had been in the family for thirty years, ever since he was a coolie boy of sixteen, had planned to go to his home to marry his little girl, who was only seven years of age but betrothed to someone in his village. We had given him a cow and his child an English doll besides other presents. That man cried for three days and wouldn't go, until my husband said, 'Why, if you don't go now Dabi, it will be too late for your child's wedding.' Such ceremonies are fixed for certain dates by their priests and cannot be postponed without fresh ceremonies, meaning months of delay. But the fellow would invariably reply, 'Sahib, I cannot bear parting with the children.'

At last he did go, and before he went away his last words were, 'Sahib, if your hearth is burning I shall hope to see you again.' Of course as long as a hearth is burning there is life, but we didn't think anything of the thought of our not being alive, so the remark went unheeded. And we saw no more of him for nearly two years. When we were staying in Cawnpore for a short time my husband sent a coolie in search of him, who brought him back an emaciated wreck. Poor man, he fell down at my husband's feet, saying, 'Sahib, how did you escape the soldiers? I never thought to see you alive again.' Then he told us in what fear and trembling he lived and how he had buried the doll we had given him for his daughter, for fear of being discovered as friendly to the English. He was such a good man.

To go back to our flight, my husband drove at a terrific pace, but had not gone far before Gardner called out, 'Tytler look back.' We cast our eyes in the direction of cantonments and saw that every bungalow and the lines were on fire. It was a sickening sight, knowing all we valued most was lost to us for ever, things that no money could ever purchase—a beloved dead child's hair, manuscripts and paintings for a book my husband was going to publish some day, all my own paintings, books, clothes, furniture, a very large carriage, horses, buggy, etc. Indeed we lost in money value, with my husband's uniform and all, some £20,000, a fortune to a poor military man in those days, and to replace even what we could buy would have cost a great deal more than this. But the one absorbing thought of flying for our lives soon made us forget that which at any other time would have been an inconsolable trial.

There was a full moon that night but the light of it was greatly obscured by the immense conflagration of cantonments. As we were hurrying on to lengthen the distance between us and the mutineers, my husband saw a dak gharree coming towards us with a lot of baggage on the top of it and, seeing a young European woman inside of it, beckoned to the coachman to stop. Then, jumping off, he went to her carriage and begged of her not to go on to Delhi as she would be sure to be killed. Her reply was, 'I don't believe you.'

'Very well madam,' he said, 'I have done my duty in warning you and I can't do more.' He returned to us and both drove off again in opposite directions. When we had got about fifteen miles from

Delhi, the poor old horse could go no further and it was necessary to get another horse from one of the staging stables as soon as we came to one.

Captain Tytler called out, 'We want a horse.'

'What company do you belong to?' came the reply.

'No company,' said my husband.

'Then we can't give you a horse.'

The two men saw from this, there being no time to lose, that one must be had by force, for every minute we expected to be followed up by the men of the mutinous 3rd Bengal Cavalry. So they jumped off the carriage and ran to the stables, my husband saying to Gardner, 'Hold your pistol at that man's head, while I loosen a horse.'

When the men saw it was no use objecting, they came forward and said, 'Sahib, we will give you a horse.'

Captain Tytler then offered them five rupees for their best horse and on we went again. It was Marie's money we used, having none of our own. Mrs Gardner said, 'Captain Tytler, you pay the man and we will settle afterwards', but she forgot all about it, leaving us to bear the burden alone and make up to Marie what we got from her later on.

We hadn't gone many miles further when all of a sudden the four wheels went into pieces leaving the body of the carriage on the road, a hopeless wreck. Of course there was nothing for it but to walk.

Each of the men carried a child and Marie another, while we two wives walked silently by their side. The moon had recovered its brightness, a moon that had beheld sights of tragedies on the road which no man would ever hear of. Men and women who had no means of escape beyond walking were killed and only known to have been killed by never being heard of again. Lieutenant Holland was cut down and left for dead on the road and his charger seized by the insurgents. Mr McWhirter of the Civil Service, who had been walking along beside my husband till his men mutinied, was also killed, and God only knows how many others.

As we trudged along, worn out by the fatigues and anxieties of the day, we met a number of native travellers going Delhi way. None spoke, but all stared respectfully, though evidently amazed at seeing Europeans travelling on foot. Of course they had no idea of the circumstances which caused us to do so.

After walking several miles, we heard the rumbling of wheels in the distance, on the Delhi side, and my husband said, 'Probably that woman has thought better of it and is coming back again.' True enough it was her. She had met someone else flying for his life who had told her the same tale, which she thus believed, and was making the best of her way back. As soon as she came up to us, my husband accosted her with the words, 'Excuse me madam, you must allow us to put our wives and children into your carriage.'

'I will do *no* such thing!' was the reply. 'Do you mean to break down my carriage?'

'Well then I won't ask you,' said he, and set to work to put Mrs Gardner, Marie and myself, with our children, inside the carriage, the men accommodating themselves elsewhere. Captain Tytler once more took the reins and drove as before for dear life. We expected to be followed up momentarily by the troopers. Had they not been engaged looting the bungalows no doubt they would have followed us up.

In this way we went on till one of the hind wheels of the conveyance rolled off. 'There,' said the young woman (she was only sixteen), 'I knew you would break my carriage. Now what am I to do?'

The two men stood there, a picture of despair, with no ropes to fasten on the wheel again!!! While contemplating the disaster, the mail cart from Delhi drove up and would have passed us, but there was a lady, a Mrs Nixon, making her escape from the city, where her poor husband had had his throat cut at the Cashmere Gate while going there out of curiosity to see what was going on. It will be ever an enigma to me why those two Mohammedans, who behaved so badly to us afterwards, should have helped to save her life. There may have been the promise of much money to make up for it.

This mail cart leaving Delhi punctually at the appointed time with the mails as if nothing had happened, showed the subtlety of the Mohammedan, or I should say the Asiatic, character. They knew the wires being cut would cause no surprise to the authorities elsewhere, because telegraphy in those days was in its infancy in India and messages were often delayed through something going wrong with the wires, but the post not arriving at the appointed time would certainly cause suspicion and enquiry. On the other hand, those drivers who allowed Mrs Nixon a seat in the cart must have known she would tell the Kurnaul* people of what had happened, making their conduct doubly inexplicable. Kurnaul at that time was a small civil station, with only one European, a civilian, and some Eurasians, so they would not have had much difficulty in disposing of them. Be that as it may.

Mrs Nixon got these post office people to give us a helping hand, such as ropes, which our husbands soon turned to account, and the mail cart drove on, the European occupant in reply to our appeal promising to send out a carriage from Kurnaul to help us forward. As soon as the wheel had been tied up, we made a fresh start, driving very carefully for fear of another mishap. But in spite of such precautions we had not gone many miles when the springs under my seat gave way and sent Marie and myself up to the ceiling, from where we had with difficulty to be extricated. There was nothing for it now but to walk, for the carriage was a perfect wreck and, as the mutineer troopers had not yet overtaken us, we could but hope they would leave us to continue our journey in peace. It was but a hope, for nothing could be less sure.

We walked several miles, nearly overcome with fatigue in the heat of a May night,[25] not knowing what was to become of us even if we escaped death for the present, for if no conveyance came to our aid we could not possibly have walked to Kurnaul that night and, if the sun had risen upon us the next day without shelter from its perpendicular rays, death must have come to our relief, from sunstroke or heat apoplexy. We kept hoping against hope that the carriage Mrs Nixon had promised to send us would come and relieve our anxieties, when happily a tumbrel came by, which was on its way to the arsenal at Delhi with a lot of odds and ends of broken arms. Happy thought—this must be seized and employed to carry us on our weary way till something better could be met with. The men hailed the driver, with a command to let us have the cart. The two natives in charge replied very nicely, 'Sahib we can't let you have it, for it belongs to Sircar.'

My husband was on the point of saying there is no Sircar when Gardner hooshed, saying, 'Don't let them know that.'

'You are right Gardner, so let us throw out the rubbish and put the women and children in.' The men, seeing the revolver and two

---

* Modern spelling is Karnal.

Europeans, thought it best in common wisdom to run away. Left to ourselves we were deposited in the springless cart. Still, it was better than walking in our exhausted condition.

The next thing was how to drive the bullocks. Neither man had ever tried their hand at this kind of Jehuism, so they tried to follow the example of the hackery wallahs[26] and each took a tail into their strong hands—too strong for the feelings of the poor creatures, for the first twist my husband gave *his* bullock's tail so startled the poor animal that he fled down an incline. On seeing this, Captain Gardner did his best to save us from immediate destruction by giving his bullock's tail a desperate twist. In self-defence the poor brute turned to his side and stopped the downward course of the other animal.

We were, thank God for his mercies, once more saved. The cartmen, seeing such ignorant handling of their animals, came running back, saying 'Sahib, Sahib, you will kill our bullocks—we will drive them if you will let us.' The two officers were only too glad to let them have that pleasure. One of them jumped on his seat, took the rope between his toes and, taking a tail gently in each hand, trotted on at the pace of some three miles an hour, our two husbands walking along by our sides. After a time they became so footsore, they had to throw off their boots and socks and walk bare-footed the rest of the way.

Our thirst was terrible, with no water to be had except greeny mire from the roadside pools which had not quite dried up. My husband would bring the children and ourselves some of this in the hollow of his hands and I used to close my eyes, hold my nose, and drink it. Such water might well do away with the theory that typhoid or enteric comes from bad water. It could not have been much worse, but thank God we did not suffer from it. Typhoid was unknown in those days, at all events by its present name and symptoms.

The cart could not have been a harder one but we were thankful for it. As day broke, about four in the morning, we fancied we saw a tiny speck in the distance, and as it got nearer, our young friend of sixteen said she thought it might be her husband coming out to meet us and so it was. When he got near enough to speak, he turned to Captain Tytler and said, 'I thank you sir for having saved my wife's life.' My husband turned his head and looked at her. Nothing was said by her, not as on previous occasions when she had said, 'I do not know what

I have to be thankful to you for', for by this time she had grasped the terrors of our situation.

We continued our journey till we reached his bungalow, about six o'clock that morning. At our request Mr O'Connor kindly ordered breakfast to be got ready, for by this time we were pretty nigh famished, not having tasted any food for nearly twenty-four hours. About eight we sat down thankfully to dall and chupattees. I forget now whether we had anything else except tea, for those who liked it.

As soon as breakfast was over, Mr O'Connor, who was in charge of the canal, brought out all the arms he could produce, such as a gun, pistols and a sword. With these the three men were duly armed and we women took knives from off the table, determined to die game if called upon to die. All these preparations being completed, we waited for the promised conveyance from Kurnaul. The waiting seemed an eternity, but at last, about nine o'clock, our eyes beheld the gladsome sight, for the same two men who had driven Mrs Nixon from her home in the civil lines of Delhi drove up, but this time armed to the teeth. Both had a double barrel gun, both had a pair of revolvers, each had a sword, and one of them had a dirk down his back.

Naturally we gave them the credit of being so armed so as to help us in case of an attack from the less loyal natives, but we soon found out our mistake. The spokesman asked us after we had been driven a very short way where the gentlemen meant to go. My husband's prompt reply was 'To Kurnaul of course'.

'Oh!' said they, 'Kurnaul is in the hands of the mutineers.'

'Then,' he said, 'we will go on to Umballa.'

'Oh! Umballa has been in the hands of the mutineers for several days. Don't you think, Sahib, you had better go across country to Cawnpore?'

For a moment it seemed as the only possible alternative under the circumstances, when suddenly it flashed across my husband's mind, and probably in the minds of the other men too, that they meant to get us off the Trunk Road and, as soon as we had got far enough from the thoroughfare, to murder us and leave our bodies there, where soon, in the heat of May, they would become skeletons and having looted us of all we possessed, even to every stitch of clothes, no one could guess that they were the bones of murdered Europeans.

How good our Heavenly Father was not to allow us to be thus

duped and then murdered by these two wretched Mohammedans. My husband's reply to their query was, 'No we won't go off the road, but take our chance with Kurnaul and Umballa.' From this time forth the conduct of these wicked men was most marked, talking to each other plainly at us all the time, looking around occasionally with an unmistakable impertinent curl of the lips, from which we could perceive their very hellish thoughts. Of course they saw we were well armed, even to the four women with their knives, which we did not care to hide from their view—two against three English men and four English women, stout-hearted ones too as we had proved ourselves that day, never to be effaced as long as memory lasted. So we went on and at last reached Kurnaul, to find no one had even heard of a mutiny until Mrs Nixon's arrival.

The postmaster was a native with an English name. My husband, the spokesman of our party, asked him for conveyances to take us to Umballa, offering to pay for the same. He heard him give these very two men orders to get some ready at once. We had arrived at Kurnaul about ten o'clock, and soon after we arrived other refugees came in—Mrs Holland with her two friends Miss Hollings and Miss Winfield, Mr Glubb of our regiment, and others. Just then came Major Shute, I think, from Umballa in a mail cart, and my husband asked him to take young Glubb back with him to Umballa to inform the authorities of what had happened in Delhi, it being so important that General Anson[27] at Simla should know of the previous day's doings without delay. So these two drove back in another mail cart at once and left us to follow in shigrams (clumsy, heavy, springless carts meant only to convey goods).

After several hours had elapsed and no appearance of the ordered carts, Captain Tytler wanted to know the reason why. The post-master said the bullocks had been taken out to graze and could not be found. After some time more had elapsed, he made similar enquiries, with the same result, but after another two or three hours of waiting he grew out of all patience and took the law into his own hands. He called the head man, one of those who had driven us in and, holding a revolver at his head, told him he would shoot him dead if he did not produce those bullocks in a quarter of an hour. Needless to say in less than that time there were the bullocks sure enough, and where had they been all this time? Only behind the walls of the post office grounds. There can be no doubt that these men hoped, by detaining us aid would come from Delhi, to kill us all before long. My husband went to see the only covenanted official, Mr Richards of the Civil Service, to tell him of the massacre, and advised him strongly to leave his post, believing as he did that he certainly would be murdered if he remained, specially as he was the collector and in charge of the treasury, a great incentive for his murder. But, poor fellow, he said much as he would like to go, he did not care to do so for fear of dismissal from the service. As it turned out it was well he did not take my husband's advice, well meant as it was, for the postmaster got all his belongings together and left the post office to take care of itself, for which we were told he had been dismissed.

Now that the bullocks had been found, the carts were got ready, but still very slowly. At last we made a start somewhere about four o'clock in the afternoon. Mrs Gardner and myself, not being very strong at the time, were through the kindness of the other ladies able to lay down. It was the hardest bed I had ever had. Her boy was placed between us, kicking my back the whole time, and I had my little Edith on the other side of me, so that I was between two fires. No one can imagine the agony I suffered. Marie, with Frank in her arms, and Mrs Holland and Miss Hollings were seated on the railings of this said delightful conveyance, while my husband and Gardner walked every inch of those seventy miles.

When we got about half way between Kurnaul and Umballa there was a cry from those ahead of us: 'The cavalry are on us.' There was no thought of any other cavalry but the 3rd from Delhi, so immediately we were dragged out and the carts upset to make a barricade, by way of defence from our enemies, but imagine our joy and surprise. Instead of the 3rd Bengal Cavalry from Delhi we learnt it was the 4th from Umballa, on their way to guard a treasury on the road, and so they passed on, saying in Hindustani to each other, 'Oh! let the poor devils go, they have but a few days to live.' For the moment it was gratifying that we had even a few days to live. Young Plowden was with them and years afterwards, when I met him after my dear husband's death, he reminded me of that occasion and told me that his men mutinied a few days later and their officers only narrowly escaped with their lives.

After this little experience, we went on without further excitement till early in the morning. I was in such agony from the kicking I had received from the two children that I implored my husband to take me out and lay me on the ground. This he did. It was heaven after the suffering of the night. I lay there for some time without a word passing between us, while the long cavalcade went slowly on. But when the last carriage made its appearance, my husband turned to me saying, 'Harrie, you must now get up.'

I replied, 'I can't. I am dying. You go and take care of the children.'

'What nonsense,' he said. 'You think I can leave you here to die alone?'

So taking me up in his arms he carried me to the last carriage and put me in. To our astonishment we found our friends the O'Connors comfortably seated in it. It was a palkee gharree like our own, the one we left Delhi in, with springs and cushions. How different from the shigrams I had suffered such agonies in. This time there was no remonstrance on the part of Mrs O'Connor.

So eventually we reached Umballa and went straight to the house of some old friends, Colonel and Mrs Ewart. They received us most kindly and put us up as best they could. Mr and Mrs O'Connor stayed there a few hours and then found some other resting place with friends. We never saw them again.

As soon as General Anson heard of the terrible news, he ordered every officer down from Simla, leaving it himself soon after to see what could be done.

Colonel Ewart was a very nervous old man and no doubt found it very trying to have a house full of refugees. Knowing all this I kept my little children all the day in our large bathroom, amusing themselves playing with the water in the gharis[28] with Marie to look after them. There they ate their meals and were as good as gold, but of course as Mrs Gardner had no servant and her boy would not remain with anybody but herself, she had to take him into meals with her. There he behaved as badly as any child could. Everything was given to pacify him, but to no purpose. He wouldn't eat this and he wouldn't eat that, till I pitied his poor mother, but what could she do with such a naughty little fellow, for he was too young to be reasoned with. Had I been in her place I would have carried him off and spanked him well, but his mother didn't, so he continued doing the same, day after day, at every meal.

No sooner had we reached the Ewarts' bungalow and our bed-room been allotted to us, than I threw myself on the charpoy and never moved the whole day to wash or eat food or drink a glass of water. So completely exhausted was I that I felt, and was to look at, a dead person. About 9 p.m. I had to rouse myself because the alarm was sounded. My husband made me jump up and we ran for our lives to the barracks of HM's 9th Lancers.[29] The moon was shining brightly so we could see our way right enough for several nights, but later on it became quite dangerous for me, tumbling about as I did several times, for every night the alarm used to sound and as often fortunately proved to be a false one.

The first night we passed in the barracks. All the soldiers' wives and their husbands surrounded Mrs Gardner and myself asking us a thousand questions as to what had taken place on the memorable 11th of May, so that we had no sleep that night. In the morning we returned to the Ewarts' house and another day of disquietude, not knowing for one moment how matters would end, but still nothing happened.

Strenuous efforts were being made by the authorities to get as many loyal soldiers to march to and retake Delhi.

After we had been at the Ewarts' three or four days, Gardner said to my husband, 'What do you mean to do, Tytler?'

'Nothing,' was his reply.

'What! Not volunteer?'[30]

'Certainly not.'

'Well, I shall assuredly.'

My husband tried to dissuade him and begged of Mrs Gardner on no account to let her husband volunteer. He said, 'I have never known a married man volunteer who did not come to grief.' He added, 'It is tempting providence'—but all without avail for poor Gardner was bent upon volunteering.

After several days, Mrs Gardner came to me and said, 'I think, Mrs Tytler, there are too many of us here, you know what a nervous man Colonel Ewart is.'

I replied, 'I know, but which of us do you think Mrs Ewart would like to go?'

She hummed and hawed a little and then said, 'I think you, as you have two children and I only have one.'

If a dagger had been thrust into me I could not have felt worse. How she could have had the heart to have seen us turned out when there was no other place to go to, after we had brought her there and after the way my darling husband had risked his life to save hers, and when one word from me would have stopped him from going, was more than I could understand. But I said with some sternness, 'Very well, Mrs Gardner, we will go.'

When Captain Tytler came in, I told him. He was very surprised, but said, 'Of course Harrie we will go, but where to I don't know.'

There were no hotels in Umballa, the dak bungalow was full, and we knew of no other friends who we could ask to receive us, but we made up our minds that we would hire tents or live in the carriage my husband had purchased from one of the shopkeepers. It was an immense long thing, about twelve feet long and four feet broad, and had been used as a crockery van to take goods up to the foot of the Hills and so had springs and a railing all round. My husband had the two end railings removed and a thick thatch put on, with the sides all enclosed with matting except two places for windows. For our bedding we had a lot of straw, and two native razais were laid on this; we had no pillows or sheets. We used to sleep in it every evening in the grounds of the 9th Lancers and be driven back again the next morning to the Ewarts' house. So if worse came to the worst we meant to live in this cart of ours.

But God was good to us, like he was to Hagar in her distress, for in the evening Captain Maisey came over and while talking to us all said, 'If any of you ladies would like to come over to my house I will be very glad to welcome you. My wife and children are away in the Hills and my house is at your service.'

This was an unexpected joy for me, so going up to him at once I said, 'Captain Maisey, do you really mean what you said just now?'

He replied, 'Of course I do.'

'Well then, may we come over?'

'Certainly, I will be delighted to have you.'

Then and there I said goodbye to Colonel and Mrs Ewart, thanking them for their kind hospitality, and took our departure. There was no packing up to delay us, for we had no clothes but what we escaped in.

Greater kindness we could not have received than we did from our newly acquired friend all the time we stayed under his roof. He even gave my husband a beautiful horse and asked him if he would like to go to Delhi with the force as paymaster to the troops, because if he would like to accept it, he thought he could get the appointment for him.[31] It was a perfect Godsend with three boys in England and everything we possessed lost in Delhi, even our last month's pay. The offer of 250 rupees per month, equivalent in those days to £25, was not to be refused. Immediately my husband decided to take us with him to Delhi, and from there send us up to our little cottage in Mussoorie. No one could foresee that we would be three and a half months retaking that city.

My husband in the kindness of his heart offered Mrs Gardner and Mrs Holland seats in this carriage, or cart as it really was. The former scoffed at the idea and persuaded Mrs Holland on no account to go with us. Poor little woman. No news had ever been heard of her husband and we all believed he had been killed trying to escape from cantonments. The last seen of him by any of us was when my husband went back for Captain Gardner. He was riding on his charger and going rather slowly for such a time. My husband called out to him, 'Holland, go faster or they will overtake you.' He replied, 'I can't Tytler, my horse has been sick.' The troopers did overtake him and cut him down, causing him to fall unconscious from his horse, after which they galloped off, leaving him for dead.

The time was now approaching for the army to start for Delhi. Captain Gardner had volunteered and had been attached to the 5th NI who, being suspected of being very disloyal, were sent out of cantonments to keep them out of harm's way. Meanwhile Mrs Gardner and Mrs Ewart started off in palankeens to Kussowlie—on the way Mrs Gardner gave birth to her little girl—but in their hurry forgot all about poor Mrs Holland, who, seeing she was left in the lurch, wrote to me a hurried few lines begging of us to take her with us. When she arrived she was dressed in a lovely pink muslin dress with pretty ribbons about it.

I exclaimed, 'Where did you get that lovely dress?'

She replied, 'Oh! didn't you see the things which were sent over to Mrs Ewart for us all?'

I replied in the negative.

She said, 'Why, there were three large bundles of every imaginable thing and amongst them two sets of baby linen.' She continued, 'I know Mrs Gardner had her choice and I got this dress and some other things. Of course I thought the remainder must have been sent to you.'

This was a second surprise for me, who knew nothing of the

world and its selfishness at that time, so I asked myself, 'How could she take two sets of baby linen, while mine will have to go without any!!!'

Meanwhile, poor Captain Gardner had no sooner got out with the 5th NI into camp than he heard the men concocting the murder of their officers, but escaped with his life, only to reach Kussowlie and die there the next day.[32]

The day after Mrs Holland joined us, the Field Force commenced their march. My husband gave up his place in the cart to Mrs Holland and slept on the ground under it. The first march he rode on Captain Maisey's horse, but the poor thing died the day following of sunstroke, after which he had to walk the whole way and sleep under the cart. But sometimes we were fortunate enough to get into a dak bungalow, specially when we had to wait for the siege guns, without which we couldn't possibly attack Delhi.

At last we reached Alipore on the 7th of June. The native soldiery had vowed General Anson should never see Delhi alive, so, poor man, he died of cholera, but I am convinced he was poisoned. He was buried in his own tent, we were told, so that the army might know nothing of it, but this could not have been true for Colonel Keith Young, in his letters to his wife, said he was at his funeral.[33]

General Barnard succeeded him and was our commander-in-chief until early in July, when he also died, but of dysentery, another form of poisoning, though his death was attributed to great anxiety. Of course this was quite possible. Brigadier Halifax very soon after we commenced our march also died of cholera.

The natives of India are experts in the art of poisoning, for I recollect, after the King of Delhi had been made a prisoner, his physician Ahsanullah Khan,[34] who was kept in close confinement under the palace we lived in, told my husband, who used often to have a chat with him, and who asked him if he could poison *ad libitum*. He replied, 'I can. Show me your victim and tell me when you want him to die. In a year? Six months? One month or a day? He shall die and, what is more, your physicians will never find out the real cause of his death.' So you can see how easy it is to put an objectionable official out of the way. I feel sure many a good upright man has died in this way, when he has made himself objectionable to either inferiors or superiors. I mean by this, of course, natives.

After the death of Brigadier Halifax, nothing more occurred, as I said before, out of the ordinary way, till the day before we reached Alipore, when I saw a poor little man (a Mohammedan baker) in clean white clothes dangling from the branch of an acacia tree (from which comes the gum arabic of commerce). From what we could gather, this poor man had been late for several days with his bread for the men's breakfast, so Tommie Aitkins threatened to hang him if this happened again and so they did. I can't understand how such a cruel deed was allowed, for they in their turn should have been hanged, but I suppose a single soldier could not have been spared, even in the cause of justice. Probably most of those who committed this deed were themselves called to account to a Higher Power during the siege to answer for their sins.

It was at once decided to attack the rebel sepoys at Badli-ke-Serai, some few miles from Delhi. They had done nothing up to this time to prepare to meet us, though Brigadier Wilson had fought two battles at the Hindun Bridge on the 30th, which was on the Meerut side of the river Jumna, where the rebels, chiefly men of the 38th, were vanquished. Evidently they must have thought it was time to make ready to coerce us on our way to Delhi. So as soon as they heard we were on our way from Umballa, they threw up some earthworks at Badli-ke-Serai and entrenched themselves, as we had taught them to do. They imagined we could never take these in under a week, by which time they would be ready to receive us on the ridge, but thank God they were fighting in a bad cause and our just God did not give them all they expected. Our troops went out early on the morning of the 8th and in two hours those who had not been killed fled for their lives back to the city.

The evening before the attack Mrs Holland and myself were sitting out with several of the officers of HM's 75th. Amongst them was a tall young Irishman of the name of Harrison and a Captain Knox, both of the same regiment. The younger, Harrison, looked sad and thoughtful, as if he had a presentiment of what might be his fate the next morning. Poor fellow, he was amongst those to fall, and Captain Knox was killed later in another engagement.[35] We saw them all lying in a row, soldiers and all, as we were on our way to join our force on the ridge. Colonel Chester too, who had given my husband his appointment, was instantly killed by a cannonball going through the body of his horse and then right up his own body. He was such a good man that death must have been his reward as a great gain to him.

As soon as the victory was won, General Barnard, in command, ordered the troops to march straight on to the ridge and take possession of it. Many of the officers under him were of the opinion that we should march in and take the city at once, as it had been entirely evacuated by every man within. Thank God for his mercy, he would not hear of it, saying, 'No, no, we will fight them in the open', and it was well he did, otherwise, though we could have got in easily enough, we would have been besieged by the very men who afterwards fought us and would have been starved out in a very short time.

About eleven o'clock permission came from the General for my husband to bring the treasure from Alipore. The order being obeyed, we had to march over the ground the sepoys had taken in their flight, numbers biting the dust from our guns as they fled. I saw some of our fine, tall, handsome men[36] lying somewhat swollen by the heat of those four hours and stark naked, for every camp follower robbed them of their gold and silver jewels, and the last comers of the clothes on their bodies, leaving the poor fellows just as God had made them. Such handsome, splendid specimens of high casted Hindus. One man had a hole as large as a billiard ball through his forehead, a perfect giant in death. I could not help saying, 'Serve you right for killing our poor women and children who had never injured you.' At any other time my heart would have been full of pity and sorrow at such awful sights, but after all we had suffered at the hands of our treacherous sepoys, pity had vanished and thirst for revenge alone remained. Such are the effects of warfare upon the hearts of gentle, tender-hearted women. May God's millennium soon come and all strife and war be at an end, which until then I fear never will be.

After a time we reached the spot where the treasure was to be located. My husband's office tent, as soon as he had purchased one, was pitched for him in front of his treasure tumbrels, over which there was a guard of sixty men from the 60th Rifles to protect it in case of the enemy's attack on it.[37] We had no home outside of our cart. There we remained night and day, eating our meals in our laps, but in the evening we all left it for an airing to sit outside for a little and, while Marie and the children walked about, our friends would come and see us and tell us all the news of the day.

On one of these occasions, just outside my husband's tent, we heard a piteous cry from a poor old man of '*Duhā'ī Sahib Kee, Duhā'ī Sahib Kee*' ('Mercy sirs, mercy sirs') and saw some of the soldiers dragging him away, evidently to hang him. I sent my husband flying after them, telling him to save the poor old man. As soon as he got up to them he said, 'Boys, what are you going to do with that poor old man?'

'Why hang him, sir, of course. He is a Pandee (a rebel). We saw him dancing before his bullocks.'

Captain Tytler replied, 'Nonsense boys, he is no Pandee, only a bullock cart driver.'

'Oh no sir, we know he is a Pandee,' ejaculated all the men.

My husband replied again, 'I see boys you only want a little fun. Let the poor old chap go and run after that dog and hang him instead.'

'I see sir, then you don't want us to hang him.'

'No indeed I don't.'

So they let him go and ran after the dog and strung him up there and then. Such is Tommie in the time of war!!!

So soon as our troops had got on the ridge, they commenced taking up positions for our defence and had to start with four batteries, the Flag Staff Tower for one, the old mosque for another, the observatory for a third and Hindoo Rao's for the fourth. Major Reid's brave little Gurkhas asked to have the most dangerous post allotted to them, which being nearest to the city was Hindoo Rao's. These little fellows throughout the siege did valiantly.[38] A Gurkha and a Sikh soldier, when led by European officers, are equal to if not better than their European comrades in arms. All three can do equal justice to the canteen, where they find much fellowship I am sorry to say.

Daily, refugees were coming in from different places where they had been hiding, till there was an undesirable number of women and children in camp, a thing that could not be allowed and which made Lord Roberts say, in his *Forty-one Years*, he could not understand how Mrs Tytler was allowed through some great negligence to stay in camp.[39] If an account of my life is ever published and he reads it, he will very soon understand why I was allowed to stay. So the order came from the authorities that we were all to hold ourselves in readiness to go on pad elephants[40] to Meerut, with an escort of European soldiers for our protection. Before this, many battles had been fought and much life lost, so it was necessary to send us away before further casualties had reduced the strength of our very small force, so inadequate to cope with the army in the city.[41]

When I heard of the mode of travelling chosen for us, I was truly appalled by the very thought of certain death to me, so I asked my husband to interview the General and beg of him to allow me to stay a little while longer, when I would be glad to go anywhere he desired. When the dear old man, who was known for his kindness to all, heard of the state of mind I was in, he said, 'Poor lady, poor lady. Let her stay.' So it was that I was allowed to stay the whole siege through, for later they couldn't spare another man for my escort. This was on the evening of the 19th, and my baby was born at two in the morning of the 21st.

Poor Mrs Holland, who had believed as we all did that her husband had been killed, had received a letter from him on our way to Alipore saying he was in Meerut. When the time came for the refugees to depart she was in high glee at the thought of seeing her husband so soon.

My baby was born with dysentery and was not expected to live for nearly a week. When out of immediate danger, the dear old doctor said, 'Now Mrs Tytler, you may think of giving him a name.' Poor child, his advent into this troublesome world, a pauper to begin with, was not a very promising one. There he lay near the opening in the cart with only a small square piece of flannel thrown over him, with the setting moon shining brightly on him, with nothing but the sound of the alarm call and shot and shell for music to his ears for the rest of the siege.

I waited till eight o'clock to have him washed, thinking of course Marie could do this, but when she took the new-born babe up by his right leg, I screamed out, 'Oh! leave him, leave him. I will do it myself.' So a brass chillumchee was brought to me. I sat up and gave my poor baby his first bath.

A week after the birth of my baby the monsoon broke with great force. Up to that time we thought the thatched roof would have kept the water out, instead of which it leaked like a sieve and in a few minutes we were drenched, baby and all, to the skin. My husband on observing this said, 'My Harrie, this will never do. I must see if I cannot get some place to protect you and the children from the rain.' Fortunately he found an empty bell of arms[42] close by, which he was allowed to take possession of, and then took our only manservant to Captain Scott's battery to bring away some fresh straw to place on the ground for us to lie on. I walked bare-footed with a wet sheet wrapped around my baby and went into that bell of arms, and there we remained till the 20th September, when we left it to go into the fort and live in Kamuran Shah's house.

After such an experience I quite expected the baby and myself would die, but through God's mercy we were none the worse and I was able to nurse my baby without the usual aid of a bottle of milk, there being neither bottles nor milk to be had for love or money. We slept on the floor with only straw and a razai under us, with no pillows or sheets to comfort us, till a poor officer who had been killed had his property sold, and my husband bought his sheets. By way of a pillow I used to substitute a few dirty or clean clothes, which we could ill spare, and so make the best of it.

The want of sufficient clothes was very sorely felt all through the siege. No native shopkeepers were in camp and with difficulty I got enough coarse stuff to make the baby a couple of petticoats. The other two children had little else but what they escaped in. I could only boast of two petticoats I had bought from my ayah and the clothes I had escaped in. While these were being washed I had nothing but a sheet to wrap myself in. My life in that bell of arms was chiefly spent in darning, from morning to night, the little we possessed, to keep them from going to pieces. Besides this a little shawl a lady sent me constituted my whole wardrobe. My husband was somewhat better off, for some of the soldiers we had brought out in the troop ship, the *Collingwood*, in '54, had put some white clothes together, and one of them brought this bundle, on hearing we had lost everything on the 11th of May, and placed it quietly under my husband's chair. Was it not a real kindness on their part? All he said, touching his cap, was, 'You will excuse us sir, but some of us thought they might be acceptable', and disappeared before my husband could see who had done this most kind deed or had time to thank them for it.

The heat was terrible and the flies were worse. Delhi had always been noted for its pest of flies, now doubled and trebled from all the carcasses of animals and dead bodies lying about everywhere. I couldn't keep Frank in the cart or bell of arms for even one hour in the day. He used to amuse himself running about in the sun, with no hat on for he did not possess one, playing with one soldier and then another. They were all very good to the boy. As for little Edith, I had to keep her in for, having just recovered from her very serious illness of abscess in the liver, she would simply have died. As it was, before she had her bath she would say, '*Mamma burra durram hai*' ('Mamma, it is very hot'),[43] when I used to say, 'Yes darling, go to the door. It will be cooler there.' But she was off in a dead faint before she could reach it. Poor child, if she escaped that she would faint in her bath. Never did a day go by without her fainting, and to keep her in the cart was so difficult that I was at my wits' end what to do. At last a bright idea entered into my head. It was rather an unique one, which was to scratch holes in my feet and tell her she must be my doctor and stop their bleeding. This process went on daily and for hours. No sooner did my wounds heal, when she used to make them bleed again for the simple pleasure of stopping the blood with my handkerchief. But it had the desired effect of amusing her for hours.

Every morning the children used to go with Marie for a walk in the camp and then, as soon as the sun got up, they used to return and have their bath and breakfast, such as it was, only remarkable for its simplicity. On one occasion Edith got ill and we sent for Dr Innes of the Rifle Brigade. The moment I laid her down for him to examine her, her terror of doctors returned. She evidently had not forgotten Dr Bruce. When he tapped her on the liver she just screamed with terror and it was all I could do to pacify her. Fortunately there was not much the matter with her, only we were anxious lest it might prove another abscess.

What a comfort it would have been in all that heat to have a greater change of clothes and how acceptable some of the clothes out of those three bundles would have been at that time. Why I never got my share will ever be a mystery to me, but God was good and brought us through all those privations only to teach us all the more that it is not riches nor two sets of baby linen which we need for our happiness. On the contrary the kindest thing after all, was for our Heavenly Father to teach us to trust in Him from day to day. The less we have of the earth's good things, the more have we to look to Him for our needs, which He provides never to overflowing, lest we should forget Him, but just enough for each day, obliging us to look to Him for more for the next day, which He gives ungrudgingly but only *enough*. This has been my experience and now I never trouble myself about anything, knowing it will all come right. But I must confess that I have been a long time coming to such a happy frame of mind. Had I known it more than fifty years ago, how much of fretting and fussing over little things would I have been spared. The following is a very applicable and sweet hymn:

Take it to the Lord in Prayer

What a friend we have in Jesus
All our sins and griefs to bear
What a privilege to carry
Everything to God in prayer.
Oh what peace we often forfeit
Oh what needless pain we bear
All because we do not carry
Everything to Him in prayer.

Have we trials and temptations?
Is there trouble any where?
We should never be discouraged
Take it to the Lord in prayer.
Can we find a friend so faithful
Who will all our sorrows share
Jesus knows our every weakness
Take it to the Lord in prayer.

Are we weak and heavy laden
Cumbered with a load of care?
Precious Saviour still our refuge
Take it to the Lord in prayer
Do thy friends despise, forsake thee?
Take it to the Lord in prayer.
In his arms He will take and shield thee,
Thou wilt find a solace there.

Before the rains had burst upon us, a shell exploded quite close to the cart my baby and myself were lying in and a huge piece fell just below the wheel, but thank God none of us were hurt. Our poor soldiers were so tired of fighting, one might say, *night and day*, that a few days after baby was born they simply refused to fight and threw themselves on the ground telling their officers they couldn't hope to cope with such odds and might just as well die then as a day or two later on. Their officers begged of them to do their duty and man the guns, all to no purpose, this at a time when some 20,000 sepoys were coming out of the Cashmere and Moree Gates to attack us. So the officers, on seeing they could not persuade the men, crammed the guns themselves up to the very muzzle with grape and shot and fired volley after volley. The rebels did not appreciate such a warm reception and luckily went back into the city. On the same day, soon after, our first reinforcements arrived. The men jumped up with joy, hurrahed the newcomers, took fresh courage and fought as well as ever again. If I recollect rightly I think this happened on the 23rd of June.[44] So once more we were saved for that day. I kept that piece of shell for years, meaning to give it to Stanley the baby when he grew up, but someone stole it.

We never knew from day to day whether we should live to see another morning or evening. On another occasion some time after this, Captain Frank Willock joined the force and, his being a connection of my husband's, came over in the evening to see us. When a shell came over the Flag Staff Tower, whizzing as it came along till it fell within the mud walls of our sepoys' lines close to where we were and exploded there, poor Captain Willock jumped up saying, 'My God, what was that?' I replied calmly, 'Oh! It is only a shell.' He was so astounded at the indifferent way I took it that he repeated it at the mess, after which it became a byword in the camp. 'Oh! it is only a shell.' Poor fellow, he did not live long enough to find out for himself how accustomed one can get to such sounds from hearing them night and day.[45] Even my baby never winked or blinked, sleeping through it all as he lay on his bed of straw. If he had lain on a feather bed in a palace he couldn't have slept more soundly.

I used to keep the baby next to the wall between it and myself for fear of his being kicked by one of the other children, till one day I observed, while bathing him, that his poor little head had grown all to one side, so I had to reverse the order of things in hopes of rectifying the evil. Thank God in due course of time it returned to its proper shape.

On another occasion some fresh straw had been brought in from Captain Scott's battery to replace the flattened old stuff. The next morning I was alone, the children being out for an airing, when I observed a *huge black* centipede, about nine inches long and about as thick as my little finger, creep out of the straw. I dashed after him with my shoe but before I could hit him, under my very eyes he disappeared like a phantom. Apparently there was not a vestige of a hole in the concrete floor in which he could have crept, so where he went to will always remain a horrid wonder. For many days I slept in terror lest he should come out and bite any of the children. If he had it would have been in all probability certain death to them. I never saw such a brute till years after, when seventy odd came out one night in Ross Island, but only one out of the whole lot managed to creep up into the upper floor. Centipedes are not poisonous that I know of, but they can nip a piece out of you and if they stick their one hundred feet into your flesh there is no way of making them loosen their hold, unless you have the presence of mind to heat a needle or any iron thing and with it touch their back, when they will curl up and then you can shake them off. But should you attempt to drag him off, he will leave all his legs in your flesh and cause blood poisoning to set in, when the limb would have to be amputated.

The flies were by this time simply too awful to bear. They nearly drove me mad. I used to try and kill every one and then sit down to mend the clothes. We had two very large apertures made in the wall for a current of air, there having been before only one outlet and that was the door. Over these apertures we had some chicks[46] put on to prevent the flies from coming in. I couldn't make out for some time how, after I had killed every one, they got in again, till at last one day I made the wonderful discovery that they came in seated upon the punkah string, for my husband had very cleverly improvised a punkah for us, boring with much difficulty a hole through the massive stone wall to pass a rope through. As soon as I discovered this I had a long cloth bag fastened to the wall outside for the string to pass through. This effectually stopped their coming in, so I had peace from these tormentors ever after. The officers used to amuse themselves laying a train of gunpowder on the mess table over which they placed some sugar and waited for the enemy. Very soon the sugar was covered with myriads of flies, when they were immediately blown up and the game repeated, but it didn't seem to lessen the flies.

One day we got a terrible fright. Marie, who used to take the children out for an airing as soon as it got cool enough for Edith and the baby to go out, was asked by a native soldier if Frank would like to have a ride. The boy was delighted and Marie saw no harm in letting him have this pleasure. At first we didn't think much about any danger but as it began to get very late and no appearance of the trooper or the child, we made sure we had lost him, thinking the trooper was an enemy and not a friend and that he had carried the child off to the city as a hostage. But thank God our surmises were wrong, for in due time he brought back the boy, safe and sound. He must have carried him off to his own lines and then brought him back, as there was no place in camp where he could have kept him riding all that time. After this Marie had strict injunctions never to let him go with any strange man.

On another occasion, a party of the rebel cavalry got into camp dressed in the uniform of one of our native cavalry then in camp. They first killed some of the native gunners who would not join them, then, unlimbering the horses, sent them flying into camp with all their trappings clattering after them. They tore in as if they were mad and passed my bell of arms. Immediately there was a cry from all our men, 'Treachery, treason.' The alarm was sounded and in a minute every man was standing, musket in hand, waiting for the word of command, some with their shirt-sleeves tucked up, others without their shoes or socks on, just as they had turned out of bed when off duty. Next moment the word of command came and they were off to meet the enemy, which they did in front of the canton-ment cemetery. That was the only battle I ever saw fought with my own eyes. I shall never forget the sight, the glistening of the bayonets even through the smoke as both sides fired. Almost in the twinkling of an eye, all was over. Leaving some fifty of their own men dead, they dashed off.

It was on this occasion that Lieutenants Tombs and Hills (both gunners) won the Victoria Cross for their conspicuous bravery.[47]

Later that day the rebels took in our troops a second time as they walked their horses leisurely on the camp side of the canal, while Hodson and his men were on the opposite side. The rebel troopers did this till they came to a bridge, when they put spurs into their chargers and dashed across it, going out of sight before Hodson and his men could recover from their surprise. Up to this time they were believed to be our own cavalry, dressed as they were in their uniform.

It was a very anxious and exciting time for me, for I knew every bullet of the enemy would come across to our bell of arms, the cemetery being exactly opposite to it, so as a precautionary measure I placed Marie and the three children against the dead wall between the two large apertures, which were about 4 feet x 2 or 2½ feet each. My anxiety for my husband's safety was so great that I did not seem to realize any danger for myself, but leant out of the aperture, straining every nerve in my body to get a glimpse of him. The bullets whizzed and pinged in the air as they hit the wall of our bell of arms, not only on each side of the apertures, but also above and below. Some hit the building not more than two inches apart and yet not one came in through the aperture or I would have been killed on the spot. If one bullet hit that building over a hundred must have done so, scooping out a piece of mortar with every thud. I have always felt sure God had placed a guardian angel to guard and protect me, by warding off every bullet destined for me. People say this is not an age for miracles, yet I cannot endorse such an opinion after all the narrow and marvellous escapes I had from the 11th of May to the end of the siege.

After all the fighting was over, visitors used to come and see that bell of arms and asked to be allowed to look at the baby who was born in such troublous times in a bullock cart. The bell of arms continued to be a sight until '77 when the Queen was proclaimed Empress[48] and Lord Lytton's camp was pitched on the very spot where twenty years before our parade grounds had stood and where so many of our people had been killed on the 11th of May. Then it was that our bell of arms lost all traces of the siege, having been turned into a dwelling room with glass windows and all traces of the bullet marks so effaced that I could in no way recognize it in its new state of grandeur as my former little home.[49]

Another time secret arrangements had been made to assault the city in the dark of the night.[50] Neville Chamberlain had the command of the party. Of course my husband knew of the arrangements through a friend at headquarters, who told him out of kindness so that we might be prepared for a reverse if the attempt failed. Secret as the plan had been, it was also known to the rebels, for as Neville Chamberlain and his men crept up to the city walls they could see the enemy alive with lights and men moving about in every direction. When our troops got nearer, a tremendous volley was fired into our poor men and Chamberlain fell seriously wounded. Seeing it was a hopeless failure, thus ended that day's episode.

On another occasion, two Afghans came into camp with a scrap of paper on which a message was written in charcoal from a Mrs Leeson, saying she had been rescued by these two men and wished to be brought into camp. Hodson read the paper and offered the men a bag containing 1,000 rupees, which they declined saying they had not saved her life for money, but for humanity's sake. They were told by all manner of means to bring her in. This it appeared they could not do for some time. At last the poor woman was brought in by one of the men, an Afghan from Peshawar and immediately was sent over to me, as the only other English woman in camp.[51]

She was dressed like a native Afghan boy, in khaki, and as soon as she arrived she asked me for a Bible. Fortunately I had one and gave it to her. From that time she never said a word but she pored over that Holy book till about three o'clock, when she asked for some water. I then ventured to ask of her history and how she had been saved. She told me she was the wife of Mr John Leeson,[52] whose father was a major in a native cavalry regiment and who my husband had known in the first Kabul campaign. She then told me that she was the daughter of the postmaster Mr Collins, who she feared with her mother and other relatives had been murdered, saying the last she saw of her parents was in a tykhana, while she and her children, with her aunt Mrs White, with her children and pupils (for she kept a little school), had passed the night elsewhere. When morning came, they tried to escape by the river side but were caught by some nujeebs, the men promising to take them to the King, who they knew would treat them well, but before doing so made them give up all the gold trinkets they had about them. No sooner had these treacherous brutes (Mohammedan of course) got them into the college grounds, they shot her first and she fell to the ground unconscious. Her baby was thrown out of her arms. The shot which had gone through the poor mother's waist had shot her babe. As soon as she regained consciousness, through the burning of her muslin sleeve, she heard her aunt Mrs White call out to her daughter, 'Kneel down my child and say your prayers before you die.' Then followed bullet after bullet till the whole party were killed. Amongst them was one of the little Beresford girls; the other sister was not with them, having hid herself in the house of a poor old native woman she knew, but who, out of fear of her own life, gave up the poor child to the rebels.

Before these treacherous miscreants had killed all the others, Mrs Leeson's little boy of about six drew close to his mother and, raising her head, put it on his lap and began caressing her face. The little girl of three, running up to her wounded mother, laid herself down by her side. The baby boy, who was shot by the same bullet, was thrown out of her arms and lay, some distance, moaning. After those soldiers of the King had butchered the rest of the family they came up to her little boy and cut his throat. She told me she was quite sure he, being a highly nervous child, must have died before the sword ever touched his poor little throat, as she never felt him even tremble. They then took the poor little girl and cut her from ear to ear through her mouth. Having performed this diabolical deed to their satisfaction they departed. That poor child was some six hours before she died, all the time writhing away, in her agony, further and further from her mother till she heard one piercing shriek and then no more, so the mother supposed somebody must have killed her outright. There the poor baby lay on the ground, picking the grass and moaning pitifully, till he died too. The poor mother was helpless and unable to move.

Before the death of the younger children, two Afghans came and felt Mrs Leeson's pulse. Finding her still living, they promised to go back and ask their parents' permission to take her over to their house, saying, 'If they allow us, we will come over in the evening and take you and your children back with us.' They then took the sheet off their shoulders and covered her up saying, 'Don't let anyone know you are living.' In the evening, true to their promise, they came out with a third man and, finding her still alive but the children dead, they picked her up and placing her over their shoulders took her home. God only knows what that poor woman suffered in that burning day of May the 12th with a broken heart and wounded body with not a drop of water to quench her cruel thirst, made doubly worse from being wounded. Oh God how can creatures made after Thine own image do such dreadful deeds? And cannot you understand how it is that I cannot tolerate the followers of Mahomet, who but for this dreadful unChristlike religion would be splendid men in other respects?

The Afghans and the women of the priests were very good to her. They begged of her only *once* to become a Mohammedan. She said, 'I cannot. You saved my life, you can take it, but I will never renounce my faith.' She begged of them to find her a Bible out of all the books belonging to Christians which were daily being burnt in the city. Not knowing English they could not discern one book from another, so all they brought were not Bibles. Poor thing, she was so terrified from the horrors of the 11th and 12th of May that nothing could induce her to come down from a little isolated room on the top of the house which was supposed to be uninhabited. It had no windows, no opening except the one leading to the women's apartments below.

After the two Afghans had received Hodson's permission to bring her into camp there was some delay in carrying out their plans to take her out, on account of which she became very impatient, poor woman. They tried to convince her of the great danger they were running, to her and to themselves, in doing so in a hurry. However, to please her they decided at last to do it. Mrs Leeson was a *little* dark but they darkened her more until she looked like one of themselves and then, having hired a covered cart, they put in their own women along with her and got a trusty friend to drive the bullocks, while the two Afghans walked on each side of the conveyance. When they came to the Lahore Gate of the city, the guard stopped them and insisted on seeing who were inside, being very suspicious of Europeans being concealed. The two men begged very hard, saying they were only their zenana (women) going to Kudam Shureef to worship at that shrine, upon which the guard made them put out their heads. On seeing they were those of native women they allowed them to pass on.

After the party had gone some distance out of the city they took Mrs Leeson and sent the cart with the other women back again through another gate. The little Kandaharee, for he was an Afghan from Kandahar, left the other two and went to see if the road was clear, while the Afghan from Peshawar and Mrs Leeson waited with anxiety for his return. Not seeing him come back they felt sure some accident had happened to him and started off by themselves, taking a most circuitous way to escape detection. Mrs Leeson, in her terror of being discovered, fell down a nullah and grazed her skin from her shoulder to her foot. She must have suffered a great deal but never did I hear a murmur from her lips, poor woman. At last, very early in the morning of the 19th of August, they reached our picket, and on producing Major Hodson's permission were allowed to enter camp.

The woman was sent on to me at once, but General Nicholson unfortunately mistook her protector for a *very bad* character, who he knew personally in Peshawar, and had him promptly put into irons. It was a very unfortunate thing for it caused an extremely bad feeling and I don't know that he ever forgave him for it. The next day General Becher came to me and said, 'Mrs Leeson must leave the camp at once as she is strongly suspected of being a spy, for General Nicholson knew the man who brought her in as being a very bad character and had him put in irons.' Poor thing, when she came to know she had to leave, she wept bitterly saying, 'All these weeks of suffering I have lived in the one hope of coming into a place of safety and now I am to be sent away to be killed on the road.' I tried to comfort her and told her how hard I had pleaded with General Becher, but could not convince him that she was *no* spy. Very soon the dak gharree arrived which was to convey her to Umballa, where she had an aunt. I heard later on of her safe arrival, much to my comfort.

The day after she left the little Kandaharee turned up and came to my window (the hole through which the bullets should have come in) and said, 'Is this the way the English treat those who save their people from death?'

I said, 'Who are you?'

'I am the other Afghan who saved Mrs Leeson and I am told Nicholson Sahib has put my friend into prison.'

I tried to pacify him by explaining to him that these were perilous times, when no one could tell friend from foe. He then enquired where Mrs Leeson was. I told her she had been brought to me but that the General Sahib had ordered her to be sent to Umballa, suspecting her to be a spy. I said, 'You darkened her so well that she looked like a native, which made her case most suspicious.'

He then said, 'Have you got anything to eat?' Replying in the affirmative, he asked me for some, saying, 'I am very hungry.'

I remarked, 'Surely you won't eat with a Christian?'

'Why not?'

'Because you are a Mohammedan.'

'Oh! no,' said he, 'that makes no difference. I will.'

So I brought out what I had and set it before him. He then asked me to eat with him. I agreed to do so (though I never took anything between meals) but just to please the poor man, who seemed so aggrieved at all that had transpired. Then he wanted water, asking me to drink out of the same cup first. This astonished me very greatly, for none of our Mohammedan servants will eat from the same plate we have eaten in, saying they would lose their caste —which reminds me of what my husband told me of Agha Khan, the Persian prince who came over with his 500 followers (nobles of Persia) in the first Kabul campaign to ask our government to reinstate him on the throne of Persia. (This request was refused, for our government had quite enough to do to fight their own battles, but Agha Khan remained with our force and fought on our side during the whole campaign and lost half his men in doing so, for he didn't dare go back to Persia.)

Agha Khan and my husband, both young then, were great sportsmen and used to dine with each other every day. One day my husband, then only an ensign, said to him, 'How is it, Agha Khan, you eat out of the same dish with me, which my servant would not do for fear of losing his caste?'

'Oh!' said the prince, 'he doesn't know his own religion. Mahomet does not forbid us to eat with any man whose religion has a written bible. The Hindus have not a bible so we can't eat with them, besides being idol worshippers' (which as we all know the true followers of Islam abhor).

Agha Khan, turning round, said to my husband's table servant, 'You dog, come here. How is it you won't eat out of your master's plate when you see I can?'

The man put up his two hands in supplication and said, 'You are master.'

Agha Khan replied, 'Get away you dog, you don't know your own religion. You are but half a Mohammedan'—and so the most part of our Mohammedans of India are, being the descendants of Hindus converted into Mohammedans by their conquerors who came from Afghanistan and who still have a harking after their old religion without probably knowing it. Excuse this digression.

Mrs Leeson's poor Afghan, being somewhat comforted, told me how he had escaped from one of their own pickets, which consisted of twelve Mohammedans and one Hindu. It appears, while he was looking about to see if the road was clear, the men of this picket espied him and taking him for a spy were going to kill him. He told them he was no spy but a disciple of one of their own priests in the city. The Mohammedans would not believe him, but the Hindu soldier said, 'Why kill him? First see if he is telling the truth or not and if he is telling the truth, then let him go, if not, kill him.' So they took the Hindu's advice and marched him off to his priest's house, and when he acknowledged him as one of his disciples, they let him go. Immediately after his release he took another road and came out again straight to the camp to find his friend imprisoned and Mrs Leeson nowhere.

After our first meeting he used to come every day and chat with me through the window. He was such a good little fellow. After some time Nicholson saw he had made a mistake in putting the other man into irons and let him go, but he could not undo the bad feeling his mistake had caused.

By this time we began to get news of all that was transpiring in other stations and the horrors of Cawnpore, though of course we could not tell how much of it was true. It was so shocking, that to be on the safe side I asked my husband to get a bottle of laudanum so that I might be prepared in case of a hopeless reverse, which we were always in dread of, for the odds against us were so great (some 50,000 trained soldiers with all the best guns at their command against our inferior ones and so few men) that I quite made up my mind to give each of my children a good dose and drain the bottle myself, telling my husband to avenge our deaths until he dropped himself. This bottle I kept close by me at night and put it out of harm's way in the day. Thank God we never had cause to partake of it.

At last the time came for Delhi to be taken. All eyes of both friends and foes were waiting for the result of that fearful day, for had we lost Delhi, every European in India would have had to die. The Nizam of Hyderabad was only backward from open rebellion by the wisdom of his prime minister, old Sir Salar Jung, one of the most able and far-seeing men India has ever known.[53] The present Nizam owes his throne to the wise policy of that nobleman. After his death his eldest son, Sir Salar Jung the second, was selected, though almost a boy, to hold the exalted position of prime minister. He was about the same age as the Nizam when an unfortunate occurrence took place. There was a woman at the bottom of it and it actually went so far to the discredit of the young nobleman as to cause him to give his master a shoe beating, the greatest insult one man can offer to another. So there was nothing for it but immediate dismissal. Sir Salar felt this disgrace very bitterly and fell on his knees, kissing his master's feet, saying, 'We played as boys together', imploring for pardon.

But the Nizam said, 'Then we were boys, now I am the Nizam and you are my subject, which makes all the difference.'

Seeing no chance of reinstatement the poor fellow took to hard drink, and when the European doctor told him he was killing himself, he replied, 'It is just what I wish to do.' The poor fellow had his wish very soon after, leaving a son of a few months old who was cared for by his mother, grandmother and great grandmother; if now alive he must be some fourteen or fifteen years old.

Sir Salar Jung's younger brother, Moonet Ul Moolk, also died very soon after from dysentery, as the doctors said, but I watched that young man from day to day and can never think otherwise than poison was at the bottom of it, slow subtle poison. Of course at the last he really died from weakness. Can there be anything more weakening than slow poisoning? Excuse this digression.

At last, everything being arranged for the capture of Delhi, there was no time to lose. Our strength was getting less every day and John Lawrence (the late Lord Lawrence) wired to say he could not send another man, the whole of the Punjab having been drained of men to the very utmost. It was a very anxious time for us all. If we failed it meant death to every Christian in India.

General Wilson was terribly given to procrastination. At last he was forced by men like the great Nicholson and others to delay no longer. My brother, a gunner, was wounded the day before the assault while laying his gun against the Cashmere Gate and was picked up for dead.[54] The Carabineers soldier who took his place was shot dead a quarter of an hour later. The next man was also shot in a few minutes, it being the most dangerous post of all. The enemy had caught a poor European soldier and crucified him on the Cashmere Gate. Thank God the poor fellow was not long in suspense for he was killed immediately from our shot and bullets. The enemy had been very brutal to their own countrymen too, for on our entering the city we found some poor fellows in a dying condition, who they had taken for spies, and pierced their bodies through and through with red-hot ramrods.

When it was discovered that my brother was not dead, he was carried to his tent. Afterwards, as soon as we heard that he had been wounded, my husband had him fetched over to his office tent, where I used to attend to his wounds. They were awful-looking ones. The piece out of his elbow had not such an appalling appearance as the one on his right side. He wouldn't let a soul dress it but myself. His morning cry used to be, 'Harrie, when will you come to me and why don't you come?' I was in the bell of arms and he was in the office tent. Well, I couldn't come sooner than I did for I had to bathe my three children in a chillumchee, which took more than usual time just because it held so little water. Their toilette on the contrary took no time, for want of clothes.

Housekeeping, too, through the siege was nil. We had our rations like any private soldier (though paying for the same), and the one servant did his best to make what variety he could out of it. It was a case of mutton curry one day, mutton koftas another day, mutton hash the third, and mutton minced the fourth. These with chupattees made our dinner, week in and week out. Breakfast was always dall and chupattees or dall and rice, supper bread and butter, such as there were, but hunger made us enjoy them all the same. Officers had their messes and many luxuries which we penniless refugees could not afford. What I felt the want of more than anything else was clean iced water. Those who drank tea, without milk of course, could not see the colour of that filthy water which came from the canal, as my husband would not allow us to drink well water for fear of its being poisoned. As the canal was the bathing place of all the elephants, camels, horses and dirty clothes of the whole camp, you may imagine what that meant, yet there was not a case of typhoid or enteric known.

One day, before the siege came to an end, a village near camp was burnt by our people. Jumal Khan our cook was a great looter and started off on his own account to see what he could find. Judge of our delight to see him coming back with a black Jumna pāri goat[55] which he named Ladoo. She was in full milk, giving us some two seers (two quarts) daily. After that we were well off for she gave most delicious milk. No one enjoyed it more than I did, who never touched tea or coffee and had to depend on any kind of water procurable.

The night of the 13th of September was one of great anxiety. My husband had our bullocks in readiness to make a start. In case things went wrong the next day, he intended to send us off in good time towards Umballa, while he would have remained with his treasure till a general rout took place. It would have been about the worst spot in camp to remain in alive, as the enemy would have made a rush to seize all the rupees they could, each man doing so for himself. Had we had a reverse, I don't believe anyone could possibly have reached a place of safety. Simla would have gone, Kussowlie would have gone, and all India would have risen in arms by one consent, though I think dear old Patiala,[56] the great grandfather of the present little Maharaja, would have stood by us. I feel we owed our very existence to that noble sovereign, for he kept the roads open for us to get our commissariat supplies by and his men (Sikhs) fought well for us all through the siege. Kapurthala and Jhind, also Sikhs, were our allies, and we owe them much gratitude for the assistance they gave us, so that really our Government, and every European too, in India, ought on all occasions to show their descendants that we have not forgotten our indebtedness to them.

The morning of the 14th rose to see the day of revenge on that doomed city. The booming of the guns was enough to show what a hard fight it was on both sides. We lost our much loved and brave General Nicholson that day. He and young Gambier of our regiment, who was his aide de camp,[57] were both mortally wounded at the attack on the Moree Gate and our casualties were over 1,100 that day.[58] But through God's mercy we were victors.

The troops on entering the city found it was almost entirely evacuated by the soldiers and populace, with the exception of some of the sepoys, who kept firing on our troops from the roofs and the houses and gateways—though the city was not really cleared of all its rebels until the 19th of September, when the King and his family escaped, by the same gates through which the rebels from Meerut entered on the 11th of May, and took refuge in Humayun's tomb, some six miles from the city.

On the 20th of September my husband received orders to bring on his treasure, with his guard of sixty men from the 60th Rifles, and we followed in our cart. What an experience it was to behold the myriads of women and children coming out of the Cashmere and Moree Gates, women who had never seen the outside of their zenana walls or walked but a few steps across their tiny courtyards, surrounded only by their own family or their slaves, now to have to face

the gaze of European soldiers as well as their own, but all strangers.
What an experience for them too, but they were not flying for their
lives as we had to do, nor had they the fear of seeing their children
brutally killed before their eyes, so I could not pity them as I
otherwise would have done. Still I was sorry for the poor things,
more specially for the poor high-casted Hindu women to whom it
was agonizing pain to be jostled along with sweeperesses and other
women of low birth and caste.

Government had very good reason for turning them out 'nolens
volens', since some of them had been found enticing our poor
soldiers to their doom by laying tables with cups of tea and liquor,
served by their young women of doubtful reputation, so that when
the poor fellows had thoroughly enjoyed themselves and got well
drunk, their men, who were hiding round the corner as it were,
would come out and kill them. I forget now but I think some nine
men were so found with their throats cut.[59] How they got the liquor
is hard to say, since one of the first orders to the officers on entering
the city was to see every hogshead or bottle of liquor destroyed in
their presence for fear of not only Tommie Aitkins, but Sikhs and
Gurkhas too, partaking too freely of such drinks, which would have
proved fatal to our whole army, for finding our soldiers well drunk
almost to a man the enemy would have returned to the city and killed
every one of them on the spot. Wine was much needed in the
hospitals, but they did not dare spare it for the few lives to be saved
against the thousands that would have been lost.

Government had issued orders against looting by men or by
officers, as the contents of the city was all to go for prize money,
which I think was a great and an unjust mistake. The men had fought
hard by the side of their officers to conquer that city and should have
been allowed to loot to their hearts' content and take all they could
get. When the prize money was distributed, it was portioned out
according to rank. General Wilson of course got a very goodly share,
and all the officers under him from the highest to the lowest,
according to their rank, but when it came to Tommie Aitkins, who
had borne the brunt and hardships of that siege, his share was hardly
enough to give him baccy for a month. I believe it would be a wise
policy and a just one to let the soldiers know they would be allowed
to loot, if not then let every man from the highest to the bugler boy
get an *equal* share of the prize money he had fought so well for. I

know some officers intimately who did loot and made a good thing of their looting in the palaces, which was done openly and winked at by their superiors.

On one occasion two Gurkhas were seen by an officer of another regiment carrying two large bags full of riches, jewels of course. This officer stopped them and told them to give it up. At once their hands grasped their kookries (Gurkhas' knives) and in a respectful way, though showing what they meant, said, 'Sahib, we do not mean to do any such thing. We have fought hard for it and we mean to keep it.' The officer saw protestation was useless; they were daring fellows not to be trifled with, so he let them go.

Another time two Sikhs in undress were carrying off similar loot when an officer met them saying, 'You give up that treasure to the prize agent or I will report you to your commanding officer.' These men, like the Gurkhas, had fought hard for it and did not see why they should obey this officer. Accordingly he did report them, but when a parade was ordered for the whole regiment to appear in undress, they looked so like each other that the man who reported them could not point out the delinquents, so they got off scot-free.

The first thing which struck me so forcibly on entering the great city of Delhi, only a few months before so crowded, was that it was now a city of the dead.[60] The death-like silence of that Delhi was appalling. All you could see was empty houses where the household hearths had ceased to burn, and not a living creature, except now and then a starved-looking cat, would show itself, and empty cages were to be seen here and there with their once-beloved occupants laid dead below. The utter stillness too, after the incessant booming of the guns and living in the midst of shot and shell the whole of those never to be forgotten days from the 8th of June to the 14th of September, was indescribably sad. It seemed as if something had gone out of our lives. Truly, living in the midst of unceasing firing, it had become music to one's ears. Even my baby on a bed of straw slept through it as soundly as the most luxurious baby could have done in a feather bed in a palace, proving how we can become accustomed to anything, even to hanging so they say.

Soon after we got into Delhi, Hodson, who was a tremendous looter, did the most audacious thing ever heard of in going out to Humayun's tomb with another officer and four men from his own regiment on his own responsibility, and unknown to his superiors,[61] to capture the Emperor and his sons. Those royal refugees, hiding in their ancestral tomb, must have thought an army in ambush was behind them, or can anyone think that men in their desperate condition would have quietly given themselves up to six men? My husband always said that Hodson ought to have been tried by a court martial for taking upon himself to do that which, if he had not met with success, might have caused great trouble to the rest of the army. Captain McDowell told me himself that Hodson, with himself and the four men, rode straight up and commanded the King and his sons to give themselves up at once, or they would know the reason why. But instead of the men coming out Zinat Mahal, the Emperor's younger wife, came out with her face covered up, saying she wished to speak to the Sahib, which Hodson allowed her to do. Now I was not there to know what she said, but through my knowledge of native character and of the woman herself, I feel sure what she must have said was, 'Sahib, if you will guarantee the King's life as well as my own and that of my son, I will get the others to give themselves up.' I have never believed that Hodson dealt treacherously with the princes he shot, in spite of his brother saying that Hodson had written to him to say he had shot these miscreants because he was afraid they would have been rescued by a mob outside of Delhi.

In the first place there were no men to be seen near Delhi so soon after its fall. Even supposing there had been, why should he suppose they would rescue the sons and not the King himself? No, it is all nonsense, for I was in Delhi and heard all the particulars of that tragedy from eyewitnesses. What I believe is this, that Zinat Mahal, having had her life and that of her son guaranteed to her along with that of her royal husband, must have told the King's sons that she had the promise of their lives also, upon the strength of which they came out and were put into country carts and brought to the city by another route, i.e. the Lahore Gate. When this cavalcade reached the Golden Temple of the Chandni Chowk (i.e. the moonlight street), Hodson called out with a stentorian voice, 'Come out you rascals to be shot', upon which the men put up their hands in supplication and said, 'Sahib, you promised us our lives.'

Hodson replied to them, 'I *never* did. I only promised Zinat Mahal, her son and your father their lives.'

It was then that he shot one and McDowell the other. I know poor Hodson was terribly abused, for having broken his word, after his

A courtyard in the Red Fort and the Lahore Gate, photographed by the Tytlers in 1858.

Formerly the mansion of a Mahratta chief, Hindoo Rao's house, 'the most dangerous post', photographed by the Tytlers after the siege.

Lieutenant Hills attacking the rebel cavalry which had entered the British camp, and winning the VC in the process. It was the only action Harriet actually witnessed. From Charles Ball's *The History of the Indian Mutiny*.

The Tytlers' photograph of the Cashmere Gate, Delhi, which was blown open during the assault of 14 September 1857.

The imposing tomb of the Emperor Humayun, to the south of Delhi, where the King and his sons were captured by Hodson on 21 and 22 September. Photograph by Harriet and Robert Tytler, 1858.

'Easy Times'. Sketch by Major Turnbull. The audience hall in the palace, Delhi, became the quarters for General Wilson and his staff.

death by the English people, but in justice to him they ought to have satisfied themselves that he had broken his word before they maligned him as England did. Mind you, I am not taking Hodson's part because he was a friend of mine, for I didn't know him personally, though I admired him greatly for his pluck.

On our entering Delhi after its capture and taking up our quarters in Kamuran Shah's palace, Mrs Leeson returned from Umballa and stayed with us until the arrival of her husband, who had escaped from Goorgaon to Agra, where he had been shut up with the rest of the Europeans, all that time in ignorance of the fate of his family. Their meeting, as may be imagined, was very sad. They went off almost at once to the college grounds, the scene of the tragedy, to search, but in vain, for the bones of their murdered children.

Towards the very end of September my husband came to tell me Government had issued an order to knock down every house inside the fort walls.[62] I exclaimed, 'What a pity no one will know hereafter what the home of the Emperors of Delhi was like. How I would like to paint it!'

'Why don't you try?' my husband replied.

I immediately said, 'What is the use when I have not a paint or brush or canvas to do it upon nor can I get any?'

Upon which remark he said, 'Never mind, you try and make the sketch and we will see about the paints and brushes afterwards.'

The truth was he wanted me to have some amusement in those monotonous days after the siege, so I got some bamboos and fixed up a sort of scaffolding in the shape of a circle six feet in diameter and six feet high. This was placed in a little hot-weather sleeping room on the second storey above the present Diwan-i-am, where the King's mother had lived and died, and was now no longer inhabited by anyone. Then I sent to the Bazaar for whity-brown paper and fixed it on the circle. Now came the rub. I had never painted a landscape in my life, though I had been taught as a child to draw and to know that everything in the way of streets had a vanishing point. So I knelt down inside the cyclorama that was to be and asked God's guidance once more. The idea then came to me that the point of sight must vanish into the horizon and I should try and see what I could do by placing a thread in the four quarters of the circle.

This I did, and, though I say it who shouldn't, it made the perspective perfect and it was God's doing. He had heard and answered my petition before, when I commenced painting General Pattle's picture, and why should He not again do so? As I held the thread and brought it down, so followed every building perfectly.

The sketch being quite finished I went to my husband and said, 'Now what am I to do?'

'Oh don't ask me,' was his reply, 'I have too much to do with my office work to think of anything else.'

The picture consequently came to a standstill, when one day Mr Rood, an artist who we had known years before and who had just been staying with us on a visit before going to Bullubghur to paint the Rajah's picture there, turned up. Never was I more surprised at this apparition, for we had heard the poor man had been murdered with all the other Europeans in Bullubghur.[63] On seeing him approach I called out, 'Oh Mr Rood, where have you come from? I thought you were dead.'

He replied, 'Yes, I was left for dead, but I had a gold plate in my mouth and, fearing the natives would see it and would smash my head to get it out, I kept it closed tightly and lay there for dead, until some friendly disposed Hindu (Jat[64]) villagers, the opposite of Gujars, found me and hid me in a haystack till the road was cleared, when I found my way here.'

'Oh!' I said, 'Mr Rood, I am very thankful you were not killed, and now will you tell me how to prepare a piece of canvas?'

'What do you want it for?' said he.

'Why to paint a picture of this very place, of which I have made a sketch, for Government is going to have it all knocked down.'

'What is the size?' was his next enquiry.

I replied, 'Eighteen by six.'

'Well I think I have a piece that will just do and I will give it to you.'

I then said in a sad tone of voice, 'But what about the paints and brushes, Mr Rood?'

It was a broad hint which he accepted beyond all my hopes, for he said, 'You shall have all mine, Mrs Tytler. I have done with this beastly country and mean to go home at once.'

There I was through God's mercy provided with everything.

The next day I set to work to transfer my sketch on to the canvas and began painting the cyclorama. As I began so on that very day the work of destruction began at the Queen's Baths, now known as the officers' mess. I had sketched out the trees very correctly, but did not attempt to paint them and left their places blank, till years after my dear husband's death, and eventually put them all in myself, while in Hyderabad, a great deal more to my satisfaction than I had ever hoped to do.

When I undertook the task of painting it, I thought I might sell it to Barnum the showman, but we did not get home for nearly three years afterwards, when the great interest in the events of the Mutiny were over, and so we thought it was no use trying. Anyhow the painting, along with our photographs taken two years later, went to Buckingham Palace for Her Majesty to see. My husband was to have explained everything to her, for I was too ill to do so myself. The day appointed was near at hand when we got a letter from the Palace to say Her Majesty had a telegram to say her mother was very ill and had at once left for Windsor. Therefore, unless the cyclorama and photos could be seen later, Her Majesty would be obliged to forgo the pleasure of seeing them. My husband had to write back and say how sorry he was, but as his leave was up and our passage had been taken to return to India the following week, there was nothing for it but to have them returned.

To return to Delhi after this long digression, I must mention that the soldiers who were left in Delhi, after so many of them had been sent off in a flying brigade,[65] began to get sick and many died of cholera. Time seemed to hang heavy on their hands, so by way of a little amusement they found time to rob Government money, which was all kept locked and sealed by my husband's own hands. To his horror, on opening one of the tumbrels and counting out the money, he discovered some of it was gone. Such being the case he had every tumbrel opened and all the money counted. Then came the appalling truth of 12,000 rupees being gone, which money he would have had to make good or stand his court martial for embezzlement. Poor fellow, he felt it so bitterly that he became dangerously ill with dysentery and was unable to attend his office work. He would not allow the native treasurer to touch a rupee of the money kept in the chests for cash payments, but gave the keys, always in his possession, to me to see the needed money counted out and the rest locked up again. I used to follow his instructions and take a receipt in triplicate and bring these to my husband, and then write it down in his military chest account book. But for such a precaution the native treasurer would probably have helped himself and given my husband a dose to finish the work anxiety had started, but thank God he did not die.

One day, as he was going through the gate of the Nobid Khana, the sentry stopped him and said, 'I hear, sir, you have lost some money.'

'Yes,' replied my husband, 'what do you know about it?'

'A great deal sir,' said the man. 'I will show you when off duty where the false keys are.'

'Say no more my man till I return.' Saying which my husband went off in hot haste to see Mr Saunders the commissioner and, finding him in his office, he said, 'For God's sake Saunders, come with me and hear what a soldier has to say about the lost treasure.'

By this time the man was off duty and took them straight to an outhouse where the false keys were buried, telling them how they opened the seals. It appears, though contrary to the rules of the service, the men were allowed to smoke while on guard, so they used to heat their penknives on the pipes they were smoking and, when thoroughly heated, lay the hot penknife under the seal and take it off without breaking it and then put it on again in the same way, so that when my husband went his round, as he did every morning to see everything was right, he was perfectly satisfied it was so, noting the seals were just as he left them. Of course my husband immediately brought all this to the notice of Colonel Jones, the officer commanding the 60th Rifles, and, at my husband demanding a court of enquiry upon himself, he became furious and said, 'The idea of you, sir, bringing discredit on my men who have behaved so nobly through the whole siege, by listening to the tale of the known worst character in the regiment.'

Captain Tytler was now in his turn angry and said, 'Evidently, sir, you would rather see an honest man ruined through the rascality of your men than have justice dealt out to all parties. Everybody knows that your men have fought well, and your own officers know too how many of them were once the most daring thieves in London.' However, it ended in a court of enquiry where my husband was honourably acquitted and Government had to bear the loss.

About the same time, some money had been brought in from some of the Collectorates,[66] but had not been made over to my husband by the men in charge, who never left the spot night or day, even sleeping under the carts, and yet these same soldiers had abstracted 20,000 rupees of that money and had never been caught doing it. Fortunately my husband could not be made responsible for money he had never received from those who were alone responsible for it. What became of the soldier who peached on his comrades or the locksmith who made the false keys we never heard, but the guard which had been on ever since leaving Umballa—another very reprehensible act on the part of the regiment—were now removed and replaced by a guard from the 61st.

On their second night the sergeant on night duty saw a soldier lying on his charpoy, very busy digging a hole with his bayonet into the wall of a locked-up room where there was more treasure. He waited quietly till he saw the man crawling in and, catching him by one of his legs, dragged him out and put him under arrest. The next morning he brought him to my husband, who said to him, 'My man, what is the meaning of this, do you want to ruin me and my family?'

The man, a private, replied, 'Bless your honour sir, we don't wish to hurt you but we look upon all this money as loot money and are entitled to some of it.'

'Oh!' said my husband, 'is that your way of looking upon it?' Then, turning to the sergeant, he said, 'You had better take your prisoner to your adjutant and let him deal with him as he thinks proper.'

After this all the guards were changed every week and no more robberies were committed in Delhi, but some of the men of the 60th Rifles were caught playing the same tricks with the Government treasury in Meerut, showing that robbery was inherent in some of these otherwise splendid soldiers. And had you seen their wives come to church, dressed in the most gorgeous of silks made up by the English milliner Mrs Ludlam at Meerut and with French bonnets that could never have cost less than £3, you would have known they never bought them out of their husbands' pay. None of their officers' wives could approach them in style or magnificence, barring their boots.

Shortly after we got a little settled in our new quarters, in the palace, I felt it was time to have our baby boy christened, for he was over three months old. So Jumal Khan, our faithful cook, had to make a cake and many officers were invited to see him baptized. The soldiers, who were devoted to the baby, were heard to say the morning he was born, 'We shall have victory now that this baby has come to avenge the deaths of the murdered children',[67] but two or three days after they soon forgot this when they laid down and refused to fight any more, such are the ways of impulsive Tommie Aitkins.

Of course before our baby was baptized there were many discussions as to what we should call him. The soldiers wanted him to be called Battlefield Tytler. I felt that would be a dreadful name to give the poor child, so I compromised the matter by naming him 'Stanley Delhi-Force'. My husband had been reading to me Marmion[68] just before the Mutiny and, recollecting Marmion's last words, 'On, Stanley, on', it struck me as being both pretty and appropriate.

It was a strange sight to see that chubby little baby with nothing but a pinafore on in the arms of our chaplain Mr Ellis, surrounded as we were with no womenkind except Marie and myself with our two little children, and all the rest generals and army men in their full uniforms. After the christening his health was drunk and kind speeches made. They all prophesied great things for the baby hero and left us to rejoice with thankful hearts that God had spared him through such trying times to be as well as he was.

Now came the signing of the baptismal certificate. This being done, Mr Ellis said he did not know what was to be done with it. He did not like to make the entry in the death book, which was all he had. 'But if you will promise me, Captain Tytler, to take great care of it, and as soon as the roads are open have it posted to the chaplain at Meerut, I will leave it with you.'

This he did, but it was put away too carefully for we never could find it to send to Meerut, so the child had to be rebaptized by Mr Rotton. He made a great many objections before giving in, when he quietened his conscience by saying, 'Well I will not ask you if he has ever been baptized before.' So he should have turned out a saint after a double baptism.

The children used to go out every morning with Marie for an airing on one of the commissariat elephants, a nice quiet creature. As soon as the road was clear I got the necessary materials from Meerut for Marie's Breton cap, but had great difficulty in getting her to make it up, which I could not then understand, for though a plain woman she looked really nice in it. After wearing it only twice when she went out with the children on our elephant, she came into my room and threw her cap on the floor saying, 'I will never wear the horrid thing again.' I was so astounded and asked her what she meant by doing so. She replied, 'All the soldiers laughed at me.'

But later on we found out the real facts, when she took me by surprise saying she was going to be married to a sergeant, a widower in the 60th Rifles. I was indeed very sorry to hear it, for she was such a faithful servant and so devoted to all the children, specially her 'petit François', for whom she had brought out a real French drum, a perfect beauty, and the child was learning to play on it. The very morning of the Mutiny, he received his last lesson from our native drum major.

After a short time the marriage took place. We gave her a silk dress and she wore the most antiquated old straw bonnet she had picked up as loot in the city and in which she looked the plainest old bride I have ever seen in my life.

About this time my husband offered Major Jack Waterfield of our regiment to buy his step, offering to pay him his portion of the purchase money as senior captain, but Waterfield would not hear of it, saying he would not go unless my husband gave him the whole 30,000 rupees.[69] This being out of the question, the matter was dropped, and shortly afterwards he, with Captain Fanshawe of the post office, went down country in a dak gharree. We were to have gone on our way to the Hills the same night, but something detained us, so we left the next evening. As soon as we reached Mussoorie we heard of the dreadful news that they had been attacked by a body of rebels crossing the road, about the very spot we would have had to pass had we been able to start as we had arranged. Poor Major Waterfield was shot dead and the carriage with his body in it burnt. Captain Fanshawe escaped by climbing a tree in the dark of the night, where the sepoys, not observing him, passed on.

This sad tragedy gave my husband his majority without having to pay what he had offered for it, a great Godsend to us after having lost everything we possessed in the world except the little cottage in Mussoorie.

All the above facts related took place from May 1857 to May 1858.

AFTERWORD

THE capture of Delhi was essential for the re-establishment of British power in India, but it was by no means the end of the sepoy rebellion. The capture of Bahadur Shah had denied the native forces their most prestigious symbol, but scattered throughout the sub-continent there were a number of lesser nobles, also dissatisfied with British rule, who were unable to resist the chance the uprising gave them to reclaim their land and powers. In the Bengal Army, all twenty native cavalry regiments and sixty-one of the seventy-four infantry regiments had mutinied, or were suspected of mutiny and had been disarmed, and many of these rallied round the native leaders.

While the Field Force under Archdale Wilson besieged Delhi, many British garrisons across the Presidencies, most notably at Cawnpore and Lucknow, were themselves besieged. In July 1857, Henry Havelock defeated the Nana Sahib, supposed perpetrator of the massacre of the entire Cawnpore garrison, to whom he had promised a safe passage, and two months later, five days after the assault on Delhi, a force under Havelock and Lieutenant-General Sir James Outram started out from Cawnpore to relieve the besieged garrison at Lucknow. But British forces were still fighting major engagements with the rebels the following year, and the last of the effective rebel leaders, Tatya Tope, was still at large with a small but efficient army early in 1859. He was eventually betrayed to the British by Man Singh, the Maharaja of Narwar, who hoped thus to win favour with the 'paramount power', and was executed on 18 April that year.

The Mutiny was only the second major campaign that British troops had been engaged in since the creation of the electric telegraph link. People in England received detailed and immediate reports of the fighting and the home government, through the East India Company, was directly involved in influencing the way the government in Calcutta went about re-establishing its power. This led, on 1 November 1858, to a step which had long been contemplated in London, the abolition of the East India Company, which had certainly been found lacking in that it had failed to predict the outbreak of the Mutiny or to suppress it quickly enough—even though the rebellion had only affected a small part of the country and the majority of native princes had remained neutral.

In the hot weather of 1858 Robert and his family went on leave for six months to their cottage at Mussoorie. From May 1859 to May 1860, he was in Calcutta closing the military accounts of the Delhi operation, and when that was finished the family left on furlough for England.

In an auction of the Delhi prizes, Robert had bought the King of Delhi's crown, which was more like a cap, set with diamonds, emeralds, rubies and pearls, around the base of which he would have worn his turban, as well as two of his throne chairs. Harriet had also 'unearthed' a number of beautiful ornaments, including a length of silk embroidered with passages from the Koran which was also thought to have belonged to the King. In London, Robert was offered £1,000 for the crown by a Bond Street jeweller, but he decided to offer it to the Queen first.

He approached Sir Charles Wood, Secretary of State for India (later Viscount Halifax), who informed him that the most Her Majesty would pay was £500. Although reluctant, Robert was persuaded to part with the crown by Sir Charles, who promised him a fine appointment on his return to India. Robert then offered him the throne chairs, which were richly covered in perforated gilt, and these too were sent to the palace. Having heard nothing for a while, Robert contacted Sir Charles and was told that Her Majesty was under the impression that the chairs were included for the £500. Afraid of making himself unpopular and therefore of losing his promised appointment, Robert let the matter drop, although he was convinced he had been swindled. 'But he was very loyal,' Harriet wrote, 'which made it very difficult for him to understand how Her Majesty could lend herself, for the sake of filthy lucre, to deprive one of her subjects, a poor military man who, she should have known, had lost his all in the mutiny.' But 'I am now satisfied that Sir Charles Wood did it all. I feel sure he either kept the chairs himself or presented them to the Queen in his own name.' Sir Charles did in fact contact the Prince Consort and on 19 January 1861 wrote, 'I cannot at all make out what the owner would expect for them (the chairs) and the skull cap.' Unfortunately no records exist detailing the price that was paid. The crown and the chairs are still in the collection at Windsor Castle.

After a stay in Bex, where their daughter Mabel was born, the Tytlers returned to India. Lord Canning, who had been made the first Viceroy in India, knew nothing of Sir Charles Wood's promise to Robert and had no suitable appointment to offer him at the time, so they left for Simla where they had bought two houses from Lord William Hay. On 7 January 1862 Robert was promoted to the rank of lieutenant-colonel with extra pay. He had been in the army for twenty-eight years.

The histories of British rule in India concentrate on the lives of the dashing fighting men who created the empire or on the tireless administrators who created the organization necessary to secure a peaceful rule. Robert Tytler was neither of these. He was a careful and thoughtful man, not as eager or determined as many of his contemporaries to rise through the ranks in battle. Promotion therefore came slowly, although he served throughout the operations in Scinde and Afghanistan in 1839–42, and in the 1st Sikh War of 1845–6. In Kandahar in 1842, Robert served as Baggage Master to the Field Force under Major-General Nott. Nott wrote to the government in Calcutta that he had given orders that a military bazaar should be established outside the town, and 'I appointed Lieutenant Tytler to the charge owing to his knowledge of the Persian and Hindoostanee languages, and to his great control of temper, which will, I hope, tend to conciliate the people bringing in supplies'.* This was the sort of post Robert held throughout his career. At the siege of Delhi, for example, he saw no action, being responsible for the Military Chest, while the majority of officers took on more hazardous work and were rewarded accordingly.

When Harriet and Robert arrived in the Hills with their family in 1862, Robert learnt that he had been offered the post of Superintendent of the Andaman Islands—an appointment 'worth having as a major, but not as a colonel', Harriet wrote, but he accepted it anyway, 'hoping that by doing so it might lead to something better'.

The Andaman Islands, in the Bay of Bengal, had been annexed by the British in 1858 and a penal colony established there, primarily to hold those mutineers whose lives had been spared. The post of

---

* *The Blue Book, Papers Relating to the Military Operations in Afghanistan, presented before both Houses of Parliament by Command of Her Majesty*, 1843, p. 306.

superintendent was held for two years and hardly seemed to be a reward, there being few people on the islands for the superintendent and his family to associate with apart from the missionaries and one or two minor officials.

Harriet and the children followed him down from Simla in October and had a long and troubled journey. Harriet did not take to the islands at all: 'I hated the place from the very first day. Neither my husband nor I liked boating, but I would have liked to have gone out shelling, only it was too dangerous, for the aborigines were very savage. They were believed to be cannibals.'

In spite of this Harriet was active, supervising the construction of roads being built with prison labour and taking an interest in civilizing the aborigines (who turned out to be far from cannibals), as well as running the 'governor's house' and looking after her family.

In running the settlement, Robert continued the policy initiated by his predecessor, Captain Haughton, which was one of leniency. He was careful in his approach to the Andamanese and went to some lengths to befriend them. One result of this was that their attacks on the settlement at Port Blair ended. During his superintendentship, a large tract of land was cleared on South Andaman Island around the highest hill, which was named Mount Harriet, a pier was constructed at Ross Island, and a small sawmill established.

All did not run smoothly during his period of office, however. On 28 January 1863 a member of the Naval Brigade by the name of Pratt was killed by the Andamanese. The report which Robert received from the rest of the party claimed that the islanders had killed him without provocation. Regarding the natives as dangerous savages, he sent out another party of Naval Brigadesmen to arrest the two men believed responsible for the murder. Alarmed by the incident, and by two attacks on the mainland that followed, during which the natives stole several cooking pots and wounded two men, Robert wrote to the government in Calcutta requesting two companies of sepoys to reinforce his position, suggesting that without them parts of the settlement would have to be abandoned.

He then learnt from one of the Brigadesmen that the natives had killed Pratt for attempting to rape one of their women, and the government in Calcutta strongly criticized him for believing the men's story. One result of the arrest of the two natives was the establishment of a little colony which grew up within the penal settlement as other natives came voluntarily to join the two captives. Officially called the Andaman Home, it was subsequently allocated a grant by the government. Its aim was to civilize the natives, whom Robert had described as a 'truly savage, treacherous, and ungovern-able race of people, devoid of civilisation, in every sense of the word'.* Evidently he changed his mind about them, because he was soon to suggest that they might be used to capture convicts escaping from the 'open' prison.

In October 1863 Major-General Sir Robert Napier, President in Council in Calcutta, arrived for an inspection of the settlement and was extremely critical of the conditions there, which had resulted in the deaths of 2,908 out of a total of 8,035 convicts. Another 612 had escaped. This was by no means Robert's fault because the convicts were housed in tents which exposed them to the heavy rains and to the heat.

Their stay in the Andaman Islands lasted for two years, and during that time Harriet laid the foundation stone for the first church in the settlement, which she named Christ's Church. Eventually Robert applied to be relieved of the post, and on 15 February 1864 he handed over the settlement to Major Ford and proceeded on sick leave, as his health was failing. Harriet was delighted: 'as far as I was concerned I rejoiced, for I always disliked the place and was ill the whole time'.

Robert was posted on general duty at Umballa, and in February 1866 promoted to brevet-colonel. Harriet left him there the follow-ing year to travel with the children to England to raise money for an orphanage she hoped to open in Simla for native children. 'Scottish people helped with contributions of money and fancy goods for a bazaar,' she remembered. 'With the money I added more things for the bazaar. I worked very hard for the Himalayan Christian Orphan-age. Once I recollect I was called upon to speak at a public meeting in Glasgow on behalf of the institution. I nearly fainted at the thought, but people were very kind and I am sure they felt for me, for they added to my already growing funds and offered further help.' Her orphanage was opened the next year. For Harriet it was the fulfil-ment of one of her lifelong ambitions. Remembering the sight of emaciated native children dying during a famine when she herself was only six, she wrote, 'I said to myself, "When I grow up to be a

* N. Iqbal Singh, *The Andaman Story*, Delhi, 1978, p. 125.

woman I will save all the little starving children and bring them up as Christians." '

On her return from England—she had left the children with friends in Scotland—she found that Robert was ill: 'I was shocked with the awful change in him. His system was so drained of its strength that he was never the same man again.' Believing that his spirits would revive if he had his family around him once more, Harriet returned to Europe to collect the children. 'I brought Stanley and the three girls out with me, expecting to give my husband so much pleasure in seeing them once more, but when I met him in Delhi, he was worse than ever. He never could take care of himself —indeed, I don't think many men can.'

In the autumn of 1870 Robert was placed under the Home Depot at Simla. He had already opened what was the first museum in the Hills and the authorities thought he would be of most use devoting himself to the 'curious and valuable' pieces on show.

In January 1871 Harriet gave birth, at the age of forty-two, to their fourth daughter, Kathleen, but the baby was never healthy and died three months later. In October the following year Robert died at the age of fifty-four, never having regained his health. 'We had been so much to each other for nearly twenty-five years and now I was left alone to battle against the world, of which I knew no more than an infant.'

Harriet had been married at nineteen and supported by Robert ever since, in the careful way that the sahibs regarded their mems in India, treating her almost reverentially. She, in return, bore him ten children, eight of whom survived. After Robert's death, however, Harriet took control of her affairs: the first thing she did was dismiss the servants and economize, for debts had been incurred when the orphanage was started. 'We have learnt a great deal worth learning from America. They have taught our women not to be ashamed to work in shops and offices, and to do their own cooking and washing. In my younger days, a girl from a respectable family would have thought it *infra dig* to earn a living in any way, except perhaps as a governess or teacher of music, and even then she wouldn't have liked doing it.' But 'I had to depend on myself and, little by little, gained the confidence necessary to do many things which would have been impossible under other circumstances'. So although she received a good pension from the government as a colonel's widow, Harriet raised more money by giving painting lessons while the children ran the household for her.

In 1875 Harriet heard that two of her sons, Frank and Stanley, were seriously ill, and immediately set out for London with Mabel and two of the other boys. As an economy they bought second-class tickets for the voyage:

I had comforted myself with the idea that at such a time of the year, none of my friends would be going home and so no one would know I had ventured this way. I hadn't even told my son-in-law. Had he known, he would never have allowed me—nor would any of my children either—but I was too proud to let them know. But alas there was not much rejoicing for me, for no sooner had I got into the P & O steam launch than a very tall man came up and said, 'I believe I have the pleasure of introducing myself to Mrs Tytler. Major Steele asked me to do all I could to help you.' My heart sank within me. I am already found out, thought I to myself.

On board, there were more people who knew her. 'Oh! thought I, all Simla is here, when I had hoped nobody would have heard of my going second class.' And when Archdeacon Gray from China heard what she was doing, he said, 'What! A countrywoman of mine amongst those roughs. It is not possible. She shall have my cabin!' and so Harriet and her children were moved into first-class accommodation.

Harriet stayed in England long enough to see her sons well again, and to nurse her other children through a bout of scarlet fever, and then returned to India with Effie. They arrived towards the end of December 1876, just in time for the celebrations organized by Lord Lytton, the Viceroy, to acknowledge Queen Victoria as Empress of India. In Delhi there was a durbar of magnificent proportions:

I believe it was the grandest sight ever seen in India since the start of our rule. I wish I had Kipling's pen to draw the scenes as I saw them. The Proclamation was indeed a wonderful sight, a sort of Arabian night and fairy scene. All the rajas were seated in a segment of a circle, each maharaja or raja or nawab vying with the others in grandeur of dress and jewels.

Lord Lytton was a very small man, but his Herald was immense in stature. He was chosen for his size to proclaim Her Majesty the Empress of India. This being done, all the regiments joined in a feu de joie, after which the bands played 'God Save the Queen' three times and a 101-gun royal salute was fired. Then the royalty left their boxes and mounted their elephants, everyone taking procedure [sic] according to his rank as a noble. It was both a lovely and a ludicrous sight. Lovely, because the elephants were so numerous, and as gorgeously dressed as their royal masters. They were followed by gaily attired horsemen, but they in turn were followed by the riff-raff, some even on donkeys. There was not a raja or prince of importance in the whole of India who was not present, by command, at that proclamation. I wonder what the effect was on the minds of those royalty to see the Viceroy's camp pitched on the very spot where the Delhi princes had been conquered by our army, which was only a fourth of the size of the present one.

In the 1880s Harriet moved to Hyderabad, where she painted and gave lessons. Obviously enjoying the city and her work there, she took a house with a young artist called George Rowlandson and stayed for several years. During this time she 'got up an exhibition of Indian arts, oil paintings of my own and art furniture of my own designs which turned out, thank God, a great success. Sir Dennis Fitzpatrick, the Resident at Hyderabad, opened the exhibition and I heard an artist who was painting the portrait of the Nizam on horseback say (he didn't know who I was, for we had never met before), "Really, this exhibition compares very well with those at home." I was very pleased to hear this, for the decoration and installation of the articles on exhibition and sale was left up to me. And all my art furniture sold on the first day.'

In 1894 Harriet was in British Columbia visiting her daughter Edith, and when she returned to India she began compiling her memoirs up in Simla. Towards the end of her manuscript she wrote:

I can never be rich and it is well that I do not crave it for myself, for there is no happiness in possessing more than you need. I will confess that I would like some money to help my children with a little, but thank God they are all good and, though there are seven boys in the family [two from Robert's previous marriage], I am not aware that any of them have disgraced their father's name so far, and I pray God they never may.

Right up to her death in Simla on 24 November 1907 at the age of seventy-nine, Harriet showed the energy and deep concern for others, tempered by her religious beliefs, that characterized her whole life. 'The reader of these pages will never know what I have suffered in these 75 years, but thank God he has brought me through them all, and if He will spare me till the fulfilment of my soul's aspiration—the founding of "Our Saviour's Orphan Home" and a convalescent home at Simla—I feel I would be the happiest and most enviable of women in this world.'

Harriet was born during the eighth year of George IV's reign and died three years before the end of Edward VII's. The changes that took place during her lifetime transformed the 'civilized' world and shaped the way we live today. But though significant changes and developments did take place in India—for the Europeans at least —traditions and beliefs survived almost intact throughout this period. In Europe and America, social values and the way of life were being changed beyond all recognition. The change would come more slowly in India but it would come all the same—Harriet was aware of that—and it is one of the special qualities of her writing that she preserved, through her memoirs, a way of life that she knew was soon to disappear.

ANTHONY SATTIN

APPENDIX

*Captain Tytler's Statement**

I was in Delhi on the 10th of May last. About 3 p.m. on Sunday, the 10th of May, I heard a bugle and the sound of carriage wheels pass my door. This being very unusual where I resided, I told a servant of mine to run out and see if any one was coming to my house. He went and returned immediately, and said it was a carriage with natives going towards the lines. My house being a corner one, the carriage was obliged to pass three sides of the grounds; so before it passed a second side, I directed the same servant to run to the lines, and give my salam to the subadar-major of the regiment, and say I wanted to see him, for it occurred to me that he and the other native officers of my regiment who had been to Meerut on court martial duty must be returning in this carriage. The servant returned shortly afterwards, and said there were a great number of natives in the carriage from Meerut, but none belonging to our regiment, by which I distinctly understood he alluded to soldiers.

On the morning of the 11th of May, I think about 9 o'clock, one of my servants rushed into the room and said, Lieut. Holland had sent over to say that troops were marching on Delhi. I put on my uniform and went over to him. He joined me and we then went together to Lieut. Gambier, the Adjutant, where we met Colonel Knyvett, commanding the regiment, Captain Gardner and the Brigade Major, Captain Nicholl; and I then learnt the mutineers were marching from Meerut on to Delhi, and I was ordered at once to proceed to the lines and take my own Company along with Captain Gardner's, completing them to the strength of 200 men, with the usual allowance of ammunition in pouch. I was then ordered to proceed to a house on the ridge above the new powder magazine outside the city, and to be very particular that no body of men crossed over from the opposite side of the river. Captain Gardner and I went immediately to the lines; we found the men of our companies rather excited, and it was with some slight difficulty that we succeeded in completing each of our companies to 100 strong. A slight delay now took place in serving out the ammunition, and after sending repeatedly to the magazine to ascertain the cause, I went myself, and the khalassies† said, 'what can we do? the sepoys about here who have come

---

* From N. A. Chick, *Annals of the Indian Rebellion,* 1859.

† Khalassies were unskilled labourers chiefly employed about ships and in the army.

for ammunition are quarrelling and squabbling with us about the cartridges and caps, and we cannot give either without counting them.' I hurried the work and returned to the company. When the cartridges and caps were being served out, many of the men seized more bundles than they were entitled to; therefore to prevent further delay at the time I had these men marked, that I might punish them afterwards. Captain Gardner also re-marked to me that the men of his company showed the same anxiety to secure more ammunition than they were entitled to. The order was now given to the companies to march. Both Captain Gardner and myself remarked the excited manner in which the men left the lines, shouting vehemently every now and then, and which neither of us could prevent. I wish here to record a circumstance that occurred on the morning of the 11th, but which I have omitted mentioning. There was a Brigade parade that morning to hear the sentence of a general court martial read regarding a native officer Ishwari Pandè at Barrackpore, when I remarked a murmur of disapprobation throughout the whole regiment. Though it lasted but a few seconds, it struck me forcibly as something extraordinary, never having witnessed any thing like it before. When we arrived at the house over the magazine, I placed sentries at different points which commanded the bend of the river. The rest of the men, after piling arms, I took into the house; it was a very hot day, and as some of our men had procured water-melons and some sweetmeats they brought them to us, and insisted on our partaking of them; both Captain Gardner and myself remarked the great attention our men were paying us. In the meantime we were called out to see fires that were every now and then appearing in the city. Shortly after this we heard a report of cannon. All this we could not account for. Captain Gardner remarked to me how lucky it was that our men seemed so well disposed, as we were convinced that there was something serious going on in the city, particularly as we remembered the fires that had broken out in Umballa and other places. We now remarked that our men were forming small groups in the heat of the sun. I ordered them to come in and not expose themselves thus. They said, 'we like being in the sun.' I ordered them in again. When I went into one of the rooms, I remarked for the first time, a native from his appearance a soldier, haranguing the men of the companies and saying that every power or Government existed its allotted time, and that it was nothing extraordinary that that of the English had come to an end, according to what had been predicted in their native books. Before I could make a prisoner of him the magazine in the city exploded, and then the men of the two companies with a tremendous shout took up their arms and ran off to the city exclaiming, 'Prithiviraj ki jai!' or 'Victory to the sovereign of the world.'

One of my old servants, a man who had been about twenty-six years in our family, was about this time going on leave, and when I urged him particularly to return, he on several occasions, with sorrowful expression, said,—'yes, Sir, provided your hearth is still in existence,' that is, provided you and your family are in a condition to give me service. He made use of these expressions about a week or ten days before the outbreak. He left me about this time and I have not seen or heard from him since.

On the men running off towards the city, and yelling out like fiends, *Prithiviraj ki jai*, both Captain Gardner and myself rushed after them, and ordered those within reach of hearing to return to their post; when orders failed, entreaties were resorted to, but proved of no avail; however thirty or forty men of my own company and about an equal number from Captain Gardner's returned; these were chiefly old soldiers that had served with me in Afghanistan. My men having thus deserted, I felt quite at a loss how to act and what to do, for we were perfectly ignorant that there was a mutiny and massacre in Delhi, so strictly did the sepoys keep all information from us, isolated as we were at this out-post. When shortly afterwards Lieutenant Mew of the 74th native infantry came to my post and said that the Brigadier required a hundred of my men to take up a position near the rear guard of the 38th native infantry, I replied we had not a hundred men with us, and now, for the first time learnt that there was a general mutiny and massacre of all Christians in the city, and that the officers, ladies and children were assembled at the flag-staff tower on the ridge. On hearing this, in a moment I formed my plan, collected my men and marched to the flag-staff tower, picking up all the troops in the shape of guards I could find on the way. On arriving at the flag-staff tower I found the tower full of ladies, children and servants; the Brigadier, European officers and civilians were congregated in front of the door facing the road leading to the Cashmere Gate of the city, from whence they expected momentarily an attack to be made on them by the mutineers in the city; in front of this body of officers, were the only two remaining guns of the Delhi brigade in position, and to their left was a cart containing the mangled remains of the officers murdered in front of the church in the city, chiefly officers of the 54th native infantry. The remnants of the native infantry regiments were to the right of the tower, sitting and standing in groups in a most sulky mood, whilst in rear of the tower stood some of the carriages and horses of the officers. After reporting the arrival of my party I made enquiries about my wife and children, for I had given Mrs Tytler positive instructions not to leave on any account our house till I returned for her, and I dreaded to hear the worst, for had she remained in the bungalow, as I had asked her to do, she would have been murdered in cold-blood, as will be shewn hereafter; but the Almighty had willed it otherwise, and she was with the rest of the ladies in the flag-staff tower. On returning to the groups of officers I shall never forget the sad and unhappy but resigned countenances of all. Gardner and myself were, comparatively speaking, fresh, for we knew nothing of the horrors of the mutiny till Lieutenant Mew told us of it, whereas those we now saw had felt all the pangs of an anticipated speedy massacre, and seemed patiently waiting with resigned Christian fortitude the result of their fate, and that from about twelve o'clock noon, the hour they had assembled at the flag-staff. The smile and scornful look of defiance and exultation in the looks of the natives were unmistakeable and unbearable, contrasted with the meek resigned Christian fortitude of our men, women and even children. The manner in which our ladies helped in passing up to the top of the tower, the muskets and ammunition, and in their entire bearing and presence of mind, showers the greatest credit on all present. No women in such peril and imminent danger could ever have been expected to act in the praiseworthy manner that those assembled in the flag-staff tower did. When I went into the tower, I found that for their better security, they had been sent into the narrow confined stair-case leading to the top, which added to their misery and discomfort, from the suffocating heat of the day. Seeing the helpless position we were all in, I at once decided that an immediate retreat was absolutely necessary; and particularly after hearing that the cavalry mutineers had left the city and were approaching cantonments from the Subzeemundee side, I went to the Brigadier, and apologizing to him for the liberty taken, recommended and begged for an immediate retreat to Meerut by a ford on the right of cantonments, which I was well acquainted with, having often been there whilst out shooting. The proposition of a retreat appeared to take all by surprise, and whilst it cheered and held out hopes to many, the majority strongly opposed it, considering it would be an act of insanity leaving the tower, feeling convinced that I had been talked over by the men, who, they said, were anxious to get us away from this position, to fall on us at once; and that we ought to stop, and defend it to the last. My views however differed, and I earnestly urged on the Brigadier the necessity for an immediate retreat, pointing out to him that the few men of the 38th that were left, were composed of the best men in the regiment, and that I felt convinced they would protect us and cover our retreat. The Brigadier, overwhelmed as he was with anxiety, fatigue and the responsibility of his painful situation, listened to my request and told me to ascertain the feelings and disposition of the sepoys of the 38th. I accordingly went to them, they were about 150 or 200 strong, besides men of the other two regiments. I begged of our sepoys not to deceive us but to tell me, would they cover our retreat to Meerut or elsewhere, whichever the Brigadier might think most advisable; they solemnly declared they would. I pointed out to them that we had been upwards of twenty-three years together, serving in Afghanistan and several other places, the character our corps had always borne, and why should they now disgrace that regiment we had always been so proud of, and join in such foul cold-blooded murders as had been perpetrated this day? I appealed to them as the best men of our regiment, telling them to tell me honestly and not to deceive us, for I stood amongst them, unarmed and in their power, would they, or would they not, protect us and cover our retreat? Most of the men came up to me and put their hands respectfully on my head, whilst with the most solemn oaths they swore they would protect us and cover our retreat, in which declaration all joined, but begged that I should take personal command of them, and that the two guns now with us should be kept in advance of, and near the infantry, for being as they declared they were disaffected, they would seize the first favourable opportunity of firing into them for protecting us. They also entreated to be taken where water could be had, as they had not tasted water since the morning. All this I promised should be done, reminding them of their solemn oath to be faithful to us. I hurried back and reported the result to the Brigadier, begging of him, as it was nearly evening, that we had not one moment to lose, but to retire at once, for I had heard that the troopers of the cavalry from Meerut, glutted with their spoil and blood-thirsty deeds, had left the city and were then resting themselves and horses near Subzeemundee, prior to their intended attack on cantonments, which would take place the moment they were refreshed. The number of voices which opposed this movement exceeded those who agreed with me, thus naturally causing the Brigadier to doubt how to act, for the responsibility of his position was fearfully great. I again and again entreated and urged the necessity for our immediate retreat, a second and a third time he sent me to ascertain the real feelings and disposition of our men, and the result was the same, and my opinion each time strengthened, that we had not one moment to lose, and that the men would protect us. Still hope clung to that solitary tower in the breasts of many, it seemed to them their only safety, and they could not be persuaded to leave but to remain, defend and die in it. What a helpless situation to be murdered in, which it would have been, had not the Almighty willed it otherwise. A small solitary building isolated from all others built on a ridge, a conspicuous object from every side, full of men, women and children, without a drop of water, or a particle of food, a frail piece of brick and mortar suffocating in itself from the intense heat in the month of May. The Brigadier, thank God! saw the necessity of acceding to my request, and said, 'Well, what is to be done?' I replied, 'Put all the ladies and children in every available carriage, the guns to follow with the infantry close behind them, the latter I will take command of'; at the same time I proposed that it would be advisable, if the European officers would keep with the infantry, thus shewing a degree of confidence in the men. This however would not be listened to, for none had any faith in the sepoys with us, having seen during the day the treachery of the others, and which I was, comparatively speaking, ignorant of. All the officers of the 38th remained with me, as well as several civilians, and we left the flag-staff tower as proposed, when I had put Mrs Tytler, my children and Mrs Gardner into my palanquin-carriage. My pay havildar Omrow Sing, and a sepoy Thakoordeen, both men that I had every confidence in, came to the carriage, and with tears in their eyes, entreated of me to make my family over to them, and that they would take them to Meerut, by hiding them from village to village amongst their people, and thus protect them. They begged and implored of me to listen to them, for they said, we had not five minutes to live, and that an escape was impossible, for that the sowars had sworn to take the blood of every Christian. I said, 'No, I am perfectly satisfied that the men of my regiment will protect us.' They then entreated of Mrs Tytler, to get me to listen to them; she spoke to me, and talked of our children, but I was too resolved; if we were to be destroyed, God's will must be done, but I would not hear of their plan. Faithful as I then considered them, still I doubted their power of assistance in a case and trial of this nature. I now returned to the infantry column, reminded the men of their sacred pledged oath, and gave the word, 'sections right shoulders forward quick march'. The sepoys moved off, steadily enough till we reached the bottom of the ridge in cantonments, when two men of our regiment, that had been on duty at the magazine in the city, at the time it was blown up, joined our party, scorched in a frightful manner. A group of at least one-third of our men surrounded them, innumerable questions were put, and replied to, the purport of which was that the English had designedly blown up the magazine for the wilful destruction of the natives, and of the native guard, and that the whole of the 38th guard were destroyed, they only having escaped. I now heard a murmur of disgust and disapprobation, and could plainly hear words to this effect uttered, 'let it be so, we will see and taste the blood of the English yet.' I was standing next to the two men, as they related their tale, and told them it was false, no Englishman would ever destroy their own guard wilfully, it must have been an accident. They said 'no we saw it ourselves, it is true, and we were all blown up.' Many of the sepoys now came up to me, and said in a sorrowful but respectful manner, 'where are the guns, Sir, that you promised should be with us?' I told them the guns were on ahead, they said, 'yes, they are on ahead, they have gone a great distance off, and we know what they will do to us for following you.' Others began to move off toward the lines as well as the bazar, and took not the slightest notice when called. Many of the old sepoys said, 'Oh, Sir, see after those guns and get them back, for without them we can do nothing for you.' I said, 'let me go to the head of the column, and see what can be done;' one or two sepoys said to me, 'Sir, we cannot follow you, the Europeans and natives are two, we fight for you, we spill our blood for you, and you treat us in return by blowing up our brothers with gunpowder. Go, Sir, go, you have been our father and mother, always kind to us, with *bahana* (misleading) we will prevent the cavalry from following you; but we cannot come ourselves.' I felt bewildered, all seemed now frustrated by the coming of these two sepoys from the city. Still my men were respectful to a degree, and I had hopes, strong hopes, that they would remain with us, if I could but get the guns, the absence of which they seemed so much to dread. I ran to the head of the column, and there saw Captain Nicholl, who told me in answer to my question, that the guns had gone on at a rapid pace on the Kurnaul road. I regretted this, and asked Nicholl if he would lend me his horse, for I was on foot, and that I would go after them, and if possible bring them back. I accordingly went after the guns, and found the last tumbril at the junction of the *cutcha** with the *pucka*† road leading to the city; this was about two miles from the tower. On calling out 'halt,' the men on this last tumbril said, 'Oh, no, no halting now, when we do halt, it shall be in the city of Delhi,' and they were insultingly insolent. I now returned with the intention of informing the Brigadier of my unsuccessful endeavour, and had reached the bridge near cantonments, when it occurred to me, one chance more remained, and that was to see Captain de Tessier, commanding the artillery, and ask him to assist me in using his influence to bring back the guns, the only chance of the infantry following; the road was now crowded with carriages and horses, and foot-men running, so I returned at a full gallop, came up to and headed the guns. Captain de Tessier was in his carriage, his horse having been shot by the men of the 38th, during the day, and this was the only means he had for going on. De Tessier told me it was impossible, the men would obey no orders, and as we were now on the Kurnaul road, perhaps it was just as well to continue on it, besides which it was now a general flight. I asked him, if he knew where my wife and children were, he pointed out the carriage. I thought they had gone the road to the ferry that I had proposed, but they had gone on with the guns. Never shall I forget the look of entreaty my wife gave me, to come into the carriage, and assist them. I saw it was a general flight, and I wavered between two duties, but my family and those I had left behind, the agony Mrs Gardner was in about her husband, and her entreaties for me to go in search of him, decided my resolution at once. My wife, I am proud to say, did not even murmur. I told them for God's sake to hurry on towards Kurnaul, and consigning them to the care of the Almighty, for I never expected to see them again, I hurried back to cantonments. The road now had the appearance of a large fair that had

* Cutcha = dust
† Pucka (here) = paved

suddenly broken up, carriages, horses, men running and screeching to each other in sad and awful confusion; poor Glubb was sick, seated on a tumbril, on another was Major Abbott of the 74th. I recognised his friendly voice, telling me to look after my family, and shew less zeal, for it was a general flight. His words were too true, he had judged rightly, it was indeed a flight of all that remained of the Delhi Brigade; still I went on through this confused crowded mass, and on reaching the bridge entering cantonments, I saw Gardner, running and walking quite faint and exhausted. I rushed up to him, and told him to jump up behind me, there was no disgrace now in attempting to save those near and dear to us. The Brigadier and his party had known the worst, so I could have nothing more to tell them. I asked several of the natives, if they knew where the Brigade-Major was; they did not know. I longed to see him, for I was on his horse. We now saw dense crowds of natives pouring into cantonments, like fiends from the Subzeemundee side, and with a heavy heart went off at a full gallop after our carriage. On passing Holland on the road, he told us, he could not go on faster, his horse was ill and had been bled that morning. Poor fellow, he took the Meerut road, and was overtaken by the sowars, and severely wounded in the back, and left for dead by them. This shews how close the sowars must have been to us, when we left the flag-staff tower; fortunately they were so taken up with the spoil in the houses on the road to cantonments from the city, that they delayed following us up, and then only came up to those that were furthest behind or unable to proceed faster. What my feelings were on this occasion, I cannot tell. God grant, I may never experience such feelings again, fleeing from that which had once been our happy, but now no longer home, with a brother officer behind me. Before we reached my carriage, now some distance on ahead, two desperate attempts were made by Goojurs to stop us; they saw I was unarmed, for my sword, the only weapon I had, had fallen out of its scabbard and was lost; Gardner had a revolver and his sword, but from his position and holding on behind me, he was unable to get out either in time; seeing this one man in particular made a dash at the reins, and an attempt to strike with his stick, but failed in both; we now reached the carriage, and I thanked God for his great mercies to us. My syce that had been driving, I put on horse-back, Gardner stood behind the carriage, and I sat on the coach-box and drove, telling the syce to keep near us. We had scarcely gone a quarter of a mile, when the syce was knocked off the horse by a blow from a Goojur's lathee, and the horse carried off; there was nothing for it, but to put him on the top of the carriage, and take him with us. We now drove at a rapid pace, my object being if possible to pass the next horse stage, or even the one beyond it, before the enormous crowd of fugitives should arrive, and my horse though old was fully capable of doing it; when we arrived at the second stage, I called out to the syce for a fresh horse; his reply was, very well, but who is the coachman; I said, never mind, but bring the horse quickly; he still persisted in not bringing it, so I went to the stable when three or four natives assumed a most insolent manner. I called Gardner, he came and the appearance of his revolver and sword had the desired effect; they gave us a good horse, and we gave them five rupees from the little money our French servant Marie had with her. We now went thankfully, though anxiously, along, having our dear families with us, but we shuddered on looking back to see the fiery glare and blaze of the bungalows in cantonments burning. I never saw such a grand sight as it appeared from the position we were in, though it added to the horror and anxiety of our feelings. We had not proceeded above two miles, when we heard the distant rumbling of a dâk garry from Kurnaul; on its reaching us, we found it conveyed a lady passenger going to Meerut, viâ Delhi; we stopped the carriage, told her, what had taken place, advising her strongly to return at once to Kurnaul; we then drove on ourselves; scarcely had we gone a mile further, when the right front wheel of our heavily laden carriage broke into pieces; to mend it was out of the question, so we got out and walked, taking the little children in our arms; it was a clear moon light night; after walking some distance, the carriage we had stopped with the lady passenger in it, again reached us; we apologised, as well as we could, and urging the necessity of present circumstances, we put the ladies and children into her carriage, taking our position on the top; I again drove. Our misfortunes were not to end here, for the carriage, which we found out to our cost afterwards was an old ricketty veritable apology for a carriage, now that it was so heavily laden, threatened to fall to pieces, and in less than an hour, the right back wheel rolled off the axle tree from the carelessness of the nuts being imperfectly screwed, the screw nuts were lost, and it was therefore impossible to secure the wheel, besides which the axle tree became slightly bent, and we were quite at a loss what to do; whilst in this helpless situation, a cart with a lady on it from Delhi, came up to us at a rapid pace; her coachman was a man who understood cases of this nature, and with our united assistance, he put on the wheel, securing it with pieces of string; the lady went on in her cart promising to send a conveyance for us from Kurnaul, and we followed driving at a very slow pace; scarcely had we gone a mile when the two front springs of this old carriage simultaneously broke, and the carriage went to pieces. We now had to abandon the carriage and walk, it was a perfect wreck; in this way we proceeded another mile, when an empty Government Magazine Cart going from Kurnaul to Delhi, came up to us; we at once took possession of it, placing the ladies and children inside; the two men in charge were inclined to be very insolent, but that we at once silenced, they left us with a malicious scowl on their countenance. Gardner and I had therefore to drive two fresh unmanageable bullocks, as well as our ignorance of such driving admitted of, and in this manner we arrived at Paneeput; prior to this, the two Government bullock drivers returned, and insolently demanded their cattle which we refused giving them. At Paneeput I went to the Thusuldar,* and asked him to assist us if possible with a carriage; he said it was quite out of his power. No carriages being obtainable, so we went on again, the ladies sitting in the cart, with the little children asleep in their laps. It was now day break in an hour or two; we observed a gentleman on horse back approaching us. This was Mr O'Connor, the husband of the lady we had stopped and brought on with us; he had heard from the lady who had passed us on the cart of our coming, and had at once sent off to Kurnaul for a conveyance which joined us soon afterwards; we now left the bullock cart and told the drivers to take it back to Kurnaul; they replied no, we are going to Delhi. During the night, we passed a party of the 38th sepoys, returning from rifle practice from Umballa; they did not recognize me, but screeched out like demons as we passed them. On arriving at Mr O'Connor's house on the banks of the canal (his post), we ate a hurried breakfast, and then hastened our departure as much as we could, for there was evidently an unnecessary attempt for delaying us on the part of the Mahomedan coachmen, everything was wanting, or not to be found. At last the carriage was ready, as well as an old cart; the difficulty in getting these two conveyances ready was beyond all conception. We separated our now large party, and went on to Kurnaul; the two coachmen were suspiciously dressed, each armed with a double barrel gun, sword and pistols, and amused us the whole way with news about Umballa having fallen, that the European Artillery guns had been seized by the native troops, and various other fabrications, advising us strongly to leave the road and strike off to the right; when they found this would not answer, they tried to separate our two carriages, as much as possible, by one driving rapidly, and the other very slow, this however, we soon put a stop to, as we were now, through Mr O'Connor's kindness, pretty well armed ourselves. This enabled us to keep a high hand with these two scoundrels, and so we arrived at the Post Office of Kurnaul, where the Post Master Mr Maddock, and his wife shewed every attention and kindness to us, and to several other fugitives from Delhi, who now began to come in in rapid succession. I met Captain Garstin, Assistant Quarter Master General, at the house of the Collector; he had just arrived from Umballa. I told him the whole tale; he asked me to accompany him to Umballa, for the purpose of making my report to the General. I would have done so, but as Glubb of my Regiment had also arrived and was ill, I asked him to take him instead, for he could report all that was necessary, telling them if possible to send out a party of European cavalry, to assist the

---

* A thusuldar was a native revenue officer in charge of a revenue sub-division of a district (a tehsil).

fugitives in their escape from Delhi, for I felt convinced the mutinous cavalry would try and follow us up (which they did, and wounded Holland), besides which the Goojurs, who had formed fresh bands, were in reality to be dreaded, as much as the mutineers. After seeing Garstin and Glubb off, I returned to Mr Maddock, where every preparation was made for the safe escort of our now very large party to Umballa; all the bullock carts and carriages he could get were collected, and we left the same evening for Umballa, which we reached the next morning. Here I made my official report to Sir H. Barnard, commanding the division, and to Brigadier Halifax, requesting if possible that British cavalry might be sent to aid the rest of the fugitives. This was impossible; the state Umballa itself was in, required every available European to be present. During our journey from Kurnaul to Umballa, we were constantly told, that the native troops had risen, and had taken possession of the European Artillery guns, and when an escort of the 4th light cavalry passed us on their way to Thanassur, some of the troopers called out to our cart-men, 'drive on, let them go, they have only three days to live.' When we arrived at Umballa, the treatment we received from Major Ewart, Assistant Adjutant General, and from Captain Maisey, the Deputy Judge Advocate General, and their families, both of whom received us into their houses, sheltered and fed us, treating us with every attention and kindness, is beyond all praise. General Anson, and his British troops, began now to arrive from the hills, and the aspect of affairs assumed a more cheerful appearance, for up to this period, since our arrival at Umballa, we were all every night obliged to leave the bungalows, and sleep in one of the barracks of the dragoon lines, protected by European Cavalry, as a rise was expected every moment in the 5th and 60th Regiments Native Infantry. When the first and second European Bengal Fusiliers arrived many touching instances of gratitude occurred, which proves the heart of an European so different to the cold blooded treachery and lies of Asiatics. Their lying and treacherous nature I well knew, having experienced it in every shape from Afghanistan to Bengal, and now that the honest gratitude of the Englishman was displayed, it contrasted so strongly with my experience of the Asiatic, that I could not but forcibly see the difference. I had brought out with me a large draft of men from England, and many of them were in the 1st and 2nd Fusiliers. When these noble poor fellows heard of the plight we were in, several came down at night, and said they wished to speak to me. On going out it was too dark to recognise the speaker, when in a feeling tone of voice he said, 'I beg your pardon, Sir, we know it is a great liberty, but you were always so kind to us, and we have never forgotten that—we have not much, Sir, but we have made up a bundle—we are sorry to hear what has happened to you and your family, we have plenty more clothes,' and before I could thank and recognize the speaker, the poor fellows had left the bundle and had hurried away. In this bundle were shirts, trowsers, sheets, stockings and every other thing their little and scanty store admitted of; how different was this to what we had lately experienced from those cut-throat-brutes at Delhi—this was not the only occasion, but one out of several which occurred whilst we were at Umballa. The army now began rapidly to form, and I was placed in charge of the Military treasure chest; the treasury was escorted by a hundred men of the 60th Native Infantry, with their due proportion of native officers; vain and continuous were the shallow attempts of these scoundrels to instil confidence in me, in hopes of obtaining the General's permission to allow the treasure to go on a day in advance of the first troops, saying the crowd was so great, and what danger could there possibly be, when *they* were our guard! Finding this would not do, I was surprised to find the next morning, that almost every sepoy had, in addition to his musket, a native tulwar. I at once ordered this irregularity to be discontinued; the native officer said, it was the custom of his regiment, whenever going on service to take swords with them; the Non-commissioned officers backed him in rather an insolent style, but I insisted, and they were put aside. When we passed Kurnaul, numbers of the city-people, chiefly Mahomedans, lined the streets, the guard of the 60th shouted out constantly Ya Hydree Ya Hossan, &c. &c., the towns people taking up the shout, and saying, 'go on brothers, it is your fate now, but bring them back prisoners,' and whenever an European soldier passed them, the insulting sound of *dhutt dhutt*, like driving away a dog, was heard; there was evidently an unmistakeable and good understanding existing between the towns people of Kurnaul, and the men of the 60th Native Infantry. When we arrived at Alipore, I brought these circumstances to the notice of the Major General (Sir H. Barnard), the guard was relieved by H. M.'s 75th, and the subsequent conduct of the 60th Native Infantry at Rhotuck* is well-known to all. The battle of Badli-ke-Serai was now fought, the 8th of June, 1857, and on the same day we encamped on the parade ground of the Native Infantry Regiments in Cantonments. Mrs Tytler had accompanied me, and so had Mrs Holland, who was most anxious to gain any information about her husband as he was supposed to have been killed, and it was not till after our arrival at Alipore that we heard of his safety at Meerut. It was owing to the kindness of the Hollands, that Mrs Tytler had been enabled to leave our bungalow at Delhi, on the 11th of May; they sent their carriage for her, and insisted on her leaving the house at once, else she would have been murdered

---

* The 60th NI had already mutinied at Umballa on 10 May, but their officers persuaded them to return to their ranks and no disciplinary action was taken. On 22 May they were sent to Rhotuck but they mutinied on the way, firing on their officers, all of whom escaped unharmed. The mutineers arrived at Delhi on 12 June but were defeated with heavy losses the following day.

by my khitmutgar, as will be seen hereafter. Mrs Laughton, the wife of the Chief Engineer also accompanied her husband. Mrs Holland went shortly afterwards over to Meerut, with an escort, to join her husband, and Mrs Laughton went to Umballa, so that Mrs Tytler was left alone, *the only lady* present in camp throughout the whole siege and capture of Delhi; our little children were with us, and Marie our French servant. God forbid it should fall to the lot of any lady ever again to be present in a camp throughout such a critical time. Our little infant son was born in our waggon on the 21st of June, 1857, under heavy cannonading and was Christened Stanley Delhiforce, in commemoration of the event. There is a very curious and remarkable coincidence connected with the birth of this child; we were anxiously looking out for, and expecting reinforcements, our losses daily were heavy, and our troops were more and more exhausted and harassed, but still no reinforcements. This little child was born early in the morning; small groups of soldiers were formed about my treasure guard, and one of them said, 'Now we will get our reinforcements, this camp was formed to avenge the blood of the innocents, and the first reinforcement sent to us is a new born infant.' Strange to say European reinforcements arrived the next day; the child was always looked upon with deep interest by the men.

NOTES

PART ONE

1 Harriet's father, John Lucas Earle, was born in Devon on 29 January 1791 and arrived in India as an ensign in the East India Company's army at the age of sixteen. He was a captain by the time Harriet was born, promoted to major in 1835, and lieutenant-colonel in 1841. He died on 12 October 1845. Harriet's mother, Mary Earle, died on 18 June 1890.

2 Regiments were regularly moved from station to station across the Presidencies in peaceful times to ensure their fighting effectiveness and to keep up morale. During wartime, regiments not directly involved in the fighting were still moved up near the troubled area as a second or third line of strength, as was clearly shown in the wars against the Afghans. 'March', in Anglo-Indian usage, meant 'move by road' and did not exclude riding on horse or elephant, or even, as Harriet Tytler records, being carried by bearers in palankeens.

3 The first railway on the sub-continent, the Indian Peninsular Railway, was opened on 16 April 1853 and ran twenty-four miles from Bombay to Tannah. The railway network was quickly developed after this.

4 A fakir was a beggar, usually a religious mendicant living on charity. Although this fakir may well have been a professional murderer, he was clearly not a member of the fraternity of 'Thugs', who were very specialized in their methods (cf. note 9 on Thugs).

5 Lindley Murray (1745–1826) practised law until the American revolution, when he made his fortune catering for the British forces occupying New York. He then retired to England, where he wrote the hugely popular *Grammar of the English Language* (1795), *English Exercises* and *Key* (both 1797).

6 Commissioned officers could obtain promotion by buying the next senior rank from an officer who was himself being promoted, or was leaving the service. Otherwise, waiting for promotion could be a lengthy business, it sometimes taking up to fifteen years to move from lieutenant to captain. The exception to this was service during war, when, because of the high fatality rate, there was a chance of rapid promotion if one survived (see p. 173).

7 Batta was an allowance paid—on a sliding scale—to all ranks for 'hard lying' or discomfort, and for extra expenses incurred while on service

away from the main stations. With batta, a soldier could double his regular pay.

8 Many sepoys in the Bengal regiments were recruited from Oudh, which was an independent state until 1856. For the recruits, service in the Company's army conferred privileges and protection on themselves and their families still living in Oudh, where there was widespread robbery and violence (cf. p. 70). The sepoys were also able to bring money back for their families at a time when poverty was widespread.

9 Harriet's account of these Thugs is quite accurate, except that there is no evidence that there were two distinct kinds. Meadows Taylor recorded the evidence of hundreds of these men after they were captured, and wrote a vivid account in *The Confessions of a Thug* (London, 1839). They all firmly believed they were fulfilling the wishes of the goddess Kali by reducing the world's population. Thuggee was stopped here and there, in isolated places, from the beginning of the nineteenth century, but no systematic attempt was made to end it until Lord William Bentinck became Governor-General in 1834.

10 Although Harriet thinks that her father took command of the 3rd NI in 1839, *Scott's Bengal Directory* for 1840 lists him as major of the 9th NI at Benares, and Major V. C. P. Hodson's *List of the Officers of the Bengal Army, 1758–1834* states that he was in command of the 2nd Recruit Battalion at Fatehgarh in 1839, and was not posted as lieutenant-colonel to the 3rd NI until 19 January 1842. She has clearly confused these two promotions.

11 The *Seringapatam* left Calcutta in December 1839.

12 Bonnets, usually tied with ribbons under the chin, pulling the sides down over the ears, were the most popular and varied form of head-dress for women until the mid-1860s.

13 Pearce & Son, Solicitors, were at 10 St Swithin's Lane (*Post Office London Directory*, 1816).

14 In fact it was Lord William Russell, posthumous son of John, 4th Duke of Bedford, and uncle to Lord John Russell, then Secretary to the Colonies. On 6 April 1840, at the age of seventy-three, he was found murdered in his bed. *The Times* (9 May 1840) reported: 'The excitement produced by this terrible event continues unabated, and during the early part of yesterday the comparatively quiet locality of Norfolk Street, Park Lane, in which the house of the deceased nobleman is situate, was crowded with spectators . . . The carriages and other vehicles of several persons of distinction filled with ladies drew up in the street, and remained there for a considerable time. . . The excitement produced in

high life by the dreadful event is almost unprecedented, and the feeling of apprehension for personal safety increases every hour, particularly among those of the nobility and gentry who live in comparative seclusion.' It transpired that Lord William's Swiss valet, François Courvoisier, a man in his mid-twenties, had committed the murder, for which he was hanged on 7 July in front of a crowd of more than 20,000 people.

15 Oxford House, St Swithin's Lane, was bought by the Salters' Company in 1641, but it was destroyed in the Great Fire of 1666. Another hall was erected on this site in 1667–8, but 'a completely new Hall, with an impressive Ionic portico by E. Carr, replaced it between 1824 and 1827. This in turn was destroyed by fire in 1941' (Weinreb and Hibbert (eds) *The London Encyclopaedia*, London, 1983).

16 Gregory's mixture or powder contains rhubarb, magnesia and ginger. It was popular, in doses of ten to sixty grains, as an antacid and purgative.

17 Captain Frederick James Raine of HM's 96th Regiment, who had served in Spain and the South of France, was barrackmaster at Birmingham.

18 It is uncertain exactly what Ann died of, but whatever it was it appears that Harriet's aunt was in some way to blame.

19 The first attempt to travel from England to India under steam was made in 1825 by the *Enterprise*, which arrived in Calcutta, after rounding the Cape, in 113 days. The P & O were granted their charter in 1840 and started the regular Anglo–Indian mail service in 1842. Before the Suez Canal was opened in 1869, there were two routes to India: via the Cape and the Overland Route. The latter, which Harriet took, involved going by steamer to Alexandria, taking a smaller boat up to Cairo, travelling overland to Suez, and then taking another boat for the final leg. She travelled on the P & O paddle steamer *Hindostan*, which, when it was built in 1842, was the most powerful ship in that company's service.

20 Captain Robert Moresby served with the Indian Navy during the earlier part of the century. With the advent of steam travel, it was necessary to find suitable harbours for use as coaling stations. Moresby charted the Laccadive Islands off the west coast of India in 1828, and in 1830 was sent to chart the Red Sea with notable success. He commanded Indian Navy steamers until 1841, when he left the service, disgusted with the lack of appreciation shown to him by the East India Company. He joined the P & O that year, and was considered the ablest commander in the service of that company. He retired in 1846.

21 Gibraltar was captured from the Spanish by the British in 1704 and

formally ceded to the Crown under the Treaty of Utrecht on the 11th of April 1713.

22 Major James Fraser CB (1800–68) saw action at Ghazni and Kabul. 'During the Affghan war [*sic*] it fell to his lot to lead a charge of native cavalry against a body of Affghan horse commanded by the Ameer Dost Mohammed Khan. The opposing forces were nearly equal. His men were splendidly mounted, and his heart beat high with the coveted opportunity of distinction. Gallantly he led them, and plunged into the thickest of the enemy, but his men failed to support him. Just before reaching the foe he cast one look towards his men, and found that, save his brother officers, there was not a man within 20 yards of him. Assailed on all sides, his reins were speedily cut, and he himself severely wounded —his sword arm being nearly severed. Of seven officers who accompanied him into action three were killed outright, two, including himself, severely wounded, and two only came out of action unscathed. He owed his own escape to the speed and vigour of the powerful English horse which carried him, and which (unguided) bore him back to camp. But he came back a maimed man for life, deeply deploring the cowardice of his men. This mischance gave a tinge of bitterness to all his future life' (*The Gentleman's Magazine*, February 1868, p. 261). For his wounds, Fraser was granted a pension and a gratuity of one year's pay. He had been on furlough since 7 January 1843 and was returning to India, where he was made an Honorary ADC to the Governor-General.

23 Malta was taken by the British under Pigot on 5 September 1800 and guaranteed to the Crown by the Treaty of Paris, 1814.

24 Samuel Shepheard was an Englishman who had arrived in Cairo in 1841 and opened the New British Hotel, which became Shepheard's British Hotel, as did his hotels in Alexandria and Suez. The Cairo hotel was famous for its style and grandeur and became the favourite hotel for royalty and the wealthy passing through Egypt. It was burnt down during the riots of 1952. 'Few hotels in the world have been so much a part of the history of their times that their destruction would symbolize the end of an era' (Kay Showker, *Fodor's Egypt*, London, 1984, p. 150).

25 The East India Company had been trading in China since 1680. Chinese tea had been brought to England twenty years before that. In 1834 the exclusive rights of the Company to trade ended and free trade ships sailed for England. This was one of the factors that contributed to the outbreak of the Opium War of 1839.

26 The Suez Canal was fully open to shipping in 1869.

27 Aden was captured by the British on 19 January 1839 and a garrison and later a coaling station for Indian steamers were established.

28 Mrs Birch's husband, (then) Captain Frederick Birch, was Superintendent of Police in Calcutta, and was raised to Senior Magistrate in 1846.
   Mrs Birch died in Multan on 9 July 1852, while he was killed by the
   mutineers at Sitapur on 3 June 1857.

29 Harriet's brother, John Earle, and her uncle Major Louis Bird were both
   serving with the 24th NI.

30 Robert Neave was Special Commissioner and Civil and Sessions Judge
   at Azimghur.

31 John Adams Tytler won his VC in action against the mutineers at
   Chorpura on 10 February 1858. When his men were beaten back by the
   rebels' fire, Tytler rushed forward on his own and engaged the gunners
   in hand-to-hand combat.

32 Sir Donald Stewart (1824–1900) rose through the army to become
   Commander-in-Chief in India from 1881–5. On his return to England,
   he was appointed to the Council of India.

33 Ann, second daughter of Major Robert Durie, 11th Light Dragoons,
   married William Beckett at Meerut in July 1824. He was adjutant of the
   9th NI when John Lucas Earle was captain. Captain Beckett died in 1844.

34 Captain Henry Siddons married his uncle's second daughter, Harriot
   Emma Siddons. Her brother, Captain William Siddons, married Harriet
   Tytler's eldest sister, Susan Earle, at Mussoorie in 1843. He was
   appointed Bhil Agent at Indore on 2 January 1851. He died on 21 September that year at Bhopawar, CI.

35 Bishop Heber of Calcutta 'died in a swimming-bath at Trichinopoly on 3
   April 1826, from bursting a blood-vessel' (C. E. Buckland, *Dictionary of
   Indian Biography*, London, 1906, p. 198). Another Bishop of Calcutta,
   Dr George Cotton, drowned in 1866.

36 The East India Company began trading under the Charter granted by
   Queen Elizabeth I on 31 December 1599. It was quickly obliged to
   maintain a force of militia to protect its trading ports or 'factories' at
   Surat, Madras, Calcutta and Bombay. From the outset they enlisted
   Indian troops, as well as those recruited in Europe, and as the forces were
   expanded the native section quickly became the most numerous. By the
   middle of the eighteenth century, they were being drilled on European
   lines to compete with the French, as competition for the lucrative Indian
   markets became fiercer. Later, regiments from the British Army were
   sent for duty in India, the first being HM's 39th, later the 1st Battalion,
   the Dorsets, whose motto was *Primus in Indis*, who arrived in Madras in
   1754.
      By the middle of the nineteenth century, the Company had created

three separate native armies in India, the Bengal, the Madras and the Bombay Armies, all officered by Europeans. There were also the Queen's regiments serving in India and the Company's Europeans. There were therefore three distinct groups of British officers serving in India.

On 1 November 1858, the East India Company was abolished and direct control of India passed to the Crown. The Company's native armies became the Indian armies and the Company's European regiments became British line regiments, although this caused much discontent and led to the so-called 'White Mutiny' of 1859.

37 The Court of Directors were appointed by the shareholders, but although the East India Company was ostensibly an independent trading organization, ultimately it was guided by and responsible to Parliament in England.

38 Lieutenant R. W. Bird, 4th Regiment of Native Infantry, was First Assistant to the Resident at Lucknow.

39 Captain G. E. Hollings was Second Assistant to the Resident. He was from Robert Tytler's regiment, the 38th NI.

40 The Imambarah was built towards the end of the eighteenth century. 'Imambarah' meant 'Patriarch's Place' and was so named by the Shiah Muslims because it was consecrated to the memory of the martyred sons of Ali, immediate descendant of the Prophet. On the tenth and final day of the 'Moharam', a Muslim festival, which was celebrated at the Imambarah, the entire building was illuminated. One observer recorded: 'The Imambarah, the mosque attached to it, and the gateways that lead to it, are beautiful specimens of this architecture (light, elegant, but fantastic). From the brilliant white of the composition, and the minute delicacy of the workmanship, an enthusiast might suppose that genii had been the artificers' (Edward Thornton, *A Gazetteer of the Territories Under the Government of the East India Company, and of the Native States on the Continent of India*, London, 1857, p. 568).

41 Robert Tytler was born in Allahabad on 25 September 1818, a grandson of Count Schneeberg. His father, Robert Tytler, was an MD in the Bengal Medical Establishment. Robert married Isabella Neilson at Meerut on 21 January 1843, but she died at Landour on 6 January 1847. He fought in the 1st Afghan War of 1840–2 and in the Gwalior Campaign. He married Harriet in Lucknow on 2 March 1848. The marriage certificate, recorded on 8 March 1848, and witnessed by Lieutenant-Colonel Louis Bird and A. F. Richmond, the Resident at Lucknow, described Harriet as 'under age'.

42 Andrew Barlow (b. 1781) reached the rank of lieutenant in the Company's service, but took furlough on 9 May 1811 and was struck off the army register after five years' absence. He was thought to have taken up service with the King of Oudh.

43 There was no prescribed age for marrying. The Prophet married Ayishah when she was only nine years old. She lived to be sixty-seven and became his favourite wife.

44 The custom of going up to the Hills was relatively new. The first European house was built at Simla in 1819 and the town was first visited by the Governor-General in 1827. The annual retreat to the more temperate climate of the Hills was soon regarded as a necessity and, by the time of the Mutiny, even the official seat of government was removed to Simla each summer to avoid the heat of the plains.

45 The kotwal would have been surprised that Robert could read the Arabic script, a rare achievement for a British officer.

46 Calomel is mercurus chloride, a white powder, insoluble in alcohol, which was used as a purgative. It was taken in doses of half to five grains. The severity of Robert's condition is shown by his need for 500 grains.

47 The regimental cadres were on the scale of the British service—1,000 privates, 120 NCOs, 20 native and 24 British officers, although this was by no means a hard and fast rule. Many British officers held posts outside their regiments, and others would be on furlough, sometimes for as long as three years, so there was often only about one-third of the British officers actually present with their regiments.

48 Rudyard Kipling, the illuminator of so much of Indian life, wrote about a Village of the Dead in a story called *The Strange Ride of Morowbie Jukes*. Harriet's description seems confused, since she claims that the children sent to the village 'never survive . . . very long' and yet they are able to marry there.

49 General William Pattle was ADC to Queen Victoria.

50 Sir George Hayter (1792–1871) became portrait and historical painter to the Queen.

51 John Zoffany (1733–1810) was born in Rattisbon of a Bohemian family. He arrived in England in 1758, and was elected to the Royal Academy in 1769. He was noted for his portraits of Garrick, Samuel Poole and other actors. He was in India from 1783 to 1790 and painted the altarpiece of the Last Supper for St John's Church in Calcutta.

52 Bengalis here suggests officers of the Bengal Army.

53 2nd Burmese War of 1852–3.

54 Lord Dalhousie (1812–60) was made Governor-General of India in 1847. Active in the 2nd Sikh War, he declared the Punjab a British Province in 1849. Under his rule, the telegraph and railways were introduced into India and the imperial postal system was organized. He continued to suppress suttee (the Hindu ritual of burning widows on their husbands' funeral pyres) and dacoits. Under his governorship, the East India Company annexed Satta'ra, Nagpur, Jhansi and Oudh. He retired the year before the outbreak of the Mutiny.

55 In his introduction to the *Dalhousie–Phayre Correspondence, 1852–1856* (London, 1932), D.G.E. Hall notes: 'A regiment of local service troops, the 38th NI, or Bengal Volunteers, as they were called, refused for caste reasons to proceed to Burma by sea. What might have proved an ugly situation . . . was saved by ordering the men to proceed to Arakan by road via Dacca' (xxiii–xxiv). The General Service Enlistment Act was brought in soon after this and obliged all recruits to enlist for overseas duty.

56 'Perfectly respectful in their language, they were firm in their refusal. Doubt and suspicion had taken possession of their minds . . . a belief was afterwards engendered among them that the English Government had a foul design to entrap them . . .' (Kaye and Malleson, *History of the Indian Mutiny*, London, 1891, vol. I, p. 339).

57 By 'fine men' Harriet means the Other Ranks, of whom, she is suggesting, only one was well enough to attend parade. It seems incredible, and it has been impossible to verify.

58 The Duke of Wellington died on 14 September 1852 at the age of eighty-three.

59 Napoleon's remains were moved there on 15 December 1840.

60 John Lempriere (1765?–1824) was a classical scholar educated at Winchester School and Pembroke, Oxford, from where he received his MA in 1792 and his DD in 1803. His *Classical Dictionary* was published in 1788.

61 Writing of the siege of Lucknow in his book *The Martiniere Boys in the Bailey Guard By One of Them* (Lucknow, 1877), E. H. Hilton wrote: 'Our active and energetic Principal, Mr Schilling, determined to do all that in him lay for the preservation of the youths entrusted to his charge' (p. i).

62 At many of the smaller military stations, the wives and children as well as the officers and men lived for considerable lengths of time in tents.

63 The circuit house was a superior form of dak bungalow where judges and other senior officials stayed when on circuit.

64 The excessive mismanagement of Oudh grew worse when Waud Ali Shah came to the throne in 1847. Colonel Sleeman, the Resident at Lucknow at the time of Lord Hardinge's visit, wrote of the King, 'I do not think that His Majesty can ever be brought to feel the responsibilities of sovereignty' (Kaye and Malleson, op. cit., vol. I, p. 96). By virtue of the treaty made with the East India Company in 1801, Oudh was annexed on the 7th of February 1856. The deposed king sent his mother and younger brother to appeal to Queen Victoria in London for the return of their lands, in August 1856, but their petition was denied.

65 This kind of blister is a condition of the skin caused artificially by the application of mustard, of various kinds of dried fly, or of any other vesicatories. The blister-flies are known as cantharides, because they produce cantharidin. When applied to the skin, they create a sensation of warmth which is followed by a blister, at one time considered beneficial for liver complaints, although it is best known now as the aphrodisiac 'Spanish fly'. The Telini 'fly' of India produces a high concentration of cantharidin.

PART TWO

1 The 38th NI had amongst its battle honours Seringapatam, Kandahar, Ghuznee and Kabul.

2 The garrison was commanded by Brigadier Harry Graves (1803–61), who had arrived in India in 1822 and had served in the 1st Burmese War, the 1st Afghan War and the Gwalior campaign. He was posted as Brigadier, 2nd Class, to the command of the Delhi garrison in August 1856. Later he was acting Brigade-Major with the Delhi Field Force from 8–30 June 1857. In 1859 he left on furlough for England, where he died, in 1861, at the age of fifty-seven.

3 Bahadur Shah II, the last King of Delhi, succeeded to the throne on 28 September 1837 at the age of sixty-one.

4 Hodson, after the recapture of Delhi, shot two of the king's sons, Mirza Moghul and Mirza Khizr Sultan, and his grandson, Mirza Abu Bakr.

5 In 1803, the Mahrattas, aided by the French, took Delhi. The British under Lord Lake recaptured it on 11 September and restored the aged Shah Aulum to the throne with a pension. The present king was his descendant.

6 Harriet's view of the natives' ability to write is somewhat unrealistic as the literacy rate amongst the native soldiers was extremely low, and presumably even lower among their relatives. However, their letters

reassured their families that they were still alive, and there was usually a scribe in each regiment and in many villages. Rather than suffering under the new postal regulations of October 1854, the native soldiers were better off. Although Harriet thinks the sepoys could send as many letters as they liked, they were in fact restricted to one letter per troop per day, which was sent free of charge. Under the new regulations they were allowed to send as many letters as they liked at the regular rate of half an anna (there were four pice to one anna and sixteen annas to one rupee). One common practice was for sepoys to send letters without paying any postage. On delivery, their families would also refuse to pay. In this way they were reassured of the continuing well-being of their relatives.

7 No one has ever explained the exact meaning or significance—if there was one—of this occurrence, which was observed in many districts of Northern India.

8 Robert Tytler's ability to speak Hindustani and his interest in his men makes him stand out from many of the officers of the time. Language was a barrier, and many English officers relied on interpreters to communicate with their men (cf. p. 72: 'When he saw that my husband could read Hindustani he was rather taken aback', and note 13). In a letter written while captive near Kabul during the Afghan War of 1839–42, Major Eldred Pottinger noted the effects of this. 'The service is excessively unpopular both with [native] officers and men . . . We no longer get the sons of respectable land-holders . . . If the Government . . . does not take some decided step to recover the affections of the Army, I really think a single spark will blow the sepoys to mutiny, for the zeal of the officers is cold . . .' (from a letter in the Gerald Sattin Collection).

9 After the Mutiny the practice of piling arms outside church was stopped and soldiers attended services with their weapons.

10 In July 1857, under the command of the Nana Sahib, mutineers at Cawnpore killed 600 Europeans who had been promised a safe passage and were embarking on boats to take them down the Ganges. The 200 Europeans who survived this attack were murdered later and their bodies thrown down a well, above which a memorial was erected.

11 Captain W. H. S. Earle of the 20th NI, which mutinied. He survived the Mutiny and reached the rank of lieutenant-colonel. Captain Earle acted as interpreter during the Native Court of Inquiry of 25 April 1857 at Meerut, which heard the objections to the use of the new cartridges and which concluded that there were no grounds on which the sepoys could object, as the cartridges with the supposed pig and cow fat had been withdrawn and the sepoys were allowed to grease the cartridges with their own tallow.

12 The Judge-Advocate-General, in summing up at the trial of the King of Delhi in January 1858, referred to Robert Tytler's evidence: 'It appears, from his statement, that a coach full of these Meerut mutineers came on Sunday evening to the lines of the 38th Native Infantry, doubtless to prepare the Sepoys . . .' (Kaye and Malleson, *History of the Indian Mutiny*, London, 1891, vol. V, p. 313).

13 A 'passed officer' was one who had passed the prescribed examination in the vernacular. It became compulsory for all officers to pass the lower standard, which was not difficult and allowed them to speak to their men, though not fluently, and with a limited vocabulary. The higher standard was very different, and the top grade of examination, as 'interpreter', which was the grade Robert Tytler had achieved, was very difficult indeed (cf. p. 72, 'When he saw that my husband could read Hindustani').

14 Tattees were grass screens placed over windows and doors, and watered to keep rooms fresh and cool. They were reckoned to reduce the temperature indoors by as much as 20°F.

15 The Delhi Almanac for 1857 shows thermometer readings of 138°F in the sun, and a high of 100°F in the shade. Another survivor, Mr Wagentreiber, the editor of the *Delhi Sketch Book*, vividly described the scene in the Flag Staff Tower: 'Here we found a large number of ladies and children collected in a round room some 18' in diameter. Servants, male and female, were huddled together with them; many ladies were in a fainting condition from extreme heat and nervous excitement, and all wore that expression of anxiety so near akin to despair . . . It was a Black Hole in miniature, with all but the last horrible features of that dreadful prison, and I was glad even to stand in the sun to catch a breath of fresh air' (Kaye and Malleson, op. cit., vol II, p. 70).

16 An officer of the 38th NI, perhaps Ensign Gambier, recorded how he and Colonel Knyvett escaped from the Flag Staff Tower and met up with this party. 'The Brigadier ordered us to retire. First went the carriages, then the guns, next the 38th, and a portion of the 74th. I cannot say then what became of the carriages. As I brought up the rear our men fell in column in order, but as we retired they streamed off right and left by hundreds into the bazar [*sic*], till at last the Colonel and I found ourselves with the colours and a handful of men. We intended to make for a ford by the powder magazine, but our men showed that they were no longer under control, took the colours, and made for their lines. The Colonel and I followed. We sounded the assembly, and there was a great hubbub. We implored the men to fall in, but they stood still and declined. The Colonel went among them, and begged they would shoot him if they

wished it. They vowed they had no ill-feeling against us. It was here I saw the last of poor Holland (since safe). His horse had not been ridden all day: it came from his bungalow. I heard Holland exclaim, "which way did the ladies and carriages go?" Some one answered, the Kurnaul road; and I watched him canter across the parade-ground to the bridge by the Company's garden. If I had had a wife or child, or any one belonging to me in the carriages, I might have done the same; but as it was I dismounted, patted Gibralter [his horse] with a kind of presentiment of evil, and sent him to my bungalow, and walked disconsolately into our quarter-guard. The Colonel did the same; somehow the idea of flight did not occur to us. I got my bed down from the bungalow and my kit, and went for some dinner. Then our men commenced urging us to escape, but we refused, and I fell asleep. I awoke, and my bearer entreated me to go, and said that the ruffians were coming from the city. Peile was also in the quarter-guard. We each took one of the colours, and got as far as the door, but the men closed on us, and jerked them out of our hands. Firing commenced behind us, and the satisfaction of being shot by one's own troops is small. I met the Colonel in the doorway and, seizing him by the wrist, forced him along over the parade-ground to the bridge by our butts. It was quite dark. We reached it untouched and scrambled on till we fell exhausted by a tree. Soon the moon rose, and cantonments in a blaze threw a glare on the Colonel's scales: my scabbard flashed, and white clothing looked like snow. We crouched like hares, and thus passed all that fearful night, now running forward, now hiding in hollows and gaps, as voices seemed in our track. We kept parallel to the road which leads to the Shalimar gardens. We crossed the Jumna canal by a ford, and drank as perhaps we never drank before. The poor Colonel was terribly exhausted; we had had nothing all day. Day broke; we were under a tree, and the Colonel tore the scales off his coat and hid them in the bushes. I was bent on making for the Kurnaul road, trusting to some conveyance meeting us, but the Colonel was set against the plan, and we made for the Jumna bank. We perceived a broken down mud hut at a little distance. Into this we crept and lay down; while there as the sun rose, we perceived a party of sepoys and others advancing towards us; they seemed to search the bushes, and the sun glittered on their arms. I cocked my pistol mechanically, but after two barrels I had no more ammunition. The Colonel had not even his sword. I remember saying, "Oh, Colonel, death is better than this horrible suspense"; God's hand was over us then as ever. The sepoys turned towards the river, as if thinking that we had taken the ford, and disappeared. Some Brahmins discovered us as they came to work, one took us to the village and put us in a tope (clump of trees), while he got us chuppaties (bread) and milk.

On the way Mr Marshall, the auctioneer and merchant, met us. He had quitted the quarter-guard immediately after the Colonel and me, together with three others, but in the morning Marshall alone remained, and where the others are, alive or dead, we know not. After giving us food our Brahmin friends took us over a ford of a branch of the Jumna, and concealed us in the long jungle grass on the other side. While there another came to me and said a party of fugitives like ourselves were in the grass at a little distance. I followed, and he led me some two miles, when I found a party of ladies and others concealed. The first person I saw was Proctor, and in my joy at seeing him, whom I had believed shot at the main-guard, I saw no one else. After the first joy of meeting him, I looked about and found Mrs Forrest, her husband, and three girls, Mr Fraser (Engineers), Mr Salkeld, Vibart, and Wilson (Artillery). I sent to the Colonel and Marshall, and this made our party thirteen: with guns and swords, we thought ourselves a match for a chance straggling party of mutineers.

'The escape of this party from the main-guard was wonderful. During the afternoon it was determined by Major Abbott at the Cashmere gate to send what ladies were there to cantonments. There were no conveyances, and they were mounted on the carriages of the guns—who knows what spirit possessed our men?—they were suddenly dislodged, and a murderous fire commenced on all there assembled. There was a rush up the ramparts into the main-guard. Osborne was shot through the thigh; he said, "I am not going to be murdered by these sepoys", and led the way, throwing himself over the wall into the ditch below; others followed. Mrs Forrest was shot through the shoulder, but over they went, one after another, dropping down what in ordinary circumstances one would say endangered life and limb, yet they reached the ditch, scrambled up the scarp, and the party I mention reached Sir T. Metcalfe's house; the servants gave them some beer and food, and led them to the river bank shortly before the house was fired. They passed much such a night as we did, with one narrower escape. As they lay concealed some men passed and saw a ribband or a bottle, and saying, "Oh, they have been here, evidently", went on. They came to the same ford, and while concealed heard me described by my eyeglass, sent for me, and thus we happily met.

'We could not stay in the grass, so that evening started, the Brahmins conducting us to a ford over the Jumna. We travelled some two or three miles up stream before reaching it. Our hearts failed, and no wonder, where ladies were concerned, as we looked at the broad swift river. It was getting dark, too. Two natives went across. We watched them anxiously, wade a considerable portion of the river; then their heads alone appeared above water. It was our only chance of life, and our brave ladies never flinched. It was so deep that where a tall man would wade a short man would be drowned. I thought it was all over when, on reaching the deep water with Mrs Forrest on my left arm, a native supporting her on the other side, we were shot down the river; however, by desperate efforts and the assistance of another native, we reached the bank in safety. I swam back once more for another of our party, and so ultimately we all got safe over. It was a brave feat for our ladies to do. We passed another wretched night, suffering fearfully from cold, and crouching close to each other for warmth; there was no noise but the chattering of our teeth. Next morning we were discovered and led to a tope, where again the Brahmins temporarily proved our friends, but they turned us out shortly afterwards with news that there were sowars behind and sowars in front. We turned wearily to the left to fall into the hands of the Goojurs. These ruffians gradually collected and with a wild howl set upon us. Our arms had been under water and useless, and they were 15 to 1. They disarmed us and proceeded brutally to rob and strip us. I think a fuqueer [fakir] here saved our lives. On we toiled all day in the burning sun, with naked feet and skins peeling and blistering in the burning wind. How the ladies stood it is marvellous, yet they never murmured or flinched, or distressed us by a show of terror. We were taken to a large Brahmin village that night and concealed in a fuqueer's hut. We were there three days, and I trust hereafter handsomely to reward our benefactors. While here we sent in a letter in French to Meerut asking for assistance. It seemed not to come, and from Bhekia we were taken to Hurchundpore at the request of an old zemindar, who had heard of our whereabouts, and treated us royally. He was a German by birth, an old man of eighty or ninety, and now native in dress, language, &c.—not in heart or religion. He sent us up clean stuff for clothes, and gave us something like civilised food again. That evening thirty sowars, under Lieutenants Gough and Mackenzie, who volunteered for the service in answer to our letter, rode in, and we enjoyed the luxurious sense of release from the almost hourly expectation of death. The old man provided carts for us, and at 10 pm the day week of our escape from Delhi, we reached Meerut.

'What a delight it was to be surrounded by kind faces and by sympathizing friends. We were truly in a deplorable condition—lame, filthy, and plundered of all; we were ashamed to look people in the face. There are many who, like ourselves, have lost everything belonging to them. I feel that thankfulness for life must counterbalance every other consideration. My losses are small, for I have lost none dear to me by relationship. I often thanked God that I had neither wife or child. All the

38th are saved, as Holland came in here alive, but with a slight cut on the back from a sabre. Poor fellow, he has been wandering seventeen days, owing his life to the kindness of villagers and others on the road' (N. A. Chick, *Annals of the Indian Rebellion*, 1898, n/e 1974, pp. 61–4). Gambier was wounded at the final assault on Delhi and died of his wounds on the 18th of September 1857.

17 Colonel Keith Young's diaries and letters were published as *Delhi —1857. The siege, assault and capture as given in the diary and correspondence of the late Colonel Keith Young, C. B., Judge-Advocate General, Bengal*, edited by General Sir Henry Wylie Norman and Mrs Keith Young, London, 1902.

18 Harriet was by now nearly eight months pregnant, as was Mrs Gardner, with whom they escaped.

19 The battle of 23 June 1757 led to the foundation of the British Empire in India. Clive, with 1,100 Europeans, 2,100 native soldiers and 10 guns, defeated Suraj-ud-Dowlah, Nawab of Bengal, and his 68,000 men and 53 guns. Clive lost only twenty-three men in the battle, aided by the treachery of the Nawab's commander.

20 Robert Tytler reported them as shouting, '*Prithiviraj ki jai*', meaning 'Victory to the sovereign of the world'.

21 Brigadier Graves' adjutant may have been Lieutenant Mew of the 74th NI.

22 The Diwan-i-am was the public hall of audience. The Diwan-i-Khas, the private hall, once housed the famous Peacock Throne. An inscription on the wall read: 'If there is a paradise on earth: It is this; it is this; it is this.'

23 Not all this group were killed under the peepul tree (*Ficus religiosa*, a large fig tree, sacred to Hindus). Mrs Aldwell, a Eurasian woman, had sent a petition to the King when she was made captive claiming that she and her children were Muslims. Accordingly, for the three days they were held in the palace with the Europeans, they were fed separately along with an 'old native Mahomedan woman'. 'On the morning of the 16th of May, some of the king's special servants, attended by a small number of infantry sepoys, came and called out to our party, that the Christians were to come out of the building, and that the five Mahomedans were to remain . . . they were taken out of my sight, and as I heard, brought under the Pipul tree by the small reservoir in the courtyard, and there were murdered with swords by the king's private servants' (Chick, op. cit., pp. 95–6).

24 Harriet thinks the Gujars were all Mohammedans, but they were mostly Hindu farmers from the North-West Provinces, although there were

some instances where they had converted to Islam. The Gujars claimed to be descended from the Rajputs (high-caste Hindus, predominantly landowners and soldiers) by women of inferior caste. They tended to be nomadic and easily fell into crime. They were generally hostile to the British during the Mutiny.

25 At night the temperature might drop to 75° or 80°F, but often not below 90°F.

26 A hackery was a native bullock cart, a wallah, the man who drove it.

27 The Honourable George Anson had been appointed Commander-in-Chief in 1856, having arrived in India in 1853. It had become the custom for the government to move from Calcutta to the Hills for the hot weather. In 1857, General Anson arrived in Simla on 1 April. The news of the Mutiny was received in Simla on 13 May, although Colonel Keith Young, who was in Simla with Anson, recorded 'bad news' in his diary on 12 May: 'Mutineers from Meerut have seized the bridge at Delhi' (Colonel Keith Young, *Delhi 1857*, ed. General Sir Henry Norman and Mrs Keith Young, London, 1902). On the 13th he wrote 'an anxious time—no dak from Umballa. Over at the Chief's and had a long talk with him; he appears to rather pooh-pooh the thing. We shall see.' The next day, Anson and his staff left for Umballa to gather a force to recapture Delhi, although the civil government had not yet moved.

28 The word 'ghari' has several meanings, including a measure of time, a time piece, and, here, a small earthen pot.

29 There had been incendiary fires at Umballa in April, which had made the Europeans in the Hills nervous. Rumours spreading through Simla included the news that the Gurkhas were going to murder them, which, in the light of their subsequent record during the Mutiny, was rather ironic.

30 Officers who were not posted to regiments were placed on the Un-attached List, presumably with loss of pay. It was generally only possible to volunteer for service during wartime and was therefore extremely hazardous, but taking part in a campaign offered the chance of rapid promotion, which was especially attractive to ambitious officers. Robert, not knowing then the full extent of the mutiny, must have believed there would be a chance of being posted elsewhere, away from the action.

31 Captain Tytler's appointment as paymaster to the Delhi Field Force, with responsibility for the military treasure chest, was approved by Colonel Chester.

32 The 5th NI were disbanded at Umballa. Captain Gardner died from his
    wounds at Kussowlie on 28 June 1857.

33 Keith Young (op. cit., p. 27) wrote on 28 May, 'We all attended poor
    General Anson's funeral last night, Chester reading the service.'

34 Ahsanullah Khan was Bahadur Shah's Hakim (physician) and adviser.
    Thomas Metcalfe, in 1843, called him 'the root of all evil' in the palace,
    but when the mutineers arrived from Meerut on 11 May the Hakim
    urged the King not to side with them. Throughout the siege he was
    disliked by the soldiers—on 20 May he had urged the King to expel them
    from the city for looting—and when a powder factory exploded on
    7 August, Ahsanullah Khan was blamed. His house was looted and he
    was arrested by Mirza Moghul, but the King threatened to take his own
    life if the Hakim was harmed. He was spared and was at Humayun's
    tomb when Hodson arrived. His account of the Mutiny is recorded in the
    Home Miscellaneous Series (India Office Records), vol. 725 (unpub-
    lished).

35 Captain Knox of the 75th Foot was killed on 12 June when the mutineers
    attacked the Flag Staff Tower piquet.

36 The 38th NI were with the rebel force that opposed General Wilson's
    advance over the Hindun on 31 May, where they suffered heavy losses.
    They were so badly cut up at the engagement near Badli-ke-Serai on 8
    June that they never kept in one body again.

37 This detachment, in fact from the 60th NI, had already been suspected of
    mutiny by the time they reached the ridge and had been replaced by a
    guard from HM's 75th.

38 Harriet wrote: 'A cousin of my husband, John Tytler, raised and
    commanded the 4th Gurkhas and was known to say that he had been
    with his men in many perilous positions but had never known one of
    them on any occasion to show any fear. Great praise from this so
    distinguished an officer who himself won the Victoria Cross during the
    mutiny at Lucknow.'

39 'Amongst the fugitives from Delhi was Captain Tytler, of the 38th
    Native Infantry, who, after a variety of vicissitudes, reached Umballa
    safely with his wife and children. When Anson's force was being formed
    for the advance on Delhi, Tytler was placed in charge of the military
    treasure chest, and through some unaccountable negligence Mrs Tytler
    was allowed to accompany him. I believe that, when Mrs Tytler's
    presence became known to the authorities, she would have been sent out
    of camp to some safe place, but at that time she was not in a fit state to
    travel . . .' (Field Marshal Lord Roberts of Kandahar, *Forty-one Years in*

India, London, 1897, vol. 1, p. 160). Major Hodson held even stronger views: 'I can see no reason strong enough to induce me to consent to any ladies coming into camp; it is true that a Captain—, who with his wife escaped from Delhi to Umbala [*sic*], has dragged the unfortunate woman back here again, though expecting her confinement, and with not a shadow of comfort or shelter except a tent. Even Mrs—(a Persian lady) and all the others of her sex have been sent back to Meerut' (Major W. S. R. Hodson, *Twelve Years of a Soldier's Life in India*, London, 1859).

40 Pad elephants had thick straw mattresses fixed over their backs on which the riders sat as best they could, rather than the more comfortable, box-like howdahs.

41 The Field Force which arrived on the ridge at Delhi on 8 June was composed of 2,800 infantry, 600 cavalry and 22 guns. By 3 July there were 6,600 men, on 14 August, 8,000, and on the day of the assault, 8,748. By the middle of August the rebel army in the city was estimated at 30,000, but Keith Young wrote on 13 September, 'The enemy, though forty thousand strong at one time, have not now more than ten or twelve thousand, so we ought to beat them' (op. cit., p. 281).

42 A bell of arms was a small, circular building, usually with thick masonry walls (although sometimes a bell-tent was used), built in a line immediately behind the sepoys' quarters. Each company had a bell of arms in which all rifles were stored after parade, and each regiment had a larger bell of arms for ammunition. A recent guidebook of Delhi noted, 'A pleasant walk may be taken through the old Cantonments, in which "bells of arms" for keeping the muskets can still be seen' (Professor L. F. Rushbrook Williams (ed.), *A Handbook for Travellers in India*, London, 1975, p. 328).

43 Harriet is quoting Hindustani baby-talk: 'durram' is a child's lisping version of 'Gurram' (hot).

44 As well as being the centenary of the Battle of Plassey, 23 June was also Ruth Juttra, a Hindu high holiday, and a new moon, a good omen for Mohammedans.

45 Captain Frank Willock of the 6th Light Cavalry was killed at Delhi on 22 August.

46 Chicks were screens or blinds made from laced split bamboo. A punkah was a fan, where cloth was stretched over a large rectangular frame which was hung from the ceiling. As Harriet suggests here, the punkah was operated by strings attached to the sides of the frame and passed through the wall. A punkah-wallah sat outside, pulling the strings, but

Harriet doesn't mention whether she had a servant to operate the punkah in their bell of arms or not.

47 On 9 July, Lieutenant-Colonel H. Tombs and Lieutenant J. Hills won their VCs. Roberts wrote: 'The moment Hills saw the enemy he shouted, "Action front!" and, in the hope of giving his men time to load and fire a round of grape, he gallantly charged the head of the column single-handed, cut down the leading man, struck the second, and was then ridden down himself . . . As soon as the body of the enemy had passed on, Hills, extricating himself from his horse, got up and searched for his sword, which he had lost in the melee. He had just found it when he was attacked by 3 men, two of whom were mounted; he fired at and wounded the first man; then caught the lance of the second in his left hand, and ran him through the body with his sword. The 1st assailant coming on again, Hills cut him down, upon which he was attacked by the third man on foot, who succeeded in wrenching his sword from him. Hills fell in the struggle, and must have been killed, if Tombs . . . had not come to the rescue and saved his plucky subaltern's life' (op. cit., pp. 188–9). In all, 182 VCs were awarded for services during the Mutiny, thirty-two to officers and men of the Bengal Army and eight of those at Delhi.

48 The durbar held in Delhi on 1 January 1877 was to recognize Victoria officially as Empress of India. The tallest officer in the Indian Army read the proclamation. The resolution had been passed almost twenty years earlier, on 1 November 1858, when the East India Company was dissolved and control of India passed directly to the Crown.

49 After the durbar, the windows were removed and, as the whitewash and mortar peeled off, the bullet marks appeared again and the bell of arms looked as it had done before.

50 Harriet seems to have confused several different events here. There were many plans to attack the city, urged on by men like Nicholson and Chamberlain, but Brigadier Archdale Wilson, commander of the Field Force after General Barnard's death, was hesitant, knowing how essential it was for him to succeed, and fully aware of the odds against him. But he was eventually persuaded. Neville Chamberlain was seriously wounded on 14 July in an attack led by Brigadier Showers, which was quite defensive in its aims. 'On the morning of the 14th July, the rebels again swarmed out, 9,000 or 10,000 strong, and made an onslaught on the British position . . . As the fire from the ridge failed to drive them off, a column moved into the Subzee Mundee about three in the afternoon, and, after a sharp struggle, forced them to withdraw their field artillery, and retire into the city. Our men pressed them so closely as

to suffer from the grape fired from the city walls . . . among the latter [wounded] being Chamberlain, whose arm was shattered by a bullet —the seventh time in which he has been mentioned in the *Gazette* or despatches as "wounded in action"' (Charles Low, *Soldiers of the Victorian Age*, London, 1880). Chamberlain saw no further action until after the capture of the city.

51 Colonel Keith Young wrote on 19 August: 'This morning a female European captive came into the camp, a Mrs Leeson, the wife of a clerk or patrol of that name; her maiden name was Collins. She was wounded on the day of the outbreak, and some friendly Afghan took her away, and has concealed her ever since, treating her, we understand, with all proper kindness and respect. She is now with Mrs Tytler, the only lady there is in our camp. Captain Tytler has been offered the run of the female wardrobe that Major Goad sent down, for the use of the young lady' (op. cit., p. 220).

The next day he wrote: 'I have seen her statement as taken down by Captain Tytler. She gives a horrible account of the massacre on the first day, and it is almost a miracle her escaping. After having been wounded and her children killed, she was left for dead on the ground, where a friendly Afghan found her, and in the evening came and put her in a charpoy and took her away to a moulvie's [Mohammedan priest's] house, with whose family she has been residing ever since, being treated by them with the greatest kindness and respect. She never went out; so beyond what occurred on the first day in the city she knows nothing. She says, however, that it is reported that there are still some thirty Europeans concealed in the city, but cannot say whether this is true or not; and that those who have Europeans in concealment wouldn't dare to acknowledge it, or to talk about it to their dearest friends, as they would be certain to be murdered if the Sepoys found it out. She leaves tomorrow, I believe, for Umballa, where she has some friends' (p. 222).

52 Brevet-Major Joseph Leeson (1796–1848) was appointed to the command of Shah Shuja's 1st Cavalry Regiment, which was named Leeson's Horse, in September 1840. In 1848 he was made Honorary ADC to Lord Dalhousie. His third son, John Leeson, claimed the title of his father's cousin-german, the 4th Earl of Milltown, on the death of the 7th Earl, in March 1891, styling himself the 8th Earl, but his claim was never recognized.

53 Nawab Sir Salar Jung (1829–83) was Prime Minister of Hyderabad during the reign of the Nizam Afzal-ud-daula. Through his influence, Central India, the Deccan and Hyderabad itself remained loyal to the Company throughout the Mutiny. On the death of the Nizam in 1869,

Sir Salar was co-regent through the minority of the young Nizam. His sudden death was attributed to poison, but there was no evidence. His son, Nawab Sir Salar Jung Bahadur II (1862–89), was made Prime Minister in 1884, but he resigned in 1887, visited England in the same year, and died at the age of twenty-seven.

54 1st Lieutenant Edward Earle of the Bengal Artillery was wounded on the 11th of September.

55 A Jumna pāri goat was literally a goat across the river Jumna.

56 Maharaja Sir Narindar Singh of Patiala (1823–62) showed his loyalty to the Company by sending an auxiliary force to Delhi, Gwalior and Dholpur, and by helping to keep the Grand Trunk Road open. As a reward he was given additional territory, titles and power, and in 1862 he was made a member of the Governor-General's Legislative Council. The Raja of Kapurthala was given a present of 10,000 rupees, two estates in Oudh and the right to an eleven-gun salute.

57 Lieutenant Gambier of the 38th died on 18 September of his wounds (see n.16, Part 2).

58 Of the assaulting force of 5,160 officers and men, 1,104 men and 66 officers were killed or wounded on 14 September.

59 Roberts wrote: 'A report was circulated that a large number of our men had fallen into the trap laid for them by the Native shopkeepers and were disgracefully drunk. I heard that a few men, overcome by heat and hard work, had given way to temptation, but I did not see a single drunk man throughout the day of assault, although . . . I visited every position held by our troops within the walls of the city' (op. cit., p. 243).

60 Roberts describes the scene at Delhi most vividly: 'That march through Delhi in the early morning light was a gruesome proceeding. Our way from the Lahore Gate by the Chandni Chauk led through a veritable city of the dead; not a sound was to be heard but the falling of our footsteps . . . Dead bodies were strewn about in all directions, in every attitude that the death-struggle had caused them to assume, and in every stage of decomposition . . . Here a dog gnawed at an uncovered limb; there a vulture, disturbed by our approach from its loathsome meal, but too completely gorged to fly, fluttered away to a safer distance' (op. cit., p. 259).

61 Harriet's account is not always accurate. Hodson did have General Wilson's 'reluctant consent' to bring in the King, and the Queen and her son, and wrote that he went 'with fifty of his troopers'. The next day, again with the General's permission, and this time with a hundred troopers, he went to search for the remaining princes, who were known

to have been more actively involved in the Mutiny than the King himself. When he found them he refused to guarantee their lives. Hodson himself wrote: 'After two hours of wordy strife and very anxious suspense, they [the princes] appeared, and asked if their lives had been promised by the Government, to which I answered "most certainly not", and sent them away from the tomb towards the city, under a guard. I then went with the rest of the sowars to the tomb, and found it crowded with, I should think, some 6000 or 7000 of the servants, hangers-on, and scum of the palace and city . . . I demanded in a voice of authority the instant surrender of their arms, etc. They immediately obeyed, with an alacrity I scarcely dared to hope for . . . I went to look after my prisoners, who, with their guard, had moved on towards Delhi. I came up just in time, as a large mob had collected, and were turning on the guard. I rode in among them at the gallop, and in a few words I appealed to the crowd, saying that these were the butchers who had murdered and brutally used helpless women and children, and that Government had now sent their punishment; and seizing a carbine from one of my men, I deliberately shot them one after another' (Major W. S. R. Hodson, *Twelve Years of a Soldier's Life in India*, London, 1859, p. 301). Kaye states that many of those who were in Delhi at the time felt that the death of the princes secured the victory that had been won, but Kaye concludes that 'in my judgment . . . the shooting of the princes still remains one of the most painful episodes connected with the Mutiny' (op. cit., vol. IV, p. 57).

62 Harriet seems to have mistaken the order. Although there was a widespread feeling that the fort should be destroyed—some wanted to demolish the entire city!—and the principal buildings which were used to quarter the victorious force (only the Diwan-i-Khas being considered of sufficient architectural interest to be preserved), the order eventually issued was for the demolition of all the buildings within a radius of 448 yards *outside* the walls, to ensure a clear line of fire in the event of an attack.

63 'Mr Carter, a railway engineer, . . . reported that a large body of insurgents had marched from Delhi towards Agra via Bullaghur (probably Bullunghur, near Pilwal) [*sic*], where Mr Roods [*sic*], the portrait-painter, is said to have been killed' (G. W. Forrest (ed.), *Selections from the Letters, Despatches and Other State Papers preserved in the Military Department of the Government of India, 1857–58*, Calcutta, 1893, p. 268).

64 Jats, unlike Rajputs, were high-caste cultivators, generally in the north-west, and believed to be hard-working and reliable.

65 This 'flying brigade' was one of two movable columns, of about 2,500

soldiers, and left Delhi on 24 September under the command of Colonel
Edward Greathed to pursue the mutineers and open up communications
between Delhi and Cawnpore. They marched along the Grand Trunk
Road, attacking the villages which were supposed to have helped the
rebels, but were diverted to Agra, which they reached on 10 October.
They found the city quiet and encamped on the parade-ground. Here
they were attacked by a body of mutineers, who were soon defeated.

66 In 1773 Parliament passed an Act, after the Company's mismanagement
of Bengal had become apparent which obliged the Company to take
responsibility for the government of the territories it controlled. As a
direct result of this, the three Presidencies of Bengal, Madras and
Bombay were established and the civil service structured. Collectorates were areas within districts, the Collector being responsible to
the District Commissioner.

67 Roberts noted: 'On 21st June, a few days after the force took up its
position under a heavy cannonade, she gave birth to a son in the waggon
in which she was accommodated. The infant, who was christened
Stanley Delhi-Force, seems to have been looked upon by the soldiery
with quite a superstitious feeling, for the father tells us that soon after its
birth he overheard a soldier say: "Now we shall get our reinforcements:
this camp was formed to avenge the blood of innocents, and the first
reinforcement sent to us is a new-born infant." Reinforcements did
actually arrive the next day' (op. cit., p. 160).

68 Harriet is referring to Sir Walter Scott's poem *Marmion*, canto VI, verse
xxxii:

> The war, that for a space did fail,
> Now trebly thundering swell'd the gale,
> And—STANLEY! was the cry;
> A light on Marmion's visage spread,
> And fired his glazing eye:
> With dying hand, above his head,
> He shook the fragment of his blade,
> And shouted 'Victory!
> Charge, Chester, charge! On, Stanley, on!'
> Were the last words of Marmion.

69 Unless a more senior officer died or left the service, the only way for
Robert to be promoted in peacetime within his regiment was to buy his
next 'step' up. What he offered Major Waterfield was the price of the
step from senior captain to major. But Waterfield wanted him to pay
for his own step from major to colonel, which would have cost 30,000
rupees.

GLOSSARY

ayah, female nurse or attendant

bearer, a palanquin-carrier or body servant

bell of arms, conical bell-shaped building used for storing weapons

charpoy, native bed

chillumchee, basin of brass or tinned copper

chupattee, small cake of un-leavened bread

dacoit, robber

dak, post or transport using relays; relay of men or horses for carrying mails etc., or passengers in palanquins

dall, split pulse, e.g. lentil

furlough, long leave of absence

gharree, horse- or bullock-drawn vehicle

ghat, steps leading down to a river

ghurra, round, porous earthen ves-sel for carrying water

havildar, native sergeant; **kot havildar,** pay sergeant

jemadar, native lieutenant

mahout, elephant driver

memsahib, a corruption of madam-sahib

nawab, viceroy; a native ruler, as raja, wali, etc.

nujeeb, a semi-disciplined infantry soldier under some of the native governments. Also, a militiaman under the East India Company's civil administration, before there were regular police

nullah, brook or watercourse

palankeen/palanquin/palkee, a litter carried on poles—also **pal-kee gharree**

pandee, name used for mutineers, after the sepoy Mungal Pandee

raj, reign

sahib, friend, sir, gentleman

razai, quilt stuffed with raw cotton

shigram, springless cart

Sircar, lord, chief, master, usually meaning Government or an officer (literally: Persian *sar-i-har*, head of whatever is going on)

sepoy, native infantry soldier

sowar, a horseman, trooper

subahdar, native captain

subahdar-major, senior native officer of an infantry regiment

Thakoor, term of respect, 'Lord'; also chief or noble, especially of the Rajput race

tumbrel, two-wheeled cart

tykhana, underground room

zenana, harem, women's apart-ments

INDEX

H = Harriet Tytler; RT = Robert Tytler